Understanding the
Sino-Indian War 1962

BY THE SAME AUTHOR

Unlearned Lessons: An Appraisal of India's Military Mishaps, New Delhi, Har-Anand Publications, 2007 (Reprinted 2010)

Srilanka Misadventure: India's Military Peace-Keeping Campaign 1987-1990 (with M.K. Gupta-Ray), New Delhi, Har-Anand Publications, New Delhi, 2008

China-Tibet-India, the 1962 War and the Strategic Military Future, New Delhi, Har-Anand Publications, 2009

Securing India's Borders: Challenges and Policy Options, New Delhi, Pentagon Press, 2011

Insurgencies in North-East India: Moving Towards Resolution, New Delhi, Pentagon Press, 2013

Understanding the
Sino-Indian War 1962

Gautam Das
高大马

Military Affairs Series
An Imprint of Har-Anand Publications Pvt Ltd

Published by Ashok Gosain and Ashish Gosain for:
HAR-ANAND PUBLICATIONS PVT LTD
E-49/3, Okhla Industrial Area, Phase-II, New Delhi-110020
Tel: 011-41603490 Fax: 011-41708607
E-mail: haranand@rediffmail.com/info@haranandpublications.com
Website: www.haranandpublications.com

Printed in India at Vinayak Offset.

Dedication

To the officers and men of the Indian Army and the Indian Air Force, who strove, braved extreme privation, fought, and died, or were wounded, and who became prisoners, or even panicked and fled, in India's ill-considered politico-military posturing and incompetent higher direction of war and senior military leadership from 1959 to November 1962.

This is the story of their honourable struggle, which was acknowledged for the first time by India's political leadership only as late as October 2012.

Military Affairs Series

The aim of the Military Affairs series is to add to a nationwide debate on the security policies of India. The intellectual pluralism that stems from this could, in turn, provide India's politico-bureaucratic elite an idea of the national mood on military issues and enable them to direct the country's policies in the right direction. Until recently a large number of India's politicians, and the people they represent, were only interested in regional issues within India's border. That has begun to change. Across India, the media, a number of academics and intellectuals have started to debate issues of national security and military affairs, especially so in an era when India faces and fights terrorism unleashed by Pakistan. This is the start of a healthy tradition in a country which only recently was said to be without a tradition on strategic thought.

South Asia is now perhaps the most heavily militarized region in the world, and nuclear India remains boxed between the region's two other nuclear powers—China and Pakistan—and, while both are in land contiguity with India, diplomatic relations with them are far from perfect. Despite this, India sadly lacks a national security establishment and its people remain inadequately informed about the military issues that concern every citizen. It is this shortcoming that the series will address.

Maroof Raza
General Editor

Acknowledgements

I am grateful to Lt. Gen. J.F.R. Jacob, PVSM (Retd.), who in 1975 gave me a detailed exposure to many of the international and diplomatic specifics of the Sino-Indian border problem when he was the Army Commander (GOC-in-C) of India's Eastern Command. I am further grateful to him for writing the Foreword to this book, in his trademark forthright and pithy style.

I am also grateful to Lt. Gen. V.R. Raghavan, PVSM, UYSM, AVSM (Retd.), for kindly agreeing to write an Introduction to the Sino-Indian War 1962 for the benefit of the readers. He has not only been a participant in the war as a regimental officer in 1962, but is perhaps the only senior Indian general who has gone on to become an acknowledged military strategist and writer.

Brig. Lakshman Singh, VSM (Retd.), then a Captain, was the Brigade Signals Officer of 7 Infantry Brigade at the battle of the Namka Chu. He has been very kind to permit me to quote extracts from his blogspot, where he describes the situation at the Brigade HQ on the evening of 19th October, the night before the battle, and from his interview to *India Today* describing the last moments of the battle on 20 October 1962.

I am grateful to Michael Dalvi for his warmth and encouragement, and for his permission to quote freely from his father's*classic work, *Himalayan Blunder.*

**The late Brig. J.P. Dalvi (1920-1974).*

I thank Maj. Gen. Ashok Kalyan Verma, AVSM (Retd.), for his permission to quote extensively from his 1998 book, *Rivers of Silence: Disaster on the River Namka Chu, 1962, and the Dash to Dhaka across River Meghna during 1971.* Thanks are also due to Gp. Capt. A.G. Bewoor, VM (Retd.), for permission to quote from his educative article "Close Air Support in the 1962 War" on the web-site www.Bharat-Rakshak.com.

The South Asian Institute of Strategic Affairs was kind to grant permission, through Naveeta Kapoor, for me to quote extracts from the interview with Lt. Gen. Ravi Eipe, PVSM, AVSM (Retd.), former Army Commander, Eastern Command, on his combat experience during the 1962 war on the Namka Chu battlefield, which is on their website on the Net.

Maj. Gen. Kuldip Singh Bajwa (Retd.) has been encouraging and kind as always, and I am grateful to him for his permission to quote him from his *India's National Security: Military Challenges and Responses* (2008) in the Military Affairs Series of my publishers, Har-Anand Publications. I am grateful to Brig. H.S. Sodhi (*4th Gorkha Rifles*), author and military analyst, for his permission to quote from his works *Top Brass—A Critical Appraisal of the Indian Military Leadership* (1993) and *Significant Battles since Independence* (2007).

I thank Neville Maxwell for writing his most informative article, *Henderson-Brooks Report: An Introduction,* (2001), which is still available on the Internet, for the benefit of most Indians, who have been denied access to the original report. In spite of due diligence in trying to obtain his current contact e-mail addresses, I have been unable to contact him at the e-mail address made available to me. I am sure that he will approve dissemination of extracts from his article.

Preface

This work is one of my various efforts to swim against the tide of Indian indifference to our history. Various strands of interest and experience have been wound together to form this book. Some derive from the humiliation of the 1962 defeat by China, some from a fascination with China, both somewhat derived from incidental exposure at an impressionable age, and some from my own military experience.

As Class 10 schoolboys at a boarding school at North Point in Darjeeling in 1962, we heard the electrifying news on 21st October that China had attacked India from Tibet. The newspapers which we saw that evening said: 'China attacks India: *Jawans* fight a desperate battle' or words to that effect. Bhutanese boys of the two senior years, the 10th and the 11th Standards (the pre-final and the final year of the school system, which then had 11 years after the KG level, not 12 as at present) were immediately called back to join their army. The 1962 defeat and humiliation of the Indian Army was to exercise a morbid fascination on me (and on the entire army and to an extent the entire country too, for that matter) for the next many years. The questions 'Why?' and 'How?' never quite left me till I spent the time to research it thoroughly for my own satisfaction, reading everything on the subject that I could lay my hands on, a habit which has continued to the present.

The Bengali 'gentleman' class of Kolkata, the *bhadralok,* had in the 1950's 'discovered' the Chinese restaurant. My parents were no exception. Living in Kolkata on Camac Street, we were conveniently close to many restaurants. I became fascinated by the entirely different décor and paintings in Chinese restaurants, such as the Peiping, close to the Park Street-Chowringhee junction. Chinese art with its unique perspective and style, in particular the dreamy mountain landscapes and the horse paintings, started a fascination for many aspects of Chinese culture. Many things Chinese continue to fascinate me today.

My involvement with the Sino-Indian boundary dispute was in the General Staff branches of HQ 15 Corps (then written as 'XV Corps,' which then dealt with the Sinkiang-Ladakh border as well as the Tibet-Ladakh border), and of HQ Eastern Command, where I dealt with the Tibet-Sikkim border as well as with the McMahon Line issue in Arunachal Pradesh.

While on regimental sevice in Sikkim I had marched on foot in 'field service marching order' (FSMO) with the infantry company I commanded, along the so-called 'Younghusband Track' all the way uphill from Kalimpong in the foothills right up to the Jelep La area, as well as lived on the Sher post right on the boundary itself, looking out at the Chumbi Valley. In the Kameng region of Arunachal Pradesh I had seen the edge of the Tibetan plateau at Bumla, the monastery town of Tawang, and the route to Khinzemane along the Nyamjang Chu, near the site of the infamous battle of the Namka Chu of October 1962, as well as the Sela massif, the Dirang Dzong valley and Bomdila. At the far eastern end of Aruncahal Pradesh I had also been to the Lohit valley leading towards Walong.

Everything in this book has come from open sources, including the unclassified and un-copyrighted 'official' history of the 1962 War which is available on the Internet. I have leaned heavily on facts given in the one complete document that gives the Indian side of events in its entirety. This is the Ministry of Defence's *History of the Conflict with China, 1962* (1992) just referred to above, which was produced between 1986 and 1990 after being given access to all the Government's records including the still-'Secret' and unnecessarily notorious Henderson-Brooks Report, interviews with all important survivors, and has used information from all published books, with one notable exception. The other authoritative work which I have used is the late Maj. K.C. Praval's demi-official *Indian Army after Independence* (1987). This work, written at the behest of the late Gen. T.N. Raina, then Chief of Army Staff, has been written as a one-man effort but with access granted to all official records, so that it stands as a second almost-official history for all India's wars from 1947 to 1971. I have consulted the one important exception to the research carried out by the official historians, viz., the late Maj. Gen. D.K. Palit's *War in High Himalaya: The Indian Army in Crisis 1962,* published in 1991. As a Brigadier, he was the Director of Military Operations at Army Headquarters in the period 1961-63, and thus an important observer and participant at centre-stage in the Army Headquarters role in the events before and during the 1962 war.

I have used the late Brig. J.P. Dalvi's first-hand account as the brigade commander of the forward-most brigade in the Kameng sector of NEFA. His book, *Himalayan Blunder* (1969), is a classic of Indian military literature and an authoritative account of the period 1960-62 , and of 7 Infantry Brigade's role and actions till it was over-run on October 20, 1962, and Brig. Dalvi himself taken prisoner by the Chinese. When he was eventually repatriated by the Chinese on May 4, 1963, the then-Chief of the Army Staff, Gen. J.N. Chaudhuri, reportedly gave him a mouthful for *'handing over his brigade on a plate to the Chinese.'* Gen. Chaudhuri had asked him to write a report for the personal information of the Defence Minister and himself, whose aim, Brig. Dalvi was told, was 'To teach ourselves how not to hand over a brigade on a plate to the Chinese in future.' This report is no longer available, but Brig. Dalvi's own account of the events that befell his 7 Infantry Brigade is the most authentic account available.

To give readers a full flavour of the situation and actions of ground level, I have quoted extensively from Maj. Gen. Ashok Kalyan Verma's painstakingly-researched reconstruction of the actions of 2nd Rajput up to and during the battle of the Namka Chu, in his *Rivers of Silence* (1998). This infantry battalion was the most critically affected battalion, subjected to the war's major opening attack by the Chinese People's Liberation Army, in the Thagla-Namka Chu area of the Kameng sector of Arunachal Pradesh (then known as the North-East Frontier Agency, or NEFA for short).

The military reader who wishes to read most of the source-material used is advised to read the following, preferably in the given order: Brig. Dalvi's *Himalayan Blunder;* Maj. Gen. Niranjan Prasad's *Fall of Towang* (1981), the pages 171-240 in the chapters that pertain to the Sino-Indian war in Maj. Praval's *Indian Army after Independence,* and the Ministry of Defence's *History of the Conflict with China, 1962,* authored by Dr. P.B. Sinha and Col. A.A. Athale, and edited by Dr. S.N. Prasad. Though some commentators have considered it self-exculpatory, Maj. Gen. D.K. Palit's *War in High Himalaya* provides a feel of the situation from the perspective of Army Headquarters.

Foreword

By
Lt. Gen. J.F.R. Jacob, PVSM (Retd.)

I missed the 1962 war since Lt. Gen. Kaul [then Chief of the General Staff at Army Headquarters] delayed my promotion to command a brigade, as I had refused to give evidence against Maj. Gen. Manekshaw as demanded by him.

The main lessons of the 1962 war were lack of political leadership, lack of preparation, lack of proper infrastructure, lack of logistics, lack of mobility, and lack of firepower.

There was poor leadership and negligence, both political and military.

There was a problem of morale as troops did not have the wherewithal to fight due to years of political negligence. Pandit Nehru, the Prime Minister, wanted to run the Army down to a total of 100,000! It was called 'PLAN 100.' I was made to work on this plan in 1950.

The military leadership too was incompetent. Lt. Gen. Kaul, then the Corps Commander in NEFA, an Army Service Corps officer who spent most of his World War II service in the *'Fauji Dilkhush'* (Troops' Entertainment), was out of his depth.

It is worth noting a page from history:

During the Seven Years War (1756-1763), Admiral Byng of England was ordered to engage the French Fleet off the island of

Minorca in the Mediterranean Sea. He withdrew. On return to Portsmouth he was court-martialled for negligence, found guilty, and executed by firing squad on his own ship's quarter-deck.

Regrettably both our political and military leadership failed in 1962.

Lieut.-General J.F.R. Jacob, PVSM (Retd.), (born in 1921, and in the Indian Army from 1974 to 1978) had been India's Eastern Army Commander (the GOC-in-C Eastern Command), from 1974 to 1978. Later the Governor of Goa and then of Punjab, he was the architect of India's military conquest in the-then East Pakistan in November-December 1971. In 1962 he was a Colonel, serving as an instructor at the Defence Services Staff College, at Wellington in the Nilgiri mountains of Tamilnadu, where Maj.-General S.H.F.J. Manekshaw, MC, was the Commandant.

He was considered by his peers and contemporaries to be a progressive professional thinker. In May 1971 as Chief of Staff of the army's Eastern Command, whose headquarters are in Fort William, Kolkata, he had planned the military operation for the invasion of East Pakistan aimed at liberating the eastern Bengal province of Pakistan. After having prepared the army logistically, he was also greatly responsible for facilitating the progress of the operations, and was personally responsible for converting what was going to be a cease-fire negotiation in Dhaka (Dacca), into a formal public surrender by Pakistan's Eastern Army Commander, Lieut-General A.A.K. Niazi.

India's Moment of Military Truth

By

Lt. Gen. V.R. Raghavan, PVSM, UYSM, AVSM (Retd.)

The war India fought, or was forced to fight in 1962, was a consequence of unilateral Chinese aggression. It manifested as a military invasion into Indian territory. China had by then settled its boundaries with all its neighbours. What prompted the Chinese decision to attack India? Analysts have attributed it to the Chinese desire to demonstrate its military power in the Asian region. It had been recently involved against the US in the Korean War and from which it had emerged with its military image dented and with losses in troops and equipment. It had also absorbed the lessons of the war in terms of well planned attacks in the mountains, supported by artillery and of employing the principle of operational manoeuvre.

India failed to anticipate the type of campaign China's military or PLA would conduct. There was strategic failure in understanding China's geo-political objectives, intelligence failure in reading the Chinese operational objectives and major failures in preparing the Indian armed forces for a modern war. The Indian military fought the war with outmoded weapons, poor logistic support and insufficient doctrinal preparedness for the war in mountains and high altitude.

Indian defeat in the war amounted to a national humiliation and led to global erosion of respect for India as a military entity. It also led to a serious reassessment of its military needs, it led to a new paradigm of civil-military relations, and in turn brought about new thinking on defence preparedness. More importantly, the defeat led to major reorganisation within the armed forces in terms of doctrine, weapons systems, training and leadership development. The Indian Armed forces of 2013 owe their high state of readiness to fight a modern war to the traumatic experience of the Sino-Indian War of 1962. As one who fought in the war and witnessed the rapid transformation of the Indian armed forces, one can point to the successful conduct of the 1965 War and the spectacular successes of the 1971 War against Pakistan.

I hold the view that due to poor state of its readiness in 1962, India did not really fight a war. There was neither a strategic plan nor an operational purpose to the Indian actions. Consequently, India fought a series of disconnected and uncoordinated military battles, albeit marked by outstanding regimental cohesion and combat valour. It was at the brigade and divisional levels that serious failures and command shortcomings were evident. My own experience was of isolated battles, fought with inadequate fire support and poor logistic back-up. Today all these shortcomings have been corrected. It has also required decades of efforts and major investment of national economy to reach the desired levels of defence readiness.

The circumstances described above make it necessary that the war of 1962, its battles, and the operational responses are analysed and reflected upon. Officers preparing to hold responsible command and staff positions in future will gain immensely by this effort. The strategic, operational, and tactical dimensions of the 1962 War, individually and collectively, provide insights into the military's responsibility to be not only prepared but seek the resources with which to fight future wars.

Equally, such a study shows up the essential strength of the Indian soldier's resilience and commitment against heavy odds, an asset to be greatly cherished.

Lieut.-General V.R. Raghavan, PVSM, UYSM, AVSM (Retd.), was commissioned into the Indian Army in 1957 and retired as the Army's Director-General of Military Operations in 1994. He was an officer of the Infantry, and belonged to the Punjab Regiment. As a regimental officer he was a participant in the 1962 operations in the Kameng sector of the eastern theatre. He is also a strategic military thinker and academic of international repute.

Contents

Appendices

Part I

The Background to the War

1

Overview and Early Tibet-India and Sino-Indian Relations

The Sino-Indian border war of October 1962 is widely considered to be a humiliating defeat for India, a military debacle of the worst kind. For a politically new country that had been independent for a mere 15 years it was a sudden and very unpleasant shock, and put an end to any military naivete. Apart from the loss of territory in both the eastern and the western theatres of the war, some of which was returned by the unilateral Chinese withdrawal in the east, what were the military casualty figures? As per various figures available, India lost 1,423 killed, 3,078 wounded, 1,655 missing believed killed, and 3,895 taken prisoner. Of these, the total casualties in the eastern theatre were 2,616, including killed and seriously wounded; of which 875 were directly attributable to enemy action. The rest were due to other causes including weather and accidents.

A Lt. Cdr. of the US Navy, James Barnard Calvin, summarized the war in his 1984 study *The China-India Border War* (1984):

> In the war that began with skirmishes in the summer of 1962, the significant fighting occurred in October and November, 1962, along three widely separated fronts. In virtually every battle the Chinese forces either outmaneuvered or overpowered the unprepared Indians. In less than six weeks of bloody fighting, the Chinese completely drove Indian forces back behind Chinese claim lines. After achieving their limited

> strategic objectives, the Chinese dramatically declared ceasefire on November 21, 1962. Following the ceasefire, China kept most of their claim in Aksai Chin but gave India virtually all of India's claim in the North East Frontier Agency [NEFA, now Arunachal Pradesh]—about 70 percent of the disputed land.

How did this military disaster actually unfold on the ground? Why did the war take place? These are the two central questions this book attempts to answer, in a brief and easy to understand narration.

An understanding of the Sino-Indian war of 1962 requires an understanding of the military situation of the time, particularly that of India. The reasons for the war are rooted in Chinese perceptions, both ancient and of the time, as well as the overall world geo-political situation. The two together set the stage for the Sino-Indian War of 1962.

China's views of the rest of the world and its dealings with the world, including with India, have always been coloured by its long-held perceptions, including those about itself. These continue to influence its thinking up to the highest levels of governance, and shape its actions on the world stage. With the advent and growth of Neo-Confucianism in the modern PRC, and as China's Comprehensive National Power continues to grow, understanding these perceptions will remain important for all countries affected by China. Its neighbours who share borders with it, all the 20 countries that adjoin it, are particularly affected. Lack of understanding of China's attitudes was greatly to blame for the occurrence of the Sino-Indian border war of 1962, as well as its unhappy results for India.

The concept of fixed, i.e., delineated and demarcated borders, resulting from agreements between nation-states, is a fairly new concept in the world, resulting from the end of monarchy and feudalism in Europe, the growth of democracy, and the creation of nation-states. The concept can be dated to as recently as the Treaty of Westphalia in 1648. The concept was imported into Asia by the colonial-era European powers, where it clashed with the pre-existing indigenous monarchical and feudalistic systems. For China, the primary system of foreign relations with its neighbouring states was the tributary system, which treated foreigners as vassals, and thus could not conceive of diplomatic parity with them. Nor did it allow, therefore, negotiations with the alleged subjects of the Chinese emperor – i.e., any country, kingdom or state with whom it had tributary relations. It was the cause for the different perceptions regarding Tibet held by the Chinese, the Tibetans themselves, and the British who ruled India mainly as a possession of a monarchy. This irredentist attitude still colours Chinese relations with its neighbours regarding the South China Sea, for example.

The core reasons for the Sino-Indian border war of 1962 are thus:

- Chinese perceptions regarding Tibet as automatically, as per Chinese thinking, a vassal state,
- their smarting under the humiliating European-style treaties forced upon them by European powers, and
- their annoyance with India regarding both its presence in Tibet and Indian Prime Minister Nehru's postures of Western-style diplomacy which assumed a diplomatic parity that China was loath to concede to a weak Asian neighbor.

In this context, it is necessary to see some of the basic Chinese perceptions regarding India, from well before their military occupation of Tibet in 1950-51.

EARLY TIBET-INDIA AND SINO-INDIAN RELATIONS

There are various perceptions regarding the earlier relationships that existed between Tibet and India, Tibet and China, and India and China. Some of these are dramatically different from each other, even on the same subject, and this account attempts to present a synthesized view, from as many accounts as possible, shorn of bias, without presenting comparative differences where they exist.

The spread of Buddhism from India to what is now the PRC was in two separate streams, independent of each other, to Tibet and to China. Though Buddhism first reached China from India in the First Century AD, it was during the Sui Dynasty in China (A.D. 581-618), when it really grew. Many Buddhist monks from India traveled to China and made it their permanent home. The Chinese name for India, 'Shendu,' a Sinification of 'Sindhu,' got changed to 'Tianzhu,' meaning 'heavenly land,' in this period. Some Chinese Buddhist monks too traveled to India to study and to collect Buddhist documents for translation. The most well-known of these was Hiuen Tsiang's visit to India, from AD 629. Indian Buddhist monks went to China by one of two routes, one overland and the other by sea. More common was the land route through today's Afghanistan, which was then a flourishing centre of Indian Buddhism, through the similarly Indian Buddhist oasis towns of today's Sinkiang, and thence into mainland Han China. The other route was the sea route from southern India via the Indian-founded Buddhist states of modern Indonesia, there being regular seaborne commerce between southern Indian ports and south-east Asia, and thence to the southern China ports.

Bodhidharma meditating in a cave beside Shaolin Temple, China. A 15th Century woodcut by the Japanese painter, scholar and Zen monk, Toyo Sesshu; an image which is commonly seen on China's famous Jing De Zhen pottery.

Chinese chronicles such as *Gaoseng Zhuan* (Biographies of Eminent Monks) and *Yuzhi Shenseng Zhuan* (Biographies of Monks with Magical Powers) written in the 6th and 16th Centuries respectively, have recorded the visit of every Indian scholar to China, such as Kashyap Matanga, Dharmaratna, Kumarajiva, Bodhidharma,[1] Amogha Vajra and Vajra Bodhi, but none who went from India to Tibet. The Indian founders of Tibetan Buddhism are not mentioned therein. Guru Padmasambhava from Kashmir, known in Tibetan as Guru Rinpoche is not mentioned. Neither Shantarakshita from India's famous Nalanda University, who introduced the Brahmi script to Tibet, nor his disciple Kamalashmita who accompanied him, find mention. There is also no mention of the famous Tantric Buddhist teacher Atisha Dipankara. It is thus clear that in this vast period of Chinese history, even in their own literature, China did not include Tibet.

The Brahmi alphabet of India which consists of vowels and consonants, was the basis of the Tibetan script, and has nothing in common with the Chinese script, which is based on characters originally derived from pictorial writing (pictograms). There has been constant cross-frontier Indo-Tibet trade in traditional items from Tibet and manufactured goods and other necessities from India, right up to September 1962. Pilgrim traffic has been both ways and constant between India and Tibet, traditionally known in India as *'Bhot'* (the people of Tibet being called *'Bhotiya' or 'Bhutia'*), from the Tibetans' own word for their country, *'Bhod.'* Thousands of Indian pilgrims every year visited the holy Mount Kailash (Tibetan *'Kang Tissu'* or *'Khang Rinpoche'*),[2] and Lake Mansarovar (Tibetan *'Mafamyu Tso'*), sacred to Indian Hindus and Tibetan Buddhists alike. Thus the people-to-people contacts between Indian and Tibet on the social and cultural plane had a volume and a quality completely unlike the practically non-existent direct contacts with 'mainland,' or Han, cultural China.

To Indians, therefore, Tibet has always been seen as a friendly and peaceful neighbouring country. There has been only one instance of a Tibetan attack on the Indian plains. Since this instance had been cited by Mao Zedong, a student of history just as much as Pandit Nehru, it is worth recounting.

The northern Indian Emperor Harshavardhana (606 – 647 AD) a great patron of Buddhism, and had established his capital at Kanauj. It was during his reign that the famous Chinese pilgrim Hiuen Tsiang visited India and stayed at his court. Harsha maintained diplomatic relations with China, sending an envoy to China in 641 who returned in 643 accompanied by a Chinese mission.[3] In 642 when Hiuen Tsiang returned to China and met the Chinese emperor, briefing him about Harshavardhana's patronage of Buddhism, the Chinese emperor decided to send another mission to India in 646.

By the time this second mission reached India, however, Harshavardhana had passed away, and since he had no son there was a period of confusion and disorder during which one of Harsha's ministers named Arjuna seized the throne. Arjuna was not well disposed towards Buddhism, and when the Chinese mission, under the Chinese envoy Wang Hiuen-tse reached his palace, it was attacked and the envoy's 30-man escort killed. Only the envoy himself and one of his ministers escaped and reached Nepal, which had come under Tibet during the reign of Songtsen Gampo, the founder of Lhasa, who was responsible for introducing state Buddhism into Tibet. When the Chinese envoy's message reached Songtsen Gampo, he retaliated against Arjuna by sending a force of 12,000 Tibetan troops and 7,000 Nepali troops, which met Arjuna's army at Hirahati in Tirhut (part of modern Bihar and north Bengal) and defeated it after a short battle.[4] Arjuna was captured and sent to China as a prisoner.[5] With the usurper deposed, the Buddhism-inclined King of

Kamrup in Assam, probably Yasovarman, was enthroned at Kanauj, and he maintained diplomatic relations with China.[6] Both Tirhut and Nepal remained subject to Tibet until 703 AD.

Chairman Mao had cited a version of this history at the enlarged Central Military Commission (CMC) meeting held on 16th October 1962 at Xishan ('Western Hills') on the western outskirts of Beijing wherein the final decision was taken to launch the attack on India.[7] During the discussions that preceded the decision and his final approval of the attack, he said that so far there had only been one-and-a-half wars against India. As per Mao, the first Sino-Indian war was in 656 AD, when a Tang dynasty emperor had dispatched troops to assist the legal claimant to the throne of an Indian kingdom (*jieri diguo*), after the other claimant had killed 30 members of a Tang diplomatic mission. The 'half-war' (of the 'One-and Half Wars') was in 1398, stated Mao at the same meeting, when Temur captured Delhi. This, though a great victory, as per Mao was a 'Half War' because Temur and his army were Mongols from both Inner and Outer Mongolia, thus making the victory 'Half Chinese,' because Mongolia was supposedly under China at the time! In point of fact, Temur himself was not a Mongol but a Barlas Turkoman born near Sakhrisabz in today's Uzbekistan. Neither Mongolia nor eastern Turkestan (now Xinjiang) were under China at the time, which was under the Ming dynasty. Both eastern Turkestan and the western part of Mongolia were then under the rule of Islamicised and Turkicised Mongols, an eastern branch of the Chaghtais, and the region they ruled was known as Mughalistan, or land of the Mongols. It was ruled by the Muslim Mongol khan, Khizr Khoja, who was opposed to Temur. Cessation of hostilities between the Mongols and Temur was reached only in 1397, by Temur's marriage to the Khan's daughter, the princess Tukal-khanum. This strategic marriage actually freed Temur's way eastwards to the prize he craved to conquer, the 'infidel' Ming China. The only element of truism could be that Temur's army that invaded India had Muslim horsemen from all over the Central Asian steppes, including no doubt some of the Turkicised western Mongols of Mughalistan.

As per Indian history, the only instance of Sino-Indian armed conflict prior to 1962 would be the clash in central Asia in the 2nd Century C.E. (AD). This occurred between the Kushan emperor Kanishka's expeditionary force and the Chinese general who first conquered Xinjiang (Sinkiang), Pan Chao (32-102 C.E.). Kanishka's capital was at Purushapura (modern Peshawar, the capital of Pakistan's former Northwest Frontier Province, now renamed Khyber Pahktunkhwa). Kanishka's campaign in Central Asia subdued the area later known as Eastern Turkestan, including Kashgar, Khotan and Yarkand, now China's Xinjiang-Uighur Autonomous Province. This brought him into conflict with the Chinese empire of the Eastern Han dynasty. He was defeated by the Chinese general Pan Chao (Ban Chao/ Pan Ch'ao) in about 100 AD.[8] There was a later Chinese re-conquest in 1759, after which eastern Turkestan was officially named as Xinjiang, meaning 'New Dominion.'

NOTES

1. Bodhidharma (Chinese: *Da-mo/Tamo, Japanese: Daruma*) is reported to have traveled to China by sea in AD 520 and died there in AD 532. He is believed to have been born a Pallava prince in Kanchipuram who became the 28th Patriarch of Buddhism in India. He is the well-known founder of 'Dhyan' Buddhism (Chinese: Ch'an Buddhism, Japanese: Zen Buddhism), and of the Shaolin martial arts school which he based on his mastery of *Kalaripayattu,* the South Indian martial art.
2. A pyramidical peak of 22,028 ft.
3. Mukherjee, L., *History of India* (Hindu Period) (27th Ed.), Calcutta, Moudal Bros., 1968, p. 187.

4. Arpi, Claude, *The Fate of Tibet,* 2001, p. 27.
5. L. Mukherjee, *op. cit.,* p. 192.
6. Claude Arpi, *op. cit.,* p. 27 and L. Mukherjee, *ibid.,* p. 193.
7. In Garver, 'China's Decision to Attack India,' in Johnson, Alastair Iain, and Robert S. Ross (eds.), *New Directions in the Study of China's Foreign Policy,* 2006.
8. L. Mukherjee, *op. cit.,* pp. 140-141.

2

The Status of Tibet and Sino-Indian Relations 1949-1962

"It is on the Roof of the World that our friendship with China will flourish or flounder."

(Acharya Kripalani, 1950)

The Sino-Indian war of 1962 is the only armed conflict during the period since Independence in 1947 that the generally-ignorant Indian public associates with a military defeat. Even the Government of India's own Historical Section of the Ministry of Defence, in its history and analysis of the conflict, acknowledges that it was a military fiasco. But its roots lay in the rivalry that developed between India and China over the question of Tibet, the high plateau lying north of the Himalayan Mountains, known to Indians as *'Bhot,'* the neighbouring country where the holy Mount Kailash and the holy lake Manosarovar are located.

During the period that followed the 1904 Younghusband expedition against Tibet, British India had established numerous concessions in Tibet, including a telegraph line from Lhasa to Kalimpong, and the stationing of Indian Army troops at Gyantse and Lhasa.

At Independence in 1947, India took the official position that it recognized Tibetan autonomy while at the same time recognizing China's suzerainty (as distinct from sovereignty).

Basically this implied a continued recognition of the old medieval and earlier Asian system of independent but vassal states, who accepted the overlordship of a neighbouring major power by paying some form of ritual tribute, which thereby prevented the major power from attacking them. It also provided some notional protection from other neighbouring powers, as long as the overlord's power was strong enough for its reputation to deter others from attacking its vassal. This position was soon to come under considerable strain.

When India became independent in 1947 it saw itself as the successor to all the treaties of the former Govt. of India with Tibet, and continued accordingly, but things changed dramatically when the Chinese Communists consolidated themselves in China after their civil war, which followed the military operations by both contending parties against the occupying Japanese. The Communist Party came to power, the Chinese Peoples' Republic was established in 1949, and on

January 1st, 1950, the Chinese People's Liberation Army (PLA) moved in to occupy Tibet, to 'liberate' it from foreign influence and to 're-unite it with the Motherland,' as the Chinese put it. On the morning of 7th October 1950, troops of the Chinese PLA's Eighteenth and Second Field Armies under General Liu Bating crossed the Yangtse River in a six-pronged attack on Chamdo, the capital of the Kham region of Tibet, most of which has since been made part of China's Sichuan (earlier spelt 'Szechwan') province. By November 1950 China's conquest, 'liberation' or 're-unification,' of Tibet was a fact.

From India's independence in 1947 to the Tibetan rebellion of 1959, the primary issue on the agenda of the two governments had been the legal status of Tibet. China's official position on this is that Tibet was incorporated into China in the 13th Century when the Mongols under Chinggis Khan's grandson Kublai Khan established the Mongol, or Yuan Dynasty (1127-1368) in China. China harks back to its own imperial past to claim any territory which was ever, howsoever remotely, under Chinese domination. C.P. Fitzgerald quoted by Francis Watson in his book, The Frontiers of China, writes, 'Territory once won for civilization must not be given back to the barbarians; therefore, territory which was once Chinese must forever remain so, and if lost, must be recovered at the first opportunity.'[1] David Scott (2011) maintains that:

> ... there are ambiguities in China's very claim on Tibet.[2] China claims that political links with Tibet go back centuries. In reality, Chinese control was first seen in the intervention of a Qing army in 1720 and arrival of a Chinese resident commissioner (*amban*). Since then, some degree of Chinese control was able to be enforced in Tibet when China was strong, but effectively lapsed (for most of the period) when China was weak.

The loss of the so-called historic 'buffer' became a fact, though Tibet had been a 'buffer' only in the context of the competition for imperialist conquest in Asia, or the 'Great Game' as it has been called. Tibet was never a buffer between India and China, for the simple reason that Indian and Chinese empires of the past had never been geographically in physical contact. An Indian empire and a Chinese one had only once very briefly been in conflict, in the time of Kanishka in AD 100, as already noted, and that too in a fringe area for both, in eastern Turkestan, which was at the time a centre of Indian Buddhist culture.

Lt. Gen. Sir Francis Tuker, India's GOC-in-C Eastern Command in 1948, in a six-page analysis had quoted the Tibetan-speaking former British Political Officer for Sikkim, Bhutan and Tibet, Sir Charles Bell, saying that *'We want Tibet as a buffer to India in the North.'*[3] He had prophetically added that:

> Tibet will afford a great central emplacement for the installation of long-range nuclear weapons.... It is India's interest to prevent the military occupation by China of the Tibetan plateau. She must always be able to forestall it by her own occupation.[4]

In 1950, when there was information available that China was about to send its troops into Tibet, some persons at the highest level in the Government of India had wanted to send Indian troops into Tibet. The subject of an Indian military intervention in Tibet on behalf of the Tibetans was actually raised at a high-level meeting held in the office of the Foreign Secretary, at which India's ambassador to China, K.M. Pannikar and the Commander-in-Chief (C-in-C) General K. M. Cariappa were present. However, Gen. Cariappa, the Indian C-in-C, had categorically stated that India had no troops to spare, and that the most that could be spared was an infantry battalion.

The Indian Army was then hard-pressed with commitments in Kashmir, and the C-in-C was clear that this battalion could go no further than Yatung, in the Chumbi valley opposite Nathu La and Jelep La in Sikkim, with at the most, a company further forward at Gyantse. At the meeting he explained that the Indian Army was neither equipped nor trained to operate at those heights, and would be seriously at a disadvantage against Chinese troops who were far more experienced in fighting in extremely cold conditions. He also stated that the PLA was better armed, having acquired large quantities of American arms left behind by the retreating Nationalist Chinese (KMT)[5] Army. During this period of imminent Chinese military operations against the ruling Tibetan regime, both the Americans and the British were ready to play a double-faced game, using India as a pawn. The American government recognized Tibet as a part of China, but President Truman was willing to provide transport aircraft to airlift a brigade of Indian troops for the defence of Chamdo, in the Kham region of Tibet.[6] The British had indicated that they were willing to replace all arms and munitions transferred by the Indian Army to Tibet, while refusing to meet a Tibetan delegation. But India's own policy was firmly against such a neo-colonialist military venture, even had it been possible, and Nehru had embarked on an active policy of bringing Communist China on to the world stage.

B.N. Mullik recorded what he felt at the time: *'What Cariappa said at that time was indeed very discouraging and disappointing because I had also favoured military intervention in Tibet to save it from China.'*[7] Which was all very well both as a policy preference and as a sentiment, but there was unfortunately the total disconnect with the reality that the C-in-C had pointed out.

Mullik's adventurous preferences, as well as his lack of understanding of military realities on the ground were to make him one of the principal advocates of the 'Forward Policy' adopted by India from after September 1951.

However, the events on India's northern-most border had actually started a chain of events that culminated in an important development, India's so-called 'Forward Policy.' This came about not as a result of China's take-over of Tibet, as is commonly believed, but as a result of Communist China's takeover of Sinkiang on September 25, 1949, when the Nationalist Chinese troops stationed there overnight changed their allegiance to Communist China.[8] With the fall of Sinkiang to the Communists, Ladakh's northern border had become contiguous to Communist China. An IB post was opened at Leh, and the first joint IB-Army checkpost was set up at Panamik/Shyok to cover the route from the Karakoram Pass to Leh. In 1950 the IB sent a proposal for the establishment of 21 checkposts to guard the passes on the Indo-Tibetan frontier, from Ladakh in the north-west to Lohit Frontier Division in the north-east.

A small committee of military experts was appointed, including a representative of the IB in Shillong, to assess the dangers in NEFA and to suggest the places near the frontiers at which Assam Rifles units should be posted. In November 1950 the Government of India appointed a larger committee headed by the Deputy Minister of Defence, Maj. Gen. Himmatsinghji. This 'North and North-East Border Defence Committee' as it was officially known (informally, the 'Himmatsinghji Committee'), was asked to 'to study the problems created by the Chinese aggression in Tibet and to make recommendations that should be taken to improve administration, defence, communication, etc, of all the frontier areas.' The committee included representatives from the Army (Lt. Gen Kalwant Singh, a Corps Commander), the Air Force, the Ministries of External Affairs, Communications and Home Affairs, and the IB. The Indian government's information was that by January 1951, there were 10,000 to 20,000 troops in the area of Chamdo.

The Committee submitted its report in two parts, the first regarding the borders with Tibet in Sikkim and NEFA, the border with Bhutan, and the eastern border with Burma, after receiving the report of the earlier committee set up for NEFA. The second part contained recommendations regarding Ladakh and the frontier regions of Himachal Pradesh, U.P. and the Nepal border, which was submitted in September 1951. Based on these recommendations, India decided to strengthen the existing border checkposts and to increase their number. By the end of 1952 there were 30 such posts set up all along the frontier, from Karakoram in Ladakh in the north to Kibithoo in NEFA in the north-east.

However, a known gap existed. In Ladakh, there were posts except in the north-eastern and northern areas, in Lingtzi Tang, Aksai Chin, the Soda Plains and the Depsang Plains. Because these areas were almost inaccessible and uninhabited, establishment of posts there was difficult, and so an alternative plan of extensive summer patrolling was worked out.

Towards end-1953, India took the initiative to try and arrive at a treaty with China, in order to create a friendly neighbour on the north. The resultant treaty, generally known as the Panchsheel Treaty, arrived at after six months of discussions, served mainly China's interests. It recognized China's possession of Tibet and, in fact, legalized it for the world. It allowed for trade with the Chinese government in Tibet, and relinquished numerous facilities which India had in Lhasa and en route between Lhasa and Kalimpong since 1904.[9] China could not have asked for more. It immediately began negotiations with the Indian government for the supply of rice and other foodstuffs via Sikkim to Tibet, for its army and the local people in Tibet, who were all facing famine because the massive Chinese PLA presence was solely dependent on local Tibetan grain surplus, which had been exhausted between September 1951 and 1954.

The treaty, however, left a misconception in its wake, at least in Indian minds. The PM, Pt. Nehru, had convinced himself that defining the passes through which the trade would go constituted definition of the alignment of the boundary, at least to the extent that the boundary passed through those passes named [Shipki La (Pass), Mana Pass, Niti Pass, Kungri Bingri Pass, Dana Pass, and Lipu Lekh Pass]. The Chinese did not believe so, believing, as they still do, that these lie within Tibet. The issue had been brought up by the Chinese negotiators prior to the signing of the treaty but since the treaty does not claim to be a boundary agreement, they eventually let it pass.

From 1954 onwards, there were cartographic claims by both India and China. India unilaterally decided to delimit its borders with China, based on the proposed Johnson-Ardagh Line in Ladakh, and on the McMahon Line in NEFA.

The McMahon line had been drawn on the principle of following the highest crest-lines, often mistakenly described as the 'watershed principle'. China's maps showed large areas of Asia as part of the China. A map in the book *A Short History of Modern China* by Liu P'ei-hua, published in 1954, showed large parts of Soviet Central Asia, both Koreas, the whole of Indo-China, Thailand, Malaysia, Burma, Bhutan, Nepal, and even large parts of India as 'lost territories of China.' Of India, it showed the whole of the north-eastern region, including Sikkim,

NEFA and Assam, parts of today's Uttarakhand state, a big chunk of north-eastern Ladakh, (including the entire Aksai Chin region), and even the Andaman and Nicobar Islands as parts of China. The Indian government had then deemed it too preposterous even to protest.[10] But some other Chinese maps showed about 36,000 sq km of territory on the north-eastern frontier and about 31,080 sq km in north-eastern Ladakh, mainly the Aksai Chin region, as being within China. The PM brought it up with his counterpart, Zhou Enlai, when he met him in October 1954 in China. The Chinese PM sought to treat those maps as of little consequence, and even in November 1956, when he visited India, he repeated the same assurance. Of course, the Tibet-Sinkiang road was then being built through Aksai Chin, but Pt. Nehru accepted those assurances in good faith.

Soon after the Chinese PM's visit, however, there were instances of Chinese troops crossing the passes named in the central sector, and China lodged a formal protest on July 17, 1954 against the presence of Indian troops in Barahoti (which they called Wu-je), three km south of what India considered to be the border in the Niti Pass area. Thereafter there were a number of instances of such complaints and counter-complaints, though the patrol encounters remained cordial, the patrol commanders of each side telling the other that this was their own territory. From then on there were such instances in the Shipki La area in Himachal Pradesh, up to September 12, 1956. Here the Chinese regularly patrolled south of the Shipki La to Hupsang Khad, about 12 km south of the pass. There were polite formal diplomatic notes exchanged on each such intrusion. The big lacuna lay in the fact that while India believed the borders had been agreed to as the line of the passes along the main Himalayan crest line as a part of the 1954 treaty, China did not believe so.

The PLA arrives on India's borders.

The Indian Prime Minister, who was the sole foreign policy decision-maker in the Indian Government, realized the position, but wanted to have his cake and eat it too. He had become a world figure, and an acknowledged statesman, and had been championing the cause of Afro-Asian solidarity and non-alignment. He thus publicly accepted Tibet as a part of China in 1954, and the 'annexation' of Tibet as an internal affair of China's, while harbouring private misgivings. The Indian mission in Lhasa and the Indian infantry detachments at Gyantse and Yatung were withdrawn. China soon laid claim to areas beyond the Indian interpretation of the McMahon Line, and their maps began to show noticeable differences between the perceptions of both countries. Chinese troops in the meantime had been setting up garrisons all over Tibet, and had reached right up to the borders with India. The period of Sino-Indian tension over Tibet and the differing perceptions of the Indo-Tibet border had begun. Outwardly, China and India remained good friends on the world stage, with India championing China's case for admittance at the United Nations, and being responsible for preventing a discussion on the annexation of Tibet. Between 1954 and 1959 tension grew slowly regarding the two main disputed areas, Aksai Chin in

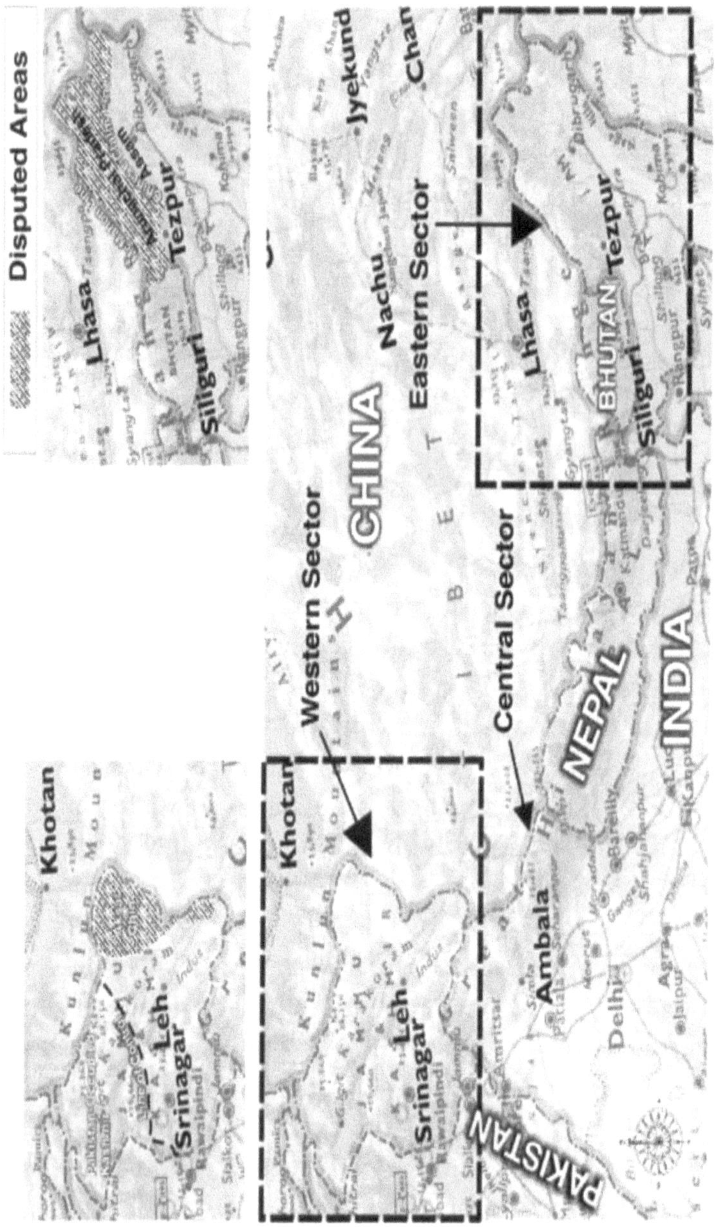

Map: Sino-Indian Border Dispute.

International borders approximate
Line of Actual Contral approximate
Chinese Claim Line approximate

Ladakh in the west, and large parts of Kameng sub-division of what was then known as NEFA (North-East Frontier Agency) and is now the state of Arunachal Pradesh. The main dispute was about Aksai Chin, which was of particular strategic interest to China, since it provided a link between western Tibet and eastern, or Chinese, Turkestan, known to the Chinese as 'Xinjiang' (Sinkiang in the older English spelling).[11]

In Tibet simultaneously the Chinese government had begun to have increasing difficulties with the monastic Tibetan Government of the Dalai Lama and the Tibetan people. India, which has had a long cultural relationship with neighbouring Tibet, (in marked contrast to the non-existent social contact with 'mainland' or Han China), and whose people have a respect for Buddhist monks, was seen as a supporter of the Dalai Lama while at the same time being a 'neo-colonial' Western-leaning Government, thus doubly annoying the Chinese communist government. After an uprising of the people in Lhasa, the Dalai Lama fled to India, and was accorded a warm welcome by the Indian people and the Government, and was allowed to stay as an exile in India.

The Chinese strategic position on the now-disputed and un-demarcated border was essentially that in the west they needed possession of Aksai Chin to push their connecting highway to Sinkiang through. Therefore they simultaneously made the road and claimed ownership. Thus most of the emphasis in whatever diplomatic exchanges took place between India and China in the pre-October 1962 period was on Aksai Chin. In the east they were prepared to negotiate, but India was not. The Chinese had a different interpretation of the 'traditional' border between Tibet and India. The Chinese claim line in Kameng, for example, was about 150 km to the south near Bomdila, and close to the plains of Assam, but India was sticking to its position that the McMahon Line was the boundary, even though the Chinese did

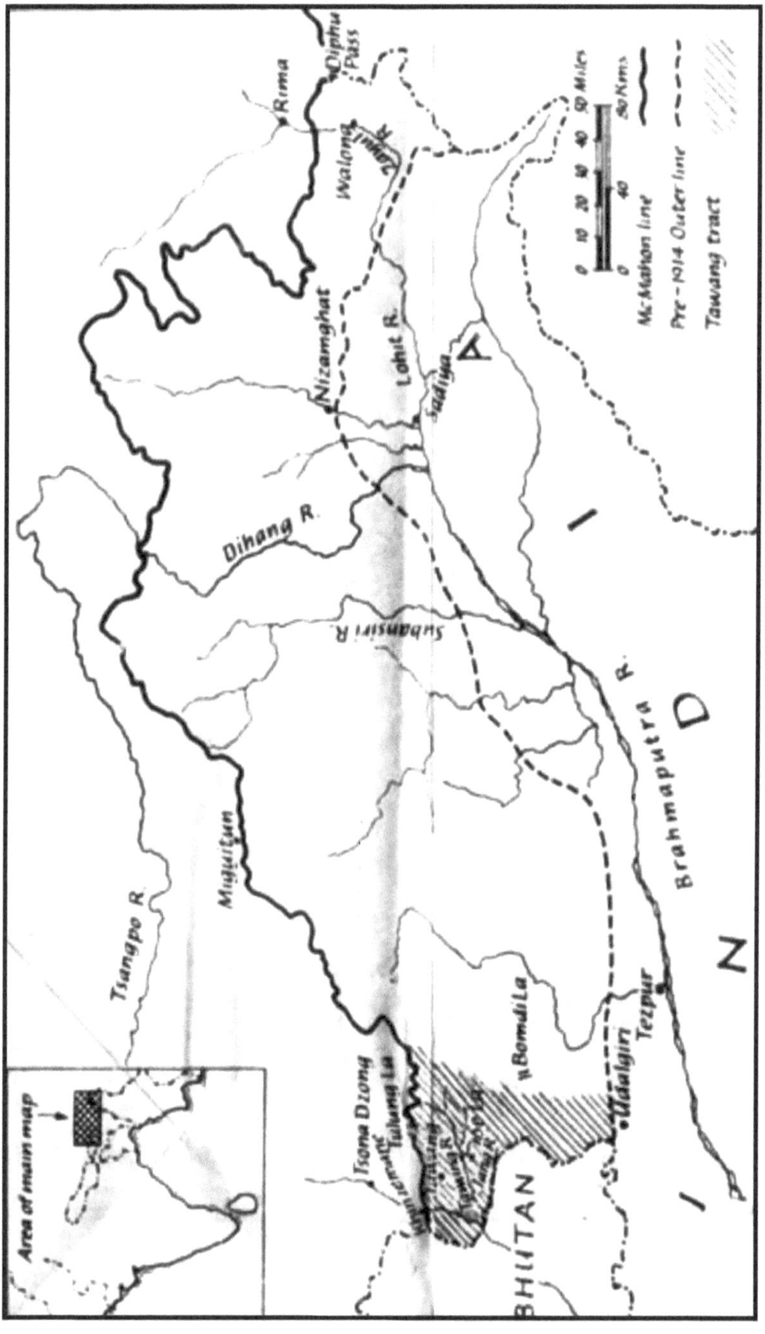

Arunchal Pradesh including the Tawang Tract.

not accept its 'legality.' India took the position that the general alignment of the McMahon Line was also the 'traditional' boundary, which had become the Sino-Indian border, though not yet a mutually-accepted and demarcated border. In that early period, the Chinese even gave feelers that they would be willing to consider an exchange deal involving a trade-off between Aksai Chin, which was of no strategic significance for India, and the Chumbi Valley, lying immediately north of Sikkim. This valley is of significance for India, as it is the area of Tibet which is nearest to the north Indian plains, with at its southern tip the two passes of Jelep La and Nathu La, leading to Kalimpong and Gangtok respectively.

A large part of the perceptual problem was that the Indian Prime Minister himself did not fully accept Chinese over-lordship of Tibet, in spite of having supported it publicly with the conclusion of the 1954 'Panch Sheel' treaty with China.[12] He was thus unable to de-link the Tibet issue from that of the border. The related problem arose from the fact that many of India's boundary areas with Tibet (as also those of Nepal with Tibet) on the southern side of the Himalayan Mountains, are peopled by Indo-Tibetan Buddhist cultures, or even purely Tibetan-type cultures, with religious allegiance to the Dalai Lama in Lhasa. Tawang in Arunachal Pradesh, for example, is the birth-place of the Sixth Dalai Lama[13] and had even been under the Tibetan religious administration at various points in time. The Buddhist 'Monpa'[14] people of the Kameng area inhabit the cool heights even fairly close to the plains of Assam, for example. Accepting a Chinese claim line so close to the plains would make it difficult to militarily defend Assam, as the British Government of India had appreciated, thus leading to the creation of the McMahon Line itself. The Indian government stuck to its belief in the validity of this line as the correct India-Tibet border, and to its own interpretation of the McMahon Line and its associated 'highest crest-lines principle' regarding the alignment of the main watershed of the Himalayan mountain range.

NOTES

1. Francis Watson, *The Frontiers of China: A Historical Guide,* 1966, p. 18.
2. M. van Praag, *The Status of Tibet: History, Rights and Prospects in International Law,* (Boulder: Westview Press, 1987); M. Goldstein, *The Snow Lion and the Dragon: China Tibet and the Dalai Lama* (Berkeley: University of California Press, 1997).
3. Tuker, Lt. Gen. Sir Francis, *While Memory Serves,* London, Cassell, 1950, p. 646.
4. *Ibid.,* pp. 641-642.
5. Kuomintang, or Guo-Min-Dang.
6. Neville Maxwell, *India's China War,* 1970, p. 71 n, citing A.B. Shah, India's Defence and Foreign Policies, 1966, p. 87.
7. B.N. Mullik, *My Years with Nehru,* 1971, p. 80. Did this imply that the Foreign Secretary had favoured this option?
8. Government of India, Ministry of Defence, *History of the Conflict with China, 1962,* 1992, p.36, and Thomas Laird, *Into Tibet,* 2002, p. 108.
9. This included the stationing of a limited number of Indian troops in Tibet, which were at Gyantse and Yatung along the route between Lhasa and India across Jelep La. The last detachments were one of 2nd Jats at Gyantse, and 'Y' Company, 1st Battalion, the Maratha Light Infantry at Yatung. The Gyantse escort consisted of 3 officers and 70 JCO's, NCO's, OR and NC'sE, including staff of the Corps of Signals, Army Service Corps, Army Medical Corps and Army Ordnance Corps. Most personnel were washed away in the great flood of 16th August 1954, including the escort's commander, Major Nagal, then Commanding Officer-designate of 2nd Jats. 'Y' company 1st Marathas was commanded by Capt. Narayan ('Nana') Pandurang Patil Thorat. The last Indian Trade Agent at Yatung in 1955 was Maj. Chibbar. The last Indian Political Officer at Yatung was Mr. Johri who was there till 1956.
10. Government of India, *History of the Conflcit with China, 1962,* 1992, p. 40.
11. Meaning *'New Dominion'* or *'New Frontier,'* having been thus renamed when it was conquered by China for the second time in 1750-51. The first time had been in the 2nd Century BC, when the famous Chinese general Pan Chao (Ban Chao), China's most-successful expeditionary general ever,

conquered, occupied, and held the area, including the repelling of two invasions by the Indo-Aryan Yueh-chi people also known as the Kushan. The second Kushan expedition was led by the Kushan emperor Kanishka himself, whose capital was at Purushapura, now Peshawar in Pakistan. The Chinese held this Buddhist area till AD 220, when the Han dynasty collapsed. The second Chinese foray into the region was in the 7th Century under the Tang Dynasty, but they were defeated and repelled by the Muslim Arabs who had invaded Central Asia after over-running Iran. The Arabs defeated the Chinese at the battle of Talas, in present-day Kirghizstan, in AD 751. However, the website of the Chinese Government and Chinese history books say that it has been a part of China since 60 BC. This is similar to the official Chinese claim that 'Tibet has always been a part of China' or that 'Tibet has been a part of China for hundreds of years.'

12. Unfortunately for India this agreement confirmed India's acceptance of China's overlordship of Tibet, at a time when much of the world had not accepted this. The agreement gave Nehru some added stature in the Afro-Asian non-aligned world, but brought India no concrete guarantees on the border issue with China.
13. A Monpa by race, and the builder of the Potala Palace in Lhasa.
14. All the various Tibetan-type Buddhist peoples on the southern side of the Himalayan watershed in India and Nepal are broadly described as 'Monpa' in Tibetan, meaning the 'ravine-dwellers,' while the entire region of Arunachal Pradesh is known as 'Mon' to the Tibetans.

3

Immediate Background to the 1962 War

India's 1962 war with China was fatally flawed both in conception and in execution. It was also totally unnecessary and avoidable. Once India embarked on what became an inevitable collision course with China, the lack of a seriously thought-out system for the higher direction of war, hampered the manner and means of preparing for it. A sycophancy-emasculated higher command system then led to amazingly dangerous decisions at the military-strategic and operational levels. The selection for pliability, as opposed to appointment on the grounds of military professional competency, also proved disastrous in respect of staffing at the Army Headquarters levels, when it appointed Lt. Gen. B.M. Kaul as Chief of the General Staff (CGS). Finally, at the business end when the right operational-level and tactical decisions were required to be taken at the right time, then and there, the nation was badly let down and thereby totally humiliated by the poor decision-making and battlefield command of the Corps Commander. He was no other than the *'Army Chief-in-waiting,'* the Prime Minister's military blue-eyed boy, the same Lt. Gen. B.M. Kaul, temporarily given command at Corps level, while simultaneously holding the appointment of Chief of the General Staff (CGS) at Army Headquarters. Below him, to compound the catastrophe, the critically affected Divisional Commander, a sudden and unwise appointment, and one of his Brigade Commanders, also a sudden appointee, let down their country, their Army, and the officers and men they were supposed to be commanding, by their conduct in the crisis. It is not surprising that India cannot forget the drubbing it received at the hands of China's methodically directed and professionally led PLA.

It was India's 'Forward Policy' that catalysed official Chinese thinking the most, described by them as 'nibbling policy' (*can shi zheng ce,* i.e., policy of nibbling at another country's territory) on the analogy of silkworms eating mulberry leaves till they are gradually consumed. This led to what has been described as the *'false war of nibbling and anti-nibbling'* from April 1961 to September 1962. In July 1962, China's Chairman Mao had himself laid down the policy for the PLA to follow in this period of tactical moves and counter-moves to counter India's 'nibbling policy.' He had ordered that: 'Never make a concession, but try your best to avert bleeding; form a jagged interlocking pattern to secure the border; and prepare for long-term armed co-existence.' The PLA headquarters' General Staff Department explained the guiding principles in greater detail, and ordered the troops to implement the rules of engagement strictly:

- If Indian troops do not open fire, Chinese frontier guards should not open fire.
- If Indian troops press on towards a Chinese sentry post from one direction, Chinese frontier guards should press on towards the Indian stronghold from another direction.
- If Indian troops encircle Chinese frontier guards, another Chinese force should encircle the Indian troops.
- If Indian troops cut off a retreat route for Chinese forces, Chinese frontier guards should cut off the Indian troops' retreat.

- Chinese forces should keep a distance away from Indian troops, leaving them some leeway, and withdraw if Indian forces permit withdrawal.[1]

Historical studies in China as recently as the 1990s still support the position that India was planning aggression in Tibet. As per all Chinese scholars, the root cause of the conflict was what they believe was India's attempt to undermine Chinese rule and seize Tibet, to turn it into a protectorate or colony of India, in order to create a buffer zone.

China's assumptions about Indian attitudes towards Tibet, whilst perhaps understandable from the Chinese perspective, are believed by most neutral observers to be fundamentally incorrect and a major contributory factor to the conflict. During the buildup to the war, the Indian government largely maintained a policy of non-violent reaction and sought Indo-Chinese friendship, even to the point of failing to prepare for military action when its military leaders were recommending such precautions.[2]

According to John Garver, a political analyst at Harvard University, USA, two of the major factors leading up to China's eventual conflicts with Indian troops were India's stance on the disputed borders and perceived Indian subversion in Tibet. There was 'a perceived need to punish and end perceived Indian efforts to undermine Chinese control of Tibet, Indian efforts which were perceived as having the objective of restoring the pre-1949 status quo ante of Tibet.' The other was 'a perceived need to punish and end perceived Indian aggression against Chinese territory along the border.' Garver argues that though the first perception was incorrect based on the state of the Indian military and polity in the 1960s, it was, nevertheless, a major reason for China's going to war. However, he argues the Chinese perception of aggression to be 'substantially accurate,' though based on China's and India's differing perceptions of their rightful boundary.[3]

Garver also observes that: ' A common tendency of humans is to attribute others behaviour to interior motivations while attributing their own behaviour to situational factors.' This human tendency can also be the reason for Gregory Clark, an impartial observer, to theorize (1967) that the Sino-Indian War of 1962 was the result of 'mutual misunderstanding.' Clark felt that 'there is good reason to believe that the hostility shown by each side towards the other was reactive rather than active: that each side was reacting to the believed hostility of the other.' Quoting Clark's detailed and erudite arguments selectively:

> The hardening of the Chinese attitude towards India in 1959 was clearly related to Tibetan developments in that year ...
>
> ... it does not seem unreasonable to conclude that the Communist Chinese sincerely believed they had a right to Tibet and that their position in the area was threatened from the direction of India. In which case they would have interpreted Indian behaviour in 1959 as an indication of hostility to which they felt compelled, or entitled, to react.
>
> By 1962, the Chinese were confronted not only by Indian agitation over Tibet, but also by two further aspects of Indian behaviour which would even more easily have been misunderstood. They were: (i) the Indian military build-up along the Sino/Indian border in 1961-2 and (ii) rigid Indian insistence that, as a precondition to border negotiations, the Chinese must first evacuate the whole of the Aksai Chin.
>
> It seems highly likely that the Chinese would be convinced of the reasonableness of their position and the unreasonableness of the Indian demand for a unilateral Chinese withdrawal from the Aksai Chin.

> Even before 1959 Nehru was being strongly criticised for his apparent refusal to take a hard line with the Chinese over Tibet and the disputed border. Thus it is possible to conclude that Indian behaviour throughout 1961-62 was influenced by a sense of wounded nationalism and wounded pride, which in turn were a reaction to the events of 1950. If, in fact, we can assume that Indian behaviour was emotionally based, we have a ready explanation of its seemingly unnecessary rigidity.
>
> If we accept that both sides appear to have been reacting defensively—the Chinese out of undue sensitivity over Tibet and fear of 'imperialist' designs against their territory, the Indians out of a sense of wounded pride and nationalism—then it would seem that neither side has taken the initiative to promote hostility: that both sides would have preferred good relations. That both sides would in fact have preferred good relations seems clear from the record of Sino/Indian relations up until 1959.

One Chinese historian of the war, Xu Yan, believes the decisive factor in the deterioration of Sino-Indian relations was Nehru's policy of 'protecting the Tibetan splittists' after the Lhasa rebellion of March 1959. That all Chinese historians point to India's 'desire to seize Tibet' is not surprising. As Garver notes, 'this is probably due to the fact that published scholarship in China is still expected to explain and justify, not criticize, the decisions of the Chinese Communist Party, at least on such sensitive matters as war and peace.'[4]

The official PLA history of the 1962 war stresses that the aim of the 1962 war was 'quickly achieving peaceful, stable borders in the west' (*ba xibu bianjiang dichu xunsu wending xialai*). This was, according to the PLA historian, the 'basic direction,' of China's border policy; to be achieved by inflicting a painful defeat on India, thus demonstrating the futility and danger of agression against borders defended by the PLA. This would force India to abandon the Forward Policy. China believed that a sharp military defeat would 'compel India to sit down at the negotiating table and solve the Sino-Indian border problem.' This too would 'achieve peaceful stability along the western borders.'[5]

Garver arrives at the conclusion that both China and India bear the onus for the 1962 war, China for misconstruing India's Tibet policies, and India for pursuing a confrontational policy on the border.[6] He also comes to the conclusion that India was unjustly accused by China for all the difficulties that Chinese rule encountered, and in fact created, from about 1959.[7]

THE FORWARD POLICY AND OPERATION ONKAR

After China's occupation of Tibet in 1950, two of India's policy responses became turning points in Sino-Indian relations. Till then, the Indian policy of appeasement towards China ensured friendly relations, though on what in retrospect can be seen to be China's own terms, or at least terms much more favourable to China. The first was the granting of asylum to the Dalai Lama in March 1959, which infuriated the Chinese leadership. The second eventually became even more controversial: the so-called 'Forward Policy' of establishing small, non-tactical military posts in order 'to show the flag' along the Indian interpretation of the international border in Ladakh, and of the McMahon Line in Arunachal Pradesh (then NEFA). The implementation of this policy in 1961-62 actually became the *'causus belli'* for the Chinese decision to actually go to war with India. This new policy was personally directed by the Prime Minister, at a high-level review meeting held on November 2, 1961. Though not officially called a 'Forward Policy' when initially directed, it had soon become known by this term.

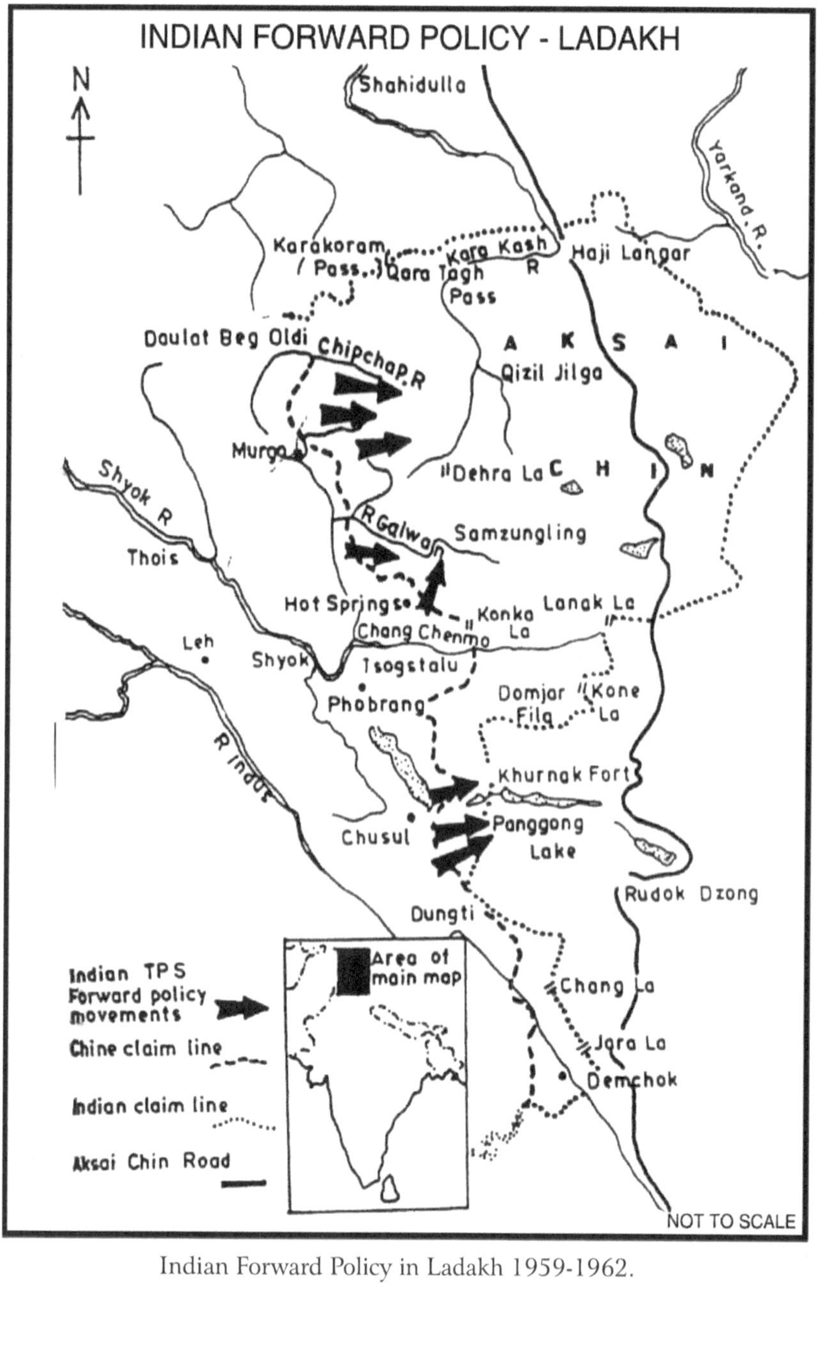

Indian Forward Policy in Ladakh 1959-1962.

The originator of this policy is unclear from the voluminous writings on the subject and on the subsequent war of 1962, with even those in the policy-making loop disclaiming responsibility in their books. However, the formal basis is undoubtedly the set of basic recommendations arrived at by the high-level and properly-constituted Committee under the chairmanship of the Deputy Defence Minister, Maj. Gen. Himmatsinghji. But circumstantially it would appear that the main proponent for the 1959-1962 forward 'push' was the head of the Intelligence Bureau, B.N. Mullik, supported by the politically-ambitious general, B.M. Kaul, whose meteoric rise was greatly due to his personal proximity to the Prime Minister.

In September 1959 China had laid formal claim to 80,000 sq. kms of territory which India believed to be hers, in Ladakh in the west and in Arunachal Pradesh in the east. In NEFA in the east, the Chinese, even though they did not accept the McMahon Line, had kept their border posts on their own side of their own interpretation of the McMahon Line. The Indian interpretation of the line, however, differed from that of the Chinese in some areas, notably in the Kameng area. There, at the Thag La ridgeline, the Indian interpretation was further 'forward' and to the north of the Chinese interpretation of it.

Beginning from end-1951, the number of Indian border check-posts were being increased. On August 27, 1959, the Army was ordered to take-over the security of the NEFA-Tibet border, and on October 24, 1959, the Army's Western Command was made responsible for the Ladakh-Tibet border.[8] In 1959, the PLA opposite the Ladakh sector was estimated at no more than one regiment (Indian brigade equivalent), so Western command projected a requirement of one brigade of five battalions in Ladakh. The downstream effects were that the Army was pushed to establish posts in the area between the two differing interpretations of either the international border in Ladakh or the McMahon Line in NEFA. This led to small confrontations with Chinese troops in several of such areas. The results of the first two clashes, both in 1959, at Longju in NEFA and at Kongka La[9] in Ladakh, should have told India that the Chinese were dead serious about what they were saying and doing, but apparently it did not.

Another of India's policy responses to the increasing possibility of military problems arising with China was to send the 4 Infantry Division, the Army HQ Reserve Division normally based concentrated at Ambala,[10] to take over the responsibility for Sikkim and NEFA. With its principal fighting component, its three integral infantry brigades, 5 Infantry Brigade, 7 Infantry Brigade, and 11 Infantry Brigade, each of three infantry battalions, it was dispatched eastwards to the Brahmaputra River valley in Assam in November 1959. 11 Brigade was sent to Sikkim, 7 Brigade was made responsible for the Kameng Frontier Division of NEFA, 5 Brigade was assigned the responsibility for the rest of NEFA.[11] This was despite the absence of any logistical set-up for deploying the division in NEFA.[12] The entire NEFA was at the time a roadless wilderness. 4 Division established its HQ at Tezpur. It was to function under 33 Corps, whose HQ was at Shillong, and which was responsible for the entire North-Eastern region: Sikkim, NEFA, the India-Burma border, the India-East Pakistan (now Bangladesh) border, and Nagaland.

'Operation ONKAR' (Op ONKAR), the name given to the plan of establishing forward posts, was originally conceived by the Ministry of External Affairs (MEA) in Delhi as a means of establishing the Indian claim to the McMahon Line and the Indian interpretation of the international Ladakh-Tibet and Ladakh-Sinkiang border. NEFA was actually administered by the MEA through the officers of the erstwhile Indian Frontier Administrative Service (IFAS) and the units of the Assam Rifles[13] which were deployed in NEFA. The Op ONKAR deployments were in accordance with the recommendations of the Himmatsinghji Committee, which has already been mentioned. In NEFA, as part of Op ONKAR, Assam Rifles posts were to be established from Khinzemane in the Tawang sector in the west, eastwards to the India-Tibet-Burma tri-junction. Theoretically, in the north-east (or the eastern sector of the Sino-Indian frontier) the Indian Army's role in Op ONKAR was to assist the Assam Rifles in setting up these forward posts. In Ladakh, it became operational when the Army was inducted into Ladakh in April 1960, with initially just a brigade HQ and two battalions of local militia, later joined by a regular infantry battalion in April 1961. 114 Infantry Brigade was then tasked as under:

- 14 J&K Militia to look after the area north of the Galwan River.
- 1/8 G.R. to hold the area between the Galwan river and Chushul.
- 7 J&K Militia to hold the area south of Chushul down to the tri-junction of the international border with two Indian states, i.e., the Tibet-J&K (Ladakh)-Himachal Pradesh tri-junction.

These posts were not strong defensible military positions as such, but were meant to show Indian 'possession,' in the belief that China was expanding its control in Tibet by militarily occupying 'vacant space,' and would stop where it saw existing 'possession.' Only in 1961 did India consider it necessary to take 'limited defensive measures to contain Chinese incursions into Indian territory.'[14] This led to numerous small clashes with

Chinese troops, Indian policemen getting taken prisoner in Ladakh, and acts of military intimidation at Khinzemane[15] and Longju in NEFA, during the period 1959-62, and set the stage for the 1962 war.

Opposite Ladakh, the Chinese reinforced their troops, and after a war-game at HQ Western Command ('Exercise SHEEL'), the command required one full division to defend Ladakh. By August 1962, however, due to logistic difficulties only four battalions could be positioned in Ladakh.

The politically-motivated 'forward' military deployment in Arunachal Pradesh (Operation ONKAR) was militarily unsound. The appropriate deployment had already been spelt out after a war-game at HQ Eastern Command ('Exercise LAL QILA') conducted in 1960 to study the Chinese threat) in the thorough formal military appreciation prepared by Lt. Gen. S.P.P. Thorat, GOC-in-C Eastern Command. Gen. Thorat had earlier been corps commander of 33 Corps, and was familiar with the ground. Till October 4, 1962, 33 Corps was the senior headquarters directly responsible for the area, with its HQ at Shillong.[16] The GOC 33 Corps in 1962, Lt. Gen. K. Umrao Singh, was completely against Op ONKAR, and had indicated that a forward deployment would require a proper administrative build-up, and thus time.

In Ladakh in particular, as a reaction to the forward deployment of an increasing number of Indian checkposts, at first the PLA simply withdrew, but eventually Chinese forces began to counter-encircle the Indian positions. This led to a tit-for-tat Indian reaction, with both forces attempting to outmanoeuver each other. However, despite the escalating nature of the dispute, the two forces withheld from engaging each other directly. Eventually, the Chinese leadership came to believe that their restraint on the issue was being perceived by

India as weakness, leading to continued provocations, and that a major counterblow was needed to stop perceived Indian aggression. At the highest level on the Indian side, there seemed to be no realization of how much this was being felt as a blow to the Chinese national pride, particularly since they had 'stood up' since 1949. Nor was there a realistic understanding of the Chinese determination to strike back if they felt they were being humiliated.

Maj. Gen. Ashok Kalyan Verma explains the significance of the differing interpretation:

> As a part of the forward policy adopted during 1961-62, the Eastern Command had asked the controlling Headquarters, 33 Corps (based at Shillong), to set up a Assam Rifles post under 7 Brigade's operational control[17] at the trijunction of India, Bhutan and Tibet. However, the Assam Rifles party that went to establish it found the site unsuitable owing to its altitude and inaccessibility and selected Che Dong instead. Somehow the post incorrectly got the name 'Dhola Post' (the Dhola feature was well South of this area). The place selected lay on the lower slope of the Tsangdhar feature, which runs Eastwards from the jumbled knot of mountains that form the trijunction. The post faced Thag La ridge in the North. Between Thag La and Tsangdhar is a mountain stream, the Namka Chu, which flows from West to East ('Chu' means river as 'La' means pass).[18]

Thag La ridge and the Namka Chu were to become the stage for the first major clash of arms between China and India.

The position of the McMahon Line in the Khinzemane-Namka Chu/Thag La area is somewhat vague, marked on the map as a straight line running from Point MM 7914 westwards to the India-Bhutan-Tibet tri-junction, ignoring the physical features on the ground. This therefore leaves the position of the Thagla Ridge somewhat ambiguous, as it undoubtedly forms the highest crest-line in the area, going by the theoretical principle of the highest crest-lines, as implied by the so-called 'watershed principle' (in reality a misnomer) of the McMahon Line. In fact, the maps that had been issued to the Army at the time showed the Thagla Ridge and the Namka Chu as lying to the north of the McMahon Line, i.e., in Tibet, and therefore not Indian territory. This had actually been pointed out in writing on July 20, 1962 by HQ 4 Infantry Division to all three of its superior headquarters, namely, HQ 33 Corps, HQ Eastern Command, and Army HQ. China, not surprisingly, believed the Thag La ridge and the Namka Chu to be part of its own territory.

Jung Chang writes that China began preparing for war in May or June 1962.[19] In May 1962 an Assam Rifles column under Capt. Mahabir Prasad of 1st Sikhs was sent westwards across the Nyamjang Chu and over the Hathung La-Karpola Ridge, to establish a post on the India-Bhutan-Tibet (China) tri-junction. The post was set up on June 4, 1962, as close as possible to the tri-junction, at a summer grazing ground named Tse Dong (Che Dong), on the south bank of the Namka Chu. The Namka Chu is a 24 km long mountain rivulet flowing eastwards from the India-Bhutan-Tibet tri-junction area, running immediately south of the Thagla Ridge to join the Nyamjang Chu (river) near Khinzemane. The post later came to be referred to as the Dhola Post. Chinese histories of the 1962 Sino-Indian border war cite this incident as the start of the war, which they show as beginning in June 1962.

The Tezpur-Bomdila-Se La-Tawang road axis was at the time being hastily prepared to permit the maintenance of a forward posture by the Assam Rifles, backed up by the Army's 4 Infantry

Division. The pressure to speed up the induction was being applied by Army Headquarters, through the intermediary formation headquarters, HQ Eastern Command, then located at Lucknow. The time-frame for the completion of this forward posture, ordered to have been completed by end-July 1962, was considered totally unrealistic by Lt.Gen. Umrao Singh, the 33 Corps Commander. He objected strongly to moving troops to what he considered to be too far forward, without adequate preparations and build-up. Lt.Gen. Umrao Singh, did not believe in the unrealistic assessment of Army Headquarters that the Chinese would not react, was therefore seen by his immediate superior, Lt. Gen. L.P. ('Bogey') Sen, GOC-in-C Eastern Command,[20] at his headquarters in Lucknow, and at Army Headquarters in Delhi, as being 'sluggish' and 'timid.'

On August 14, 1962, the Director Military Operations (DMO) at Army HQ, Brig. D.K. ('Monty') Palit, visited the 4 Infantry Division's HQ at Tezpur. The progress of Op ONKAR and the issues regarding the McMahon Line in the Namka Chu-Thagla Ridge area were discussed. Army HQ' aim was to see how the forward deployments desired by the Prime Minister could be speeded up. Till fairly recent himself the Commander of 7 Infantry Brigade, during its induction period into the Kameng Division and the Tawang sector, Monty Palit was the only person in the General Staff (Operations) branch of Army HQ who had any idea of the terrain, and of the practical difficulties involved in implementing Op ONKAR.

Writes Brig. Dalvi: 'In August 1962, 4 Division issued orders for the implementation of a limited policy of re-siting of regular troops locations, and the establishment of additional company localities forward of Towang. The aim was to locate them nearer the McMahon Line to be more readily at hand to assist Assam Rifles posts. There was no plan to counter a full-scale invasion.'[21]

He further comments: 'The Chinese, in 1962 had prepared both for war and for talks, if India appreciated the futility of fighting for her rights. India was prepared neither for fighting nor for talking.'[22]

COMMUNICATIONS AND LOGISTICS IN THE KAMENG SECTOR, NEFA

Logistics is the major constraint of military operations in the Himalayan mountains. It was a major determinant of the armed Sino-Indian conflict in the Kameng sector.

Maj. Gen. Ashok Kalyan Verma comments on the admistrative and morale aspect of the induction of 7 Infantry Brigade to the Tawang Sector:[23]

> In the ordering of the induction of 7 Brigade into the area, no thought was given to the problems of movement in the mountains, or to the logistic support of the troops being inducted. The morale of the troops being diverted from their eagerly awaited peace tenure was given no note at all.

For the readers, who are unlikely to have an idea of the difficulties of the terrain and the poor communications in October 1962, it needs to be borne in mind that up to 1960 only a jeepable track existed up to Bomdila, ahead of which all movement was on foot. For logistics build-up, the road-track situation in September-October 1962 in Kameng Frontier Division of NEFA, from Tezpur in the Assam Valley to the Namka Chu valley (about 415 km), was:

- Tezpur (in the plains)–Bomdila-Dirang Dzong: 167 km.
  All-weather 3-ton road up to Bomdila, fair-weather 3-ton road thereafter. (Basically, no mechanical transport were able to

carry troops forward of Bomdila, and the troops had to march thereafter).

- Dirang Dzong–Se La-Jang: 106 km; Fair-weather 1-ton road.
- Jang –Tawang: 39 km; Fair-weather jeep track, these vehicles being only available to senior commanders.
- Tawang – Lum La: 16 km; Fit for Army mules (GS mules) and for local hill ponies.
- Forward of Lum La to Lumpu (the administrative base selected for the forward deployment of 7 Infantry Brigade along the Namka Chu): 84 km; Fit for local ponies only.
- Lumpu to the Namka Chu valley: 15-35 km; Fit only for porters.

All movements of units were on 'man-pack' or 'mule-pack' basis. The troops themselves, as well as porters, engaged for the purpose, had to carry all the stores, rations, etc, that were required to be moved forward before so that troops could live and fight from prepared defences.

Porters could deliver only limited amounts of stores or rations where the delivery points were far. For example, local porters could deliver a 'useful' load of 15-20 kg at the end of a 3-day march, i.e., excluding their own food and blankets which they also needed to carry for the journey. Road labour engaged by the Border Roads Organisation, when employed as porters, could deliver only 5-8 kg each at the end of 3 days.

Infantry movement over the steep mountain terrain was perforce slow, a body of troops could at best cover 16 to 20 km a day along the narrow foot-tracks. For personnel not carrying loads, the 7 Brigade administrative base at Lumpu was a hard four days' march from Tawang. Many of the troops involved in the Namka Chu battle had actually marched all the way up from Foothills, at the edge of the Assam valley, 370 km away.

With the winter rapidly approaching and in the already severe cold, maintaining 7 Infantry Brigade in the Namka Chu area was not possible for more than a few days. Whether the Chinese remained comfortably dug-in on the Thagla Ridge or withdrew, and even if they had not attacked, 7 Infantry Brigade would have had to be withdrawn from the Namka Chu—Dhola area within a few days for logistical reasons alone. The troops had less than 3 days' rations available, and only 50 rounds of ammunition for each man's personal weapon.

Maj. Gen. Verma amplifies on the administrative and logistical problems:

> On 9 September 1962, Defence Minister Krishna Menon ordered the eviction of the Chinese facing the Assam Rifles post at Che Dong (Dhola). In spite of almost three full years of having been responsible for defences of NEFA, 4 Division was quite incapable of undertaking any serious operations. By September 1962 the one-ton road was just built up to Tawang.... The total distance from the foothills to Tawang was only 291 kilometres, but it took several days days to cover. Considering the necessity for acclimatisation of troops inducted from the plains, quick buildup of reinforcement of the sector was impracticable. Also, till then no staging facilities had been set up on the route and there were no replenishment dumps. . . Beyond Tawang, ponies, mules and porters were the only mode of transport. These too were usually difficult to get in large numbers.[24]

Xu Yan, a prominent Chinese military historian and professor at the PLA's National Defense University, gives an account of the Chinese leadership's decision to go to war.[25] By late September 1962, the Chinese leadership had begun to reconsider their policy of "armed coexistence," which had failed to address their concerns with the forward policy and Tibet, and consider a large, decisive strike. Mao's own weakening position within the Chinese leadership was also a significant factor in the decision to go to war, as he wanted to re-assert himself, after he had been openly criticised in January 1962, by Chinese President Liu Shaoqi who had denounced his Great Leap Forward policy before a large party conference.[26]

NOTES

1. Chen Feng and Larry M. Wortzel, 'PLA Operational Principles and Limited War,' in Mark A. Ryan, David Michael Finkelstein, Michael A. McDevitt (Eds.), *Chinese Warfighting: The PLA Experience since 1949,* pp. 180-181 (New York, M.E. Sharpe, 2003.
2. From Wikipedia, citing James Barnard Calvin, *The China-India Border War;* April 1984, on the Internet at http://en.wikipedia.org/wiki/Sino-Indian_War, accessed on June 21, 2008.
3. From Wikipedia, *ibid,* citing John W. Garver, *'China's Decision for War with India in 1962,'* accessed on June 21, 2008.
4. Garver, *ibid.,* p. 9.
5. Garver, *ibid.,* p. 63.
6. Garver, *ibid.,* p. 3.
7. Garver, *ibid.,* p. 5.
8. Ministry of Defence, *History, op. cit.,* p. 39.
9. As per the Chinese, this pass is one point on the 'traditional' boundary.
10. Once hostilities began in October 1962, the remaining Indian formations in the Punjab facing Pakistan, i.e., 5 Infantry Division, 27 Infantry Division, and the Western Command Reserve, 17 Infantry Division which was now at Ambala, had to be hurriedly pulled out and sent to the east, leaving the Punjab totally defenceless and exposed to a potential Pakistani attack for some time, till overall re-adjustments could be made. (D.K. Palit, *War in High Himalaya, 1991,* pp. 255, 295).
11. Maj. K.C. Praval, *Indian Army since Independence,* 1987, p. 171.
12. Ministry of Defence, *History,* p. 66.
13. The para-military Assam Rifles units were officered by Indian Army officers on deputation to this force.
14. Government of India Publication, *Chinese Aggression in War and Peace,* 1962.

15. 'Kejielang' or 'Kechilang' in Chinese accounts.
16. Till the sudden creation of a '4 Corps,' without any additional fighting troops or administrative resources, given to Lt. Gen. B.M. Kaul to command.
17. Though it was only later, on or about 12th September, that the 5th Assam Rifles in this sector were formally placed under the Army.
18. Ashok Kalyan Verma, *Rivers of Silence,* 1998, p.30.
19. John Garver, *op. cit.*
20. The appointment is generally referred to as the 'Army Commander, Eastern Command'.
21. J.P. Dalvi, *Himalayan Blunder,* 1969, p. 134.
22. *Ibid.,* p. 138.
23. Verma, *op. cit.,* p. 33.
24. *Ibid.,* p. 31.
25. Xu Yan, *History of the Sino-Indian Border Self-Defensive War,* 1993.
26. John Garver, *op. cit.*

4

The Key Actor and the Stage

Lt. Gen. B.M. Kaul played such an important role in the events of 1962 that it is necessary to describe him in some detail, in order to understand his importance. D.R. Mankekar explains the significance of Lt. Gen. Kaul in the period preceding the outbreak of war with the Chinese:

> Mao's rude intervention in India's destinies in the autumn of 1962 shot down a meteoric career.
>
> Had it not been for that signal event, Lt. Gen. B.M. ('Bijji') Kaul would have gone very far—possibly, farther even than the the post of the Chief of Army Staff, and carved a niche for himself in the country's history as a great soldier-politician, if not a soldier-statesman.... Until that sudden jerk and fall in October 1962, Kaul's progress up the ladder of success was dazzling, jet-propelled, almost dizzy. There was no knowing, but for Mao, where that tide in the affairs of

> Kaul would have swept him on to ... he had the ambition and as well as other essential qualifications—an extra-ordinary drive and energy, intense patriotism, a bumptious self-assurance, a vainglorious egoism and political sense, besides right contacts in the country's public life and a growing following among the younger officers in the Army.[1]

Kaul was unique among the senior officers of his time, and is well-described by Mankekar:

> Lt. Gen. 'Bijji' Kaul was a general among politicians, and a politician among generals. That was his unique advantage—and, ultimately, that also proved his undoing, for while the generals were jealous and disdainful of his extra-curricular activities in the Capital's political lobbies, the politicians distrusted an ambitious military leader hobnobbing with the mighty. As long as he was at the top, everything went fine. His circle of admirers swelled, and so did his following within the Army ranks.
>
> Brought up in the British Army tradition of avoiding politics like the plague, senior armed forces officer felt jarred and embarrassed by Kaul's political manouevres. And later, when he began to wield undue influence in the affairs of the Army H.Q. over the heads of his seniors, their embarrassment gave place to resentment. They vaguely felt that such conduct was a breach of the military code—and that, at any rate, put them at a disadvantage vis-à-vis Kaul.[2]

Mankekar describes some of his abilities and his personal status among his peers in the officer cadre:

> Kaul had the advantage of being perhaps the only one among the Indian Army senior officers who was well-versed in, and had an aptitude for, politics—nay, nursed political ambitions....

> That apart, as an organizer and executive, Kaul was brilliant, a 'go-getter' who could hack through a thick, tropical jungle of red tape and get things done....[3]

Lt. Gen. Kaul had already had some experience of the Chinese even before he became CGS and later also the Corps Commander facing the Chinese in NEFA. As GOC 4 Infantry Division, the Army's showcase division, he had given a demonstration of the division's firepower to a visiting Chinese delegation, headed by the Chief of the PLA. But his experience in Korea was much more extensive, as Mankekar states:

> When he went to Korea as Chief of Staff to Gen. K.S. Thimayya, Chairman of the United Nations Neutral Repatriation Commission, Kaul hit the headlines in a big way and became a controversial figure. The Indian contingent in Korea soon became divided into pro-Chinese and pro-American groups, and Kaul headed the former and Gen. Thimayya, said to be friendly with the Americans, headed the latter.
>
> It was apparent that Kaul got on famously with the Chinese, who invited him to tour their country as a State guest, and he went around China and was received warmly everywhere. He was also accused of reporting to the Prime Minister on Gen. Thimayya's allegedly pro-American activities, and on that account courted much unpopularity in Army circles. Indeed, had it not been for the intense personal interest taken in him by Nehru and Krishna Menon, the army hierarchy would not have allowed Kaul to go beyond the rank of Major-General.[4]

Kaul's good qualities did help the army in some ways, as Mankekar explains:

> It was against the wish of Gen. Thimayya, then COAS, and on the insistence of Krishna Menon, Defence Minister, that Kaul was promoted to Lieutenant-General, and then appointed QMG at the Army Headquarters. According to Lt. Gen. L.P. Sen, then CGS, Kaul was not selected by the Selection Board for the post of QMG. 'But Menon would not look beyond Kaul, and Thimayya was forced to accept him, but only after a very serious showdown.'
>
> As QMG, however, Kaul was an outstanding success and saw through a crash programme of building roads along the northern borders—though the programme was overtaken by the Chinese attack in 1962.[5]

The persona of Kaul was also entirely different from all the other generals of the Army. Mankekar amplifies:

> But, from the beginning, Kaul was different from them and took pains to underline that difference. Unlike his fellow-officers who were the prototypes of their British foreeunners and counterparts, Kaul did not drink or smoke, was not interested in gaiety and westernized social life and cocktail and dance parties. His flamboyant, melodramatic, frisky personality compelled attention.... He got on extremely well with the Press; he was good, friendly and confiding, and provided 'copy.'[6]
>
> Rommel believed that a successful leader of men should cultivate a legend about his personality. So did Montgomery. Kaul also fostered a legend around his dymanic energy, adventurous spirit, fearless courage and austere living. Being something of an exhibitionist, he quite often flaunted his influence with the Prime Minister and Defence Minister, in the faces of his brother officers, to the latter's extreme irritation.

That Kaul was a confidant of the Prime Minister who had since Independence entrusted him with important missions —Kaul was sent to Srinagar to supervise Sheikh Abdullah's arrest—placed him in a unique position both in the political and military circles. And in no time, many careerists and opportunists in both spheres flocked to him.

Kauls' other disqualification, in the eyes of his fellow-officers, was that he was a great 'bull-shitter' (in army parlance one who talked tall and bragged too much).[7]

Sukhwant Singh describes him from an Army officer's point of view:

> Kaul, though a King's Commissioned Indian Officer (KCIO), was unlike other KCIOs. He neither smoked nor drank, played no games, not even polo or golf, did not dance, was not seen in the capital's social haunts, and unlike his ilk, was openly and fiercely nationalistic in outlook.
>
> Due to his Army Service Corps and public relations background, he was not considered much of a soldier. But he had a burning personal ambition, to the extent that he saw himself as a man of destiny on the Indian horizon. By skilful manoeuvring of promotions and appointments he had managed to establish a considerable personal following of favour-seekers in the Army.[8]

Maj. Gen. Sukhwant Singh sums up the effect of the quadrangular Prime Minister Nehru-Defence Minister Krishna Menon-Army Chief Thimayya-Kaul relationship:

> Gen. Thimayya, affectionately known as 'Timmy,' was then Chief of Army Staff.... The troops loved him, and he inspired

> more confidence among the ranks than any other general of his time....
>
> Thimayya projected a dual threat from China and Pakistan. Menon[9] dismissed this as a fantasy....
>
> When Thimayya recommended certain higher command appointments, Menon vetoed them and brought in Lt. Gen. B.M. Kaul, another controversial figure, as Quarter-Master General. This is said to have been done to erode the Chief's influence in the Army. All this apparently had the full accord of Nehru....[10]

Thus Lt. Gen. B.M. Kaul was already a highly controversial figure in 1962. Lt. Gen. Kaul was a go-getter and a man of action, but he was unlike the other senior officers of the time.

Coming from an educated, middle-class Kashmiri Brahmin family, B.M. Kaul was commissioned in July 1933 into the infantry branch of the Indian Army from the Royal Military Academy at Sandhurst, in England. He joined what would thereafter have been his parent battalion, 5th Battalion, The Rajputana Rifles, at Razmak, Waziristan (NWFP).

After just three years in the infantry, he asked for and got himself transferred to the Army Service Corps (ASC) for financial reasons in 1936, as mess expenditures were far less there than in an infantry battalion, and it was possible to make some savings from the monthly salary. He claims to have made several attempts to return to his old battalion, or to the infantry as such, over a period of years, but was denied by Army Headquarters, which appears doubtful.

During the Second World War (1939-45) he was in various appointments of a non-professional nature for either infantry or for his own service, the ASC, being in charge of an entertainment troupe meant for raising the morale of troops. Had he wanted to return to the infantry during the war there had been ample opportunity to do so. He claims he was selected for command of an infantry battalion in 1946, but was sent instead as Secretary of the Committee to Sir Gopalaswamy Iyengar, Chairman of the Armed Forces Nationalisation Committee, and then sent to the USA as independent India's first Military Attache. He then was selected by the Prime Minister, Pandit Jawahar Lal Nehru, to be the Military Adviser to the Indian Delegation to the U.N. Security Council on the Kashmir Case.

He claims he was again selected to command a regular infantry battalion on his return from the USA in April 1948, when infantry officers were in short supply, since the bulk of the infantry's officers had been British, almost all of whom left in or soon after August 1947. He was instead given command over the irregular J&K Militia battalions, apparently at the request of the Kashmir Government. As a Brigadier he held the unimportant staff positions of Director of Organisation at Army HQ, and Director of the Territorial Army.

In a clear breach of the Army's selection criteria and professional norms, thanks to his personal influence with the Prime Minister, he was appointed General Officer Commanding (GOC) of 4 Infantry Division then located in Ambala, on promotion to Maj. General, an appointment tenable only by a suitable officer of the combat arms. Kaul's achievement in this position was getting the famous division, then the show-case division of the Indian Army, to build 'self-help' accommodation using troop labour. He was promoted to Lt. Gen. and brought to Delhi in July 1959 as Quarter-Master General (QMG) at the Army HQ, in preference to two suitable officers who were the Army's own first and second choices, Maj. Generals P.S. Gyani and P.P. Kumaramangalam, who were both senior to Kaul. This appointment was the cause of the difference of opinion between Gen. K.S. Thimayya, the Army Chief, and the Defence Minister, in which the Prime Minister supported Krishna Menon and humiliated the Army Chief by his statements in Parliament. By this time his personal influence was far beyond that of his actual appointment in the army.

From this time onwards the Menon-Kaul era in Indian defence policies began, and the Chief of the Army Staff was marginalised. Thereafter, again breaching service norms, in March 1961 he was made the Chief of the General Staff (CGS), the very important appointment at the head of the General Staff, dealing with all the operational matters, and over-riding all other staff branches, superseding at least six qualified officers, even though he was completely unqualified to hold this post.

Sukhwant Singh amplifies:

> Thimayya's retirement gave Menon the much-sought-for opportunity to overhaul the entire military higher command according to his wishes. The politically acceptable Kaul emerged as the power behind the throne. He installed the mediocre [Gen.] Thapar as puppet Chief and himself became Chief of General Staff (CGS), responsible for all policies and planning for operations, intelligence and training in the Army.[11]

This move set up the stage for Nehru's 'Forward Policy,' whose military architect is said to be Lt. Gen. Kaul, and which had been opposed by all the competent and 'non-political' generals concerned with practicalities.

With a compliant Army Chief in General D.N. Thapar, Kaul's wish prevailed in Army HQ since it was well-known that he had direct personal access to the Prime Minister. During this period Lt. Gen. L.P. Sen took over from Lt. Gen. S.P.P. Thorat as the Eastern Army Commander (GOC-in-C Eastern Command) and Lt. Gen. Daulet Singh went to Western Command.

As CGS, Lt. Gen. Kaul was in a position to order a game of military chess in the barren mountains of Ladakh. The far-flung posts designed to contest Chinese presence could only be maintained by air at considerable expense. The Western Army Commander, Lt. Gen. Daulet Singh, objected to this deployment policy on military grounds. He pointed out that it was necessary to build up depth tactical areas in strength should the Chinese react. At that time Western Command had neither the resources nor the capability, and thus the forward posture was militarily unsound. Sukhwant Singh says:

> Much against Daulet Singh's judgement, Kaul's will, with the full backing of [Prime Minister] Nehru, prevailed and set India on a course of collision with China.[12]

In the Kameng sector of NEFA, 7 Infantry Brigade was in the process of being inducted. Brig. J.P. Dalvi, Commander 7 Infantry Brigade, writes:

> In August 1962, 4 Division issued orders for the implementation of a limited policy of re-siting of regular troops locations, and the establishment of additional company localities forward of Towang. The aim was to locate them nearer to the McMahon Line to be more readily at hand to assist Assam Rifles posts. There was no plan to counter a full-scale invasion. As there was no immediate threat, and for various administrative reasons, this re-deployment was to be phased over two working seasons; the first phase to be completed by 30th November 1962, and the second during 1963. . . . On 8th September, both 1 SIKH

(who had relieved 1/9 Gorkhas) and 9 PUNJAB were in the process of establishing these new localities.

7 Brigade continued to be responsible for the operational tasks of 11 Infantry Brigade, East of Sela Pass, as this formation was still in Nagaland. This role was in addition to the existing tasks of the Brigade and the new deployment arrangements that had been freshly ordered.[13]

Wg. Cdr. Hoshang Patel (Retd.) was then the Senior Air Staff Officer with the IAF Tactical Air Centre (TAC) attached to HQ 4 Infantry Division in Tezpur, and was present when Lt. Gen. Kaul visited as CGS. He says (after describing a visit to Brig. Dalvi's brigade Headquarters at Tawang with the GOC 4 Infantry Division, Maj. Gen. Niranjan Prasad):

> Soon afterwards, General Kaul came to visit us. Gen Kaul blew the hell out of Niranjan Prasad because at that time, the Prime Minister, or the Defence Minister, had given the "Forward Policy," of placing troops right on the border and Kaul was trying to get an explanation from Gen Prasad, in front of all of us, on why the forward troop movement had not been completed.
>
> If a man like me, a non-army man, could understand what the problem was, why couldn't Gen Kaul understand? To put people right on the MacMahon Line—which is inaccessible—to supply them rations, to look after them medically, to manage their rotations. I told the General that our air force didn't have so wide an organisation to supply all these people in small pockets, and give them food, and for casualty and altitude-sickness evacuation. And if he was going to put our people there, even if it was border security force under an Army officer, the logistics problem would be

colossal. I could understand all this, but I don't know why this was not explained to General Kaul.

So anyway, he blew his top and said, "I want this thing done!" And everybody got up and out and as I was leaving the room with two or three divisional staff officers I just blurted out. "You do that, and make just one bloody mistake and the Indian carpet will be rolled down the Himalayas!"

Niranjan Prasad thwacked me on the back saying, "Shut up, Pat, they'll hear!" I said. "Let them hear!!"[14]

NOTES

1. D. R. Mankekar, *The Guilty Men of 1962,* 1968, p. 97.
2. *Ibid.,* p. 98.
3. *Ibid.,* p.99.
4. *Ibid.,* pp. 99-100.
5. *Ibid.,* p. 100.
6. *Ibid.,* p. 98.
7. *Ibid.,* pp. 97-100.
8. *Ibid.,* p. 16.
9. Krishna Menon, the Defence Minister.
10. Sukhwant Singh, *India's Wars since Independence,* Vol. III, 1982, p. 13.
11. *Ibid.,* pp. 14-15.
12. *Ibid.,* p. 16.
13. Dalvi, *op. cit.,* p.134.
14. Wg. Cdr. Hoshang K. Patel (Retd.), *Independence and the China War;* on the Internet at www.Bharat-Rakshak.com, 'Chinese Checkers.'

Part II

The War

5

Operation LEGHORN

7 Brigade was originally tasked with the defence of Tawang, situated a mere 37 km from the Tibetan border at Bumla. Its official tasking was to:

(a) Defend Tawang—the primary role;
(b) Prevent any penetration of the McMahon Line;
(c) Establish Assam Rifles posts; and
(d) Assist Assam Rifles posts.[1]

Brig. Dalvi writes:

> The roles of assisting the Assam Rifles and defending Towang were prima facie contradictory. To achieve the first I would have to disperse my command; to achieve the second I would need to concentrate the whole brigade at Towang.[2]

On September 8, 1962 an infantry battalion's worth of Chinese troops surrounded the Dhola post in NEFA which was held by an Assam Rifles platoon, and told them to leave Chinese territory. As a reaction, on 8th September 1962 itself the Eastern Army Commander, Lt. Gen. Sen, issued orders for the move of 7 Infantry Brigade, then in the process of concentrating in Tawang, to the Namka Chu area over 100 km away in the west.

Brig. John Parshuram Dalvi, Commander 7 Infantry Brigade, was a highly-regarded and professionally well-qualified officer, who had been commissioned into the Baluch Regiment and served with his battalion, the 5th/10th Baluch, in the Burma

campaign of 1944-45 during WW-II. As a Lt. Col., he commanded 4th Guards from January 28, 1952 to September 23, 1956, and later commanded 1st Guards from July 29, 1959 to January 1960. He had been a Lt. Col. in Military Operations Directorate in Army Headquarters and had later been Brigadier-in-Charge-Administration (Brig-ic-Adm) of 15 Corps which was responsible for the Ladakh sector, in addition to the rest of the state of J&K. He was thus familiar with the administrative issues related to Op ONKAR. As Brig-ic-Adm 15 Corps he had even had official dealings on this subject with Lt. Gen. Kaul, then Quarter-Master General (QMG) at Army HQ, prior to Kaul's being made CGS.

In Delhi on September 9, at a meeting presided over by the Defence Minister, V.K. Krishna Menon, it was decided that the Chinese must be evicted from south of the Thag La ridge, and by force if necessary. The meeting was attended by the Chief of Army Staff (COAS), Gen. P.N. Thapar, GOC-in-C Eastern Command, Lt. Gen. L.P. Sen, the Cabinet Secretary, S.S. Khera, H.C. Sarin, Joint Secretary in the Defence Ministry, the Director IB, B.N. Mullik, and a few others. Gen. Thapar accepted the decision, and a signal was sent to Eastern Command accordingly.

The operation was code-named 'Operation LEGHORN.'[3]

The fateful note to the Army Chief, quoted in the Defence Ministry's official History of the war, is reproduced below:

> The decision throughout has been as discussed at previous meetings, that the Army should prepare and throw the Chinese out as soon as possible. The COAS was accordingly directed to take action for the eviction of the Chinese in the Kameng Frontier Division of NEFA as soon as he is ready.

The DMO, then-Brig. Palit describes the decision, as verbally conveyed to him:

> ... that, as a result of the Dhola crisis 7 Infantry Brigade had been peremptorily ordered to move from Towang and concentrate post-haste at the bottom of the Thag-la ridge, with the task of chasing the Chinese up the mountain and across the watershed.[4]

The change in orders for 7 Brigade was in compliance with the Indian Government's decision to retake possession of the disputed Thagla Ridge area, which was physically occupied by an entrenched Chinese brigade, a militarily impossible task even if it had been logistically possible. 9th Punjab of 7 Brigade was ordered to occupy the southern bank of the Namka Chu river-line facing the Thag La ridge, which rose above it to its north.

At the time the order to deploy to the Namka Chu was received, only 9 PUNJAB was located forward, at Tawang. It had had a gruelling time, having been inducted at the height of winter, without adequate shelters in Tawang. 1 SIKH was located at Dirang Dzong, between Bomdila and Sela, as it could not be maintained in Tawang.

Maj. Gen. Ashok Kalyan Verma explains the predicament for 7 Infantry Brigade:

The tasks given to 7 Brigade responsible for the Kameng Frontier Division had no relationship to its capability. Its primary role so far was spelt out was the defence of Tawang. Even this role it could not really be expected to perform. Tawang being on the lower slopes, the heights rising to the boundary watershed along which the McMahon Line ran, was by the very nature of its location, indefensible ... it had in September 1962 two battalions with it in the general area—9 PUNJAB and 1 SIKH. The brigade's third battalion, 1/9 GR, were already concentrated at the railhead at Misamari, having completed their three-year tenure in NEFA, awaiting their railway train to take them to Yol. 1/9 GR was to be replaced by 4 GRENADIERS who were expected to come in by the same train that would take the Gorkhas out on its return journey. Like 1/9 GR, ... 2 RAJPUT were waiting nearby at Charduar. This battalion ... was waiting to move to Mathura having done their three years at Walong.

Since 7 Brigade was operationally controlling the Assam Rifles forward posture deployment, it was tasked to 'evict the Chinese investing the Che Dong (Dhola) Post.' Considering that the McMahon Line in Kameng stretched for more than 150 kilometres, this solitary brigade was woefully inadequate for these tasks. Besides, the Che Dong (Dhola) Post area was in a remote North-Western corner of the district, only approachable by a pony track that petered out into a footpath, over a distance of more than a hundred kilometres. From Tawang the track followed a Western loop, initially moving along the slopes of the Tawang Chu and then wheeling North along the Nyamjang Chu Valley. The distance would take from four to five days to cover for a fit man.[5]

Brig. Dalvi writes:

> 7 Brigade was required to guard three approaches with no laterals. In fact nothing more than a string of outposts, with regular troops at intervals could be deployed.[6]
>
> 7 Brigade had only two battalions and a battery of mountain guns. The guns and artillery mules could not be moved forward of Towang and therefore the Brigade would have to confront the Chinese without artillery support.

On September 12, 1962, Lt. Gen. Sen visited the 4 Infantry Division's HQ at Tezpur and issued orders for 'Operation LEGHORN' (Op LEGHORN), the operation intended to carry out the Prime Minister's directive to 'drive out' the Chinese from the Thagla Ridge, which the Government of India believed to be Indian territory. The remainder of NEFA was taken away from the 4 Division's area of responsibility. 7 Brigade was relieved of the responsibility for the defence of Tawang from the direction of the Indo-Tibetan border at Bumla. The responsibility for the defence of Tawang was given to 4 Division's Artillery Brigade Commander, Brig. Kalyan Singh, who was given the battalion 1st Sikh who were hitherto under 7 Brigade.

9 PUNJAB had been moved forward towards Lumpu on 11th September. On the evening of 13th September it was ordered to hurry as fast as it could to the Namka Chu, without any specific aim or task being given. The nature and scope of the operation had not been decided at the time; the only object at the time was the relief of the Dhola post.[7] The battalion reached Bridge II at about 08.30 hours on the 15th September, and found a company of Chinese troops on both sides of the river. ('Bridge II' and all the other bridges across the Namka Chu were merely log bridges consisting of two or three logs tied together and slung across the

fast-flowing river to enable herders and their cattle to cross to the high Thagla pastures.) The Chinese troops had interpreters who told them in Hindi that the area was Chinese territory, and to leave. 9 PUNJAB then deployed along the river-line, facing the Chinese positions, in places only a few metres away from each other.

The Namka Chu is a very fast-flowing, boulder-strewn mountain stream which is not a military obstacle, being unfordable for short periods only, after torrential rains or when when the snow is melting in the Thagla massif and Tsangdhar-Hathungla heights. It is about 8 m (24 ft) at its narrowest and 40 m (120 ft) at its widest. Its source is a group of small lakes at a height of 14,000 ft, and it drops 8,000 ft in about 25 km. It flows from west to east and joins the Nyamjang Chu near Khinzemane. The Namka Chu valley is extremely rugged, with precipitous, thickly-wooded slopes. Down at the edge of the river the visibility was very limited, from a minimum of 30 metres to a maximum of 100 metres. There was no room for manoeuvre.

With Chinese and Indian troops now in contact in the Kameng sector of NEFA, the operational situation had become a live one. Brig. Dalvi writes:

> The Namka Chu from Bridges I to IV had become the de-facto military boundary. The Chinese had control of the whole of Thagla Ridge, which was ours. Unfortunately, the Punjabis (*9th Punjab*) were pinned down over 7 to 9 miles in small localities, maintaining flag-posts to prevent minor incursions. Their localities had no mutual support, limited fields of fire and no room for manoeuvre. They had only pouch ammunition[8] and two 3-inch mortars.[9]

On September 18, 1962, an Indian Government spokesman informed the Press that the Army had been instructed to drive the Chinese out of the Dhola area in the Kameng region of NEFA. It appears no thought had been given to the serious problems of administration and morale. Maj. Gen. Ashok Kalyan Verma comments:

> In spite of the Army having had several years experience of operating in high-altitude areas, both in Ladakh and at certain places in NEFA, the effect of sudden exposure to rarefied oxygen in the atmosphere was given little official consideration. In a general sense it was known that mountaineers carry out careful acclimatization, but nobody in 1962 gave much consideration to this...
>
> Acclimatization is an inescapable requirement and any deployment above 7000 feet above sea-level requires from 7 to 15 days' carefully monitored preparation. Physical activity leading to hard breathing has to be carefully controlled as the dissolved oxygen in the blood cannot be easily replaced in the rarified atmosphere owing to lack of oxygen and reduced atmospheric pressure.
>
> Apart from the grave risk to life due to pulmonary edema, there are other well-known problems of mountain sickness that set in. It is thus very necessary to induct troops very carefully into altitudes where this risk exists. It is not enough to merely cater for warm clothing. Apart from this even the mental ability to think clearly and act rationally is impaired in some cases. Mental depression sometimes sets in and fluid intake needs careful watching.[10]

Brig Dalvi himself moved forward on reconnaissance and met the CO 9 PUNJAB, Lt. Col. R.N Misra, at the Namka Chu on 19th September. He continues the narrative:

At this time I was handed my copy of the most fantastic order issued between the 8th of September and the 20th of October 1962. The signal with a Military Operations Directorate file number (which I knew by heart after four years) was from the Chief of Army Staff to the entire chain of command. The gist of the order was:

> '9 PUNJAB will capture Thagla, contain Yumtsola and Karpola II by 19th September.'

> This was not a feasible order based on an estimate of the situation. It was another slogan sent as a result of political pressure. Apart from the gross impropriety of issuing orders directly to an infantry battalion, Gen. Thapar could have misled the Government into thinking that the operation could be carried out. Politicians do not expect their military chiefs to agree to undertake impossible tasks. A threat of resignation might have sobered the political bosses at that early stage. Gen. Thapar owed it to the nation to have done so.

> 9 PUNJAB was pinned down opposite the Chinese posts and could not mount an attack without altering their positions and forsaking their original task. An attack cannot be mounted under enemy observation.

> I flatly refused to obey this order and informed Division HQ accordingly. GOC agreed and protested to XXXIII Corps, who in turn asked Eastern Command to have the order countermanded. I ordered Misra to ignore the signal and await orders from me. There was all-round relief. Indian troops are obedient and disciplined. They would have given their lives if ordered.

Army Headquarters in Delhi, however, knew that the plan for evicting the Chinese had already been altered at the Eastern

Command Headquarters in Lucknow. The DMO, then-Brig. D.K. Palit, writes:

> In mid-September Jogi[11] informed me that Bogey Sen had revised his plan and decided, after all, to use the whole of 7 Brigade for the attack. He had, therefore, postponed the date of attack, estimating that the operation could not be launched before early October.
>
> I knew that no amount of air effort at Lumpu could enable logistics to catch up with the requirements for a whole brigade. (MO-I had calculated that the tonnage required for a brigade attack including an air-drop of four pack artillery pieces and a minimum stockpile of ammunition would by themselves amount to 560 tons).[12]

Brig. Dalvi continues the narrative:

> The Gorkhas and the Rajputs fetched up at Lumpu by about 26th September. Both the units were not 'fit for war' in their present state. This then was the 'brigade' being assembled in the 'requisite area' to keep the rash promise made at Delhi. [*The two battalions had only 350/400 men each, instead of their full complement of over 800, since they had already commenced their moves to their respective 'peace' stations, when they were hurriedly inducted.*]
>
> Thus was the name and title of 7 Infantry Brigade given to the miscellany of troops hurriedly marshalled for what was thought would be a limited show of force. Having been caught napping Army HQ sought to restore the position by collecting the first unfortunate units they could lay their hands on. The so-called 7 Brigade did not have any affiliation, no collective training and no time to get to know each other. It normally takes months of joint training as a formation to mould a team,

develop mutual trust and confidence and to practise battle drills. Three battalions grouped together at the eleventh hour do not form a fighting brigade.[13]

7 Brigade of 4 Infantry Division could thus in no way be compared to what it was as part of 4 Infantry Division during the Second World War, when the division had become famous in North Africa as the 'Red Eagles.' Nevertheless, the 7 Brigade as it was then stood fast at the line of non-tactical outposts and 9 PUNJAB fought back hard when the first incidents of firing between them and the Chinese broke out.

After the outbreak of firing at the Namka Chu from September 20 onwards, Gen. Thapar asked for the decision regarding Op LEGHORN to be reconsidered. The meeting was held on September 22, presided over by Deputy Defence Minister, K. Raghuramaiah in the absence of both Nehru and Krishna Menon. The Foreign Secretary re-iterated the Prime Minister's views, and after some discussion it was decided that as a matter of policy there was no alternative but to evict the Chinese from the Dhola area. Gen. Thapar requested for a written order of the government to that effect.[14] As a result, he received a note signed by the Joint Secretary, Ministry of Defence, stating:

The decision throughout has been as discussed at previous meetings, that the Army should prepare and throw the Chinese out as soon as possible. The COAS was accordingly directed to take action for the eviction of the Chinese in the Kameng Frontier Division of NEFA as soon as he is ready.

11987/JS(G)/62
COAS of 22-9-62

Sd/- (HC Sarin)
Joint Secretary
22-9-62

The tasks given to Maj. Gen. Niranjan Prasad, GOC 4 Infantry Divison, to carry out the above were:

(a) You will evict the Chinese from the North bank of the Namka Chu.

(b) You will contain Thagla.

(c) You will patrol towards Tsangle.[15]

THE OPERATIONAL LOGISTICS SITUATION

When the Brig. Dalvi was given the order for 9 PUNJAB to capture Thagla, and thus evict the Chinese, he realized that what was being required of him was to mount an offensive to clear the Thagla ridge, a task well beyond his force's capability. He started planning for a probe in strength to secure Tsen-jong, a small feature on the Thag La forward slope. As the logistics support for the plan, he asked for the stockpiling of 30 days' rations, three first lines of ammunition, snow clothing and other equipment, artillery fire support, helicopters for evacuation of casualties, and porters for the loads from Tsangdhar forwards. He made it clear that unless the logistic base could be made ready within two weeks, the operation could not be carried out before April 1963.[16]

7 Brigade's administrative base at Lumpu was a hard four days' march from Tawang. With the winter rapidly approaching and in the already severe cold, maintaining 7 Infantry Brigade in the Namka Chu area was not possible for more than a few days. Whether the Chinese remained comfortably dug-in on the Thagla Ridge or withdrew, and even if they had not attacked, 7 Brigade would have had to be withdrawn from the Namka Chu—Dhola area within a few days for logistical reasons alone. The troops had less than 3 days' rations available, and only 50 rounds of ammunition for each man's personal weapon.

The operational logistics situation of 7 Brigade, an emergency collection of unprepared infantry battalions, was frightening. Far from being able to drive out the Chinese from the Thagla ridge, they were in grave danger of being defeated by 'General Winter.' With one battalion (1/9 GR) in summer cotton uniforms and already affected by cases of pneumonia, and the others not much better off, the brigade was in imminent danger of starving and/or freezing to death, or, without sufficient ammunition, being decimated by the well-prepared, warmly-clothed and well-fed Chinese troops dug in on the Thagla Ridge.

Therefore there had come about a plan to air-drop supplies and ammunition on the flat-topped Tsangdhar feature, which was a potential dropping zone for Dakota aircraft. Tsangdhar was, in the press of events, given to the Air Force as a full-sized dropping zone, forcing them to use Fairchild Packets (C-119s) to try and drop the vast tonnages required, within nine days. Most of these drops, including artillery guns and ammunition, fell into deep, inaccessible ravines and could not be recovered. These air-drops, made right in front of the Chinese positions on Thag La, further gave the Chinese higher command that India was building up for offensive action.

The DMO of the time, then-Brig D.K. Palit, VrC, comments:

A large proportion (nearly 50 percent by some accounts) of the (recycled) parachutes failed to open; of those that did a goodly number were wafted over the precipices to the steep valleys below; of those among the latter that were eventually located, many loads were found to be too heavy to be manhandled up the steep slopes. Little wonder that my Summary ruefully recorded:

> However, in spite of all efforts, the build-up achieved by 17/18 October was still far short of minimum targets for the

sustenance of operations. Against a target of 5 first lines of ammunition and 15 days supplies only the following reached the forward troops:

(a) Tsang Dhar
   (i) Supplies: 8 days
   (ii) SAA (small arms ammunition): 1/16 first line
   (iii) 4.2 in mortar: 3/4 first line
   (iv) 75 mm: 0.5 first line
(b) Lumpu
   (i) Small arms ammunition: about 0.5 first line
   (ii) Supplies: about 5 days
(c) Towang
   (i) Small arms ammunition: 2 first lines
   (ii) 4.2 in mortar: 1 first line
   (iii) 3.7 in: 1.5 first lines
   (iv) 25 pdr: 2 first lines

For the benefit of readers unacquainted with military terms, the definition of a first line scale is the amount of ammunition required for just one day's fighting when in contact with the enemy. Thus, all that had been dropped at Lumpu and Tsangdhar by the time the Chinese attacked at Namka-chu was barely sufficient for about an hour's battle—and that only if all air-dropped items were located, retrieved and transported to the troops, which would have been impossible, as neither mules nor porters were available.[17]

Lt. Gen. Umrao Singh, the 33 Corps[18] Commander, was in Lumpu from 26th to 28th September to discuss the plans of the GOC 4 Infantry Division and the 7 Brigade Commander for evicting the Chinese from the slopes of the Thag La ridge. He seemed to have little confidence in what was being planned.

Because of the precarious logistics situation, he gave clear orders that there was to be no further concentration of troops forward of Lumpu till the bare minimum of stock-piling at Tsangdhar was achieved.

The 7 Brigade Commander comments on the administrative arrangements in the induction period:

> In the mountains, administration is the critical principle of war.... The burden of porterage was a serious embarrassment to a battalion which was in contact with the enemy [9 PUNJAB].
>
> Collection of drops was the responsibility of the Brigade and 200 men each from the Rajputs and the Gorkhas were employed daily on this chore. The primitive and improvised set-up made a deep impression on [Lt.] Gen. Umrao Singh, the Corps Commander, and was the primary reason which emboldened him to defy the general clamour for evicting the Chinese, regardless of the other factors. He was insistent that we should adhere to the basic principles of administration and was emphatic that there would be no concentration in the Namka Chu until the necessary administrative stock-piling had been achieved.
>
> While the Punjabis were being stocked, we were trying to equip the Rajputs and the Gorkha to full scales of weapons, ammunition, wireless sets, winter clothing and other unit stores. These units should never have been sent to Lumpu without these basic items which could have been provided at a rail or roadhead, instead of being despatched by air. For days they were merely eating up valuable rations when the available airlift could have been used for building up reserves.

There was a frantic effort to air-drop the necessary equipment and supplies at Tsangdhar, as well as to move as much as possible up by the one-ton road to Tawang. The air-lift capacity at Guwahati (Gauhati) was increased from 20-30 tons per day to 60-70 tones per day by mid-October. 80 more one-ton vehicles were moved up to augment the road-lift capacity.[19]

A re-organization of sectors was done in the Corps Zone in this period, because of the orders for the move of 7 Brigade westwards away from Tawang. The Nyamjang Chu sector was put directly under command of HQ 4 Infantry Division. By October 2, 4 Division's Tactical Headquarters (Tac HQ) had been established at Zemithang, in the Nyamjang Chu valley about 10 km south of the Khinzemane border post. It was now therefore commanding widely-dipersed sub-units echeloned back from the Namka Chu-Nyamjang Chu confluence, as well as the Hathungla track from Zimithang forwards. (Theoretically, it still had operational control over 5 Infantry Brigade nearly 500 km away in the Walong Sector to the east). 7 Brigade's Tac HQ was at Rongla, further forward on the Hathungla-Namka Chu axis.

When Lt. Gen. Umrao Singh opposed the impracticalities of the haste to move units forward without adequate logistic build-up, Kaul as CGS at Army Headquarters felt that he was dragging his feet. The next step taken was to divest Lt. Gen. Umrao Singh of the responsibility for NEFA. Therefore the Defence Minister and the Army Chief, who had wanted to remove Gen. Umrao Singh without appearing to do so, so that Operation ONKAR could be speeded up, created a 'special' 4 Corps, a formation in name only, which took over the responsibility for NEFA. Lt. Gen. Umrao's responsibility for the area was terminated by truncating the area of responsibility of his command, the 33 Corps Zone. The NEFA, Assam and Nagaland sector was given to the new, suddenly-created 4 Corps, leaving 33 Corps responsible thereafter only for the Indo-Tibet border in Sikkim and Bhutan (in the latter of which no Indian troops were ordinarily meant to be deployed, but for the defence of which India had a treaty obligation).

Umrao Singh was made to step aside, and Lt. Gen. Kaul was appointed task force commander in the field. Thus a new 'phantom' 4 Corps was created in name for Lt. Gen. Kaul to command. In reality, he was sent to push the forward brigade (7 Infantry Brigade) onwards, both directly in person, and through its immediate superior, Headquarters 4 Infantry Division. At his taking over a Corps under Eastern Command, his superior, the General Officer Commanding-in-Chief Eastern Command (GOC-in-C), Lieut.-General L.P. Sen, in practice gave up command over the new 4 Corps. Gen. Sen was well-aware that this new 4 Corps under Kaul was dealing directly with Army Headquarters in Delhi, by-passing his own headquarters.

Sukhwant Singh comments:

> For this [to speed up Op ONKAR], as also to stifle the whispering campaign against him for not being a fighting soldier, he decided to take up personal command in the field. It was made clear that this arrangement was only temporary as his place as CGS was not filled. Dhillon, a hanger-on in Kaul's court, took over in an officiating capacity....
>
> Kaul was given unprecedented powers, to the extent that on his arrival in NEFA he sent Umrao and his headquarters packing elsewhere and raised another corps headquarters with hand-picked staff for himself.[20]

On October 3, 1962, Army HQ replaced HQ 33 Corps with HQ 4 Corps. On October 5, 1962, the Government informed the Press that Lt. Gen. B.M. Kaul, the CGS at Army Headquarters, had been given the command of a new corps in NEFA, and that he had already left for Tezpur. On 5th October itself, while 4 Division's GOC waited to receive him at the Tawang helipad, Lt. Gen. Kaul flew straight to Lumpu, where he personally gave orders for the move forwards of the whole brigade, not to the Brigade Commander who had gone forward, but to the operational staff officer of the brigade headquarters, the Brigade Major (BM), thus completely by-passing the appropriate chain of command from Corps to division to brigade.

Brig. Dalvi comments:

> Gen. Kaul arrived at Tezpur on 4th October and amazingly was received at the airport by his Army Commander [*Lt. Gen. L.P. Sen*]—an extraordinary reversal of military protocol. The armies of the world are usually very fussy about such matters. This is not intended to be a petty barb. It is to illustrate Kaul's power and prestige—material factors which were to gravely influence the course of events in the succeeding days. Anyone exercising authority beyond his rank is bound to stifle disagreement, discourage frank discussions and brow-beat subordinates.
>
> The operational situation at Tezpur on 4th October was that there was a deadlock between Sen and Umrao. Gen. Sen was in a quandary. His immediate subordinate was adamant. His logistical build-up was behind schedule. He had no hope of achieving his targets even by 10th October, if ever ... Gen. Sen was rescued from his predicament by the arrival of Kaul. The heavy burden of reconciling the formidable problems posed by the Himalayas, the objections of his forward commanders and an insistent Government was taken off his weary shoulders.[21]

Brig. Dalvi observes:

> The abrupt dismissal of Gen. Umrao Singh was a pivotal decision. Many devious arguments have been adduced to explain the overnight change in the command structure but none of them have the ring of truth. This, the most serious blunder on the part of the Government and the Army Chief, cannot be buried under a heap of unconvincing administrative reasons. The biggest 'if' of the NEFA War of 1962 must surely be whether there would have been an actual shooting war if Kaul had not been nominated to command, with a personal mandate from the Prime Minister. The impossible task, blithely offered to Kaul, was merrily accepted by him.
>
> When Kaul accepted the assignment he knew that his so-called corps was a political gimmick in so far as his force bore no relation whatsoever to a corps as this term is commonly understood in modern armies. He had nothing but the two committed brigades – 5 and 7 Brigades.[22]

Sukhwant Singh continues:

> With his characteristic drive, he [Kaul] pushed the leading brigade located at Tawang forward to the Namka Chu and deployed them in penny packets along a thin line of about eight miles frontage. He had neither the resources nor the time to build up in the rear.[23]

The Indian attempt to hold the McMahon Line by physically sitting on it, an unrealistic deployment in an impossible time-frame, was being insisted upon by Army HQ. This was in spite of the protests of Brig. J.P. Dalvi, the Commander 7 Infantry Brigade, those of the GOC 4 Infantry

Division, Maj. Gen. Niranjan Prasad, and those of the former corps commander responsible, i.e., GOC 33 Corps, Lt. Gen. Umrao Singh. Army HQ was also insisting on an even more impossible task: that of evicting the Chinese already dug-in on the Thagla Ridge. This was most probably on the advice of Lt. Gen. Kaul (the CGS) himself, who till his arrival in person in NEFA as the Corps Commander, had been acting as the unofficial military adviser to the Prime Minister.

On October 6, the Chinese Central Military Commision (CMC) was convened in Beijing in order to plan for the coming conflict. The participants were Mao, Zhou, Marshal Lin Biao, Marshals Ye Jianying and Liu Bocheng, PLA Chief of Staff Senior General Lou Ruiqing, Vice-Chief of Staff Full Gen. Yang Chengwu, head of the PLA General Political Department Full Gen. Shao Hua, head of the PLA General Logistical Department Full Gen. Qiu Huizuo, Tibet Military Region Commander Lt. Gen. Zhang Guohua, and Sinkiang Military Region Commander Maj. Gen. He Jiachan. CMC Deputy-Chairman Marshal Lin Biao reported that PLA intelligence units had determined that Indian units might assault Chinese positions at Thag La on October 10. Earlier, probably the same day, Mao, Zhou and Lin Biao had already decided in principle upon war, after meeting to review the situation.[24] China's aim was much more than repulsion or pre-emption of Indan moves. It was decidedly punitive: to launch a large-scale attack to severely punish India for the perceived military aggression. It had been decided that India must be taught to respect China's power.

Mao and the Chinese leadership issued a directive to the PLA laying out the objectives for the war. A main assault would be launched in the eastern sector, which would be coordinated with a smaller assault in the western sector. All Indian troops within China's claimed territories in the eastern sector would be expelled, and the war would be ended with a unilateral Chinese ceasefire and withdrawal to prewar positions, followed by a return to the negotiating table.

Diplomatically, Mao acknowledged possible diplomatic isolation as the Soviet Union, the United States, the Republic of China and other 'misinformed countries' would oppose China's actions. India led the Non-Aligned Movement, Nehru enjoyed international prestige, and China, with a larger military would be portrayed as an aggressor. However, he said that if China fought successfully and in an awe-inspiring (*wei feng*) way, it *'will guarantee at least thirty years of peace with India,'* and determined the benefits to offset the costs.[25] The CMC staff was directed to draw up detailed operational plans for a campaign to expel Indian forces from the area north of the 'traditional, customary line,' i.e., the Chinese claim line in the southern foothills of the Himalayas. It was in the process of this staff-work that the idea of a unilateral Chinese halt, ceasefire, and withdrawal was developed. The operational plan developed proposed that after achieving military objectives, Chinese forces would quickly disengage and end the fighting as quickly as possible.[26]

Capt. Lakshman Singh was the 7 Brigade Signals Officer at the time. He wondered whether the Brigade Commander was allowed to exercise command at all:

> In their wisdom, the higher-ups ensured that Dalvi remained divorced from his HQ, staff and communications. He was either on the move or sitting in the wilderness with his GSO 3, the intelligence officer, the rover radio-set operator, the cipher operator and the radio mechanic for company for days together. The man pack Radio Set No 62[27] which could be operated only when static on the Brigade Command net was his sole link with the outside world. He was denied any decision making authority. Even the brigade was moved

forward from the concentration area at Lumpu to Tsangdhar and the valley of River Namka Chu without his knowledge by the new Corps Commander.[28]

On 7 October 1962, both the two available battalions of 7 Brigade, 2 RAJPUT and 1/9 GR, marching as fast as they could, climbing upwards, reached Tsangdhar by 1700 hours. At 14,500 feet it was very cold, and the inadequately clothed men had to bivouac at night in the open, three men under two groundsheets. On 8 October 1962, both the battalions commenced concentrating above Bridge III on the forward slopes of the Tsangdhar feature. In spite of the dire logistical and manpower situation, 7 Brigade attempted to obey its orders and carry out its tasking, those given to the Division, and prepared to attack to 'evict the Chinese from the North bank of the Namka Chu.'

Lt. Gen. Kaul as Corps Commander had virtually taken over personal command of 7 Infantry Brigade, dictating the locations of deployment of the companies, making the Brigade Commander and the Divisional Commander redundant, and dictating terms to the Commanding Officers of the battalions, tolerating no objections even to utterly impractical tactical movements, to implement his theoretical 'positional warfare.' Brig Dalvi states:

> Kaul was in personal command of 7 Infantry Brigade. We now had one General, two Lt. Gens., one Maj. Gen., and one Brigadier[29] to preside over the activities of this ill-starred formation. All that these generals were doing was to improvidently hound, harry and hustle this one formation to achieve the unattainable.[30]

Brig. Dalvi, who had become almost a hapless spectator as command of his own brigade was taken-over by the new Corps Commander, tellingly comments:

> At that stage Ground, Relative Strengths and Administration were not matters of bickering—they were overwhelmingly decisive. They could not be ignored at the risk of certain disaster. If Gen. Kaul intended to take a calculated risk in ignoring these time-honoured principles then there is little point in shifting the blame of the subsequent failure to the Army as a whole. He tried to do what others opined could not be done. He replaced Umrao who believed in 'bickering' when his professional conscience told him to do so. Why was Umrao sacked?
>
> If Gen. Sen removed Umrao on grounds of professional incompetence then he should have been made to relinquish command of XXXIII Corps. Discredited Corps Commanders do not retain their ranks and appointments.
>
> It has also been insinuated that the burden of commanding Assam, Nagaland and NEFA was too heavy for one commander. This is perhaps the most unconvincing argument of all.... In any case the solution obviously lay in appointing another commander for the Assam and Nagaland sectors and freeing Umrao to concentrate on the NEFA operations with which he was familiar. Would Government have removed Umrao if he had agreed to have a crack at the Chinese without harping on military prudence?[31]

Brig. Dalvi, writing later, pondered another matter with serious implications:

> The last puzzling question is why Government did not appoint Kaul to command XXXIII Corps and create a phantom corps for the dormant Assam and Nagaland Sectors. XXXIII Corps was a running organisation, had a tuned up staff under an extremely capable Brigadier and the

necessary corps troops for the maintenance of troops in combat.

The unavoidable conclusion is that Delhi was afraid of making an issue of removing Umrao lest the truth about the divergence of opinions within the Army and with the politicians leaked out, thereby shattering the morale of the nation. Umrao wanted more time and time was the one commodity Government did not have. The Indian public was breathing down its neck. There is no other explanation for the Prime Minister's personal intervention in the selection of a 'corps commander' to command one brigade to evict an allegedly small, non-violent, intruding Chinese force. Kaul was no ordinary general to be wasted on a minor assignment. I remain convinced to this day that Umrao was placed on the sideline ungracefully because he refused to collaborate with those who insisted on steering a collision course to the Chinese on the Thagla ridge. Someone who would play the politicians' game was urgently needed and Kaul was the obvious choice as the pro-consul. He was the principal military advocate of the Forward Policy which others had resisted. When called by Government Kaul could not very well refuse to practice his theory of "positional warfare" and vindicate his strategy.

We became the laughing-stock of the world when it became known that Kaul had no corps to command. The Chinese seized upon our premature disclosure of a 'task force,' as well as the uninformed jubilation in the Indian press about an impending offensive to tell the world that we had prepared for years for such an operation. We had paid for ignoring the old Japanese saying that countries should 'wage war silently and anonymously.' It was difficult even for our friends to believe our professions of peace and that the

> Chinese attacked us treacherously when we ourselves announced to the world that we were determined to evict the Chinese (albeit from what we claimed was our territory) and had selected India's outstanding General to do so. Those responsible did India irreparable harm and a great disservice. History cannot be kind to them.[32]

On October 8, China's CMC ordered several additional divisions to prepare to move into Tibet from the Chengdu and Lanzhou Military Regions. All these forces were veteran, high-quality forces. Most had previously participated in anti-rebel operations (against the Khampa resistance) in Tibet, and were therefore accustomed to combat operations at high altitude.

On 8 October and 9 October the new Corps Commander, the GOC of the division, the Brigade Commander and the three Commanding Officers (COs) of the battalions (including Lt. Col. Mishra of 9 PUNJAB) met at Bridge IV as an Orders Group and had discussions on the operational situation before them.

Brig. Dalvi narrates the landmark event of 9th October 1962:

> Gen. Kaul then threw the bombshell with which he had come from Delhi. He said that in spite of the stark facts and irrefutable arguments against military action, he had no option but to make some move on 10th October, as this was the last date acceptable to the Cabinet whatever the cost. He went on to say that the Army Commander (Sen) had advised Government that he would evict the Chinese on 29th September; then changed the date to 1st October; and later to 5th October. There was a feeling in Delhi, conveyed by Gen. Sen, that the forward troops were stalling and that was why he (Kaul) had been sent to speed up operations before

the onset of the snows and to ensure that the Chinese were evicted immediately....

As a direct assault on Thagla was ruled out, he decided to do a 'positional warfare' manoeuvre, and occupy Yumtsola—to the west of Thagla peak, which was not at that time, occupied by the Chinese. Kaul said that he hoped that this action would satisfy Government that "the Army had done its best to carry out its orders." He kept emphasising that this "operation" had to be started on 10th October, as he did not have the latitude to postpone it....

The need to concentrate 7 Brigade by 9th October and the move of this ill-armed brigade, with pouch ammunition and hard scales were now clear.... Kaul then ordered 2 Rajputs to move to Yumtsola, to sit behind the Chinese, on 10th October 1962.

This order was given when the Rajputs were still recovering from their gruelling march over Karpola I Pass. Despite the known critical shortages and the adverse tactical situation, Gen. Kaul ordered the concentration of both 2 Rajputs and 1/9 Gorkkhas to the Namka Chu.[33]

The plan decided upon by the Corps Commander was as follows:

- One platoon of 9 PUNJAB from Bridge IV under an officer to cross over to the North bank of the Namka Chu and take up a position at Sinjan, with a section at Karpo La II. This action to be completed by last light on 8 October 1962.
- 2 RAJPUT less a company (their 'B' Company was deployed at Bridge I under the command of 9 PUNJAB, having been sent earlier from Lumpu) to move and occupy Tsangle, Muksar and Sinjan, in the first phase

- In the second phase, 2 RAJPUT to attack the Thag la feature from the West, clearing the enemy to as far as possible.
- On 2 RAJPUT being halted by the enemy, 1/9 GR to pass through and continue clearing the enemy from West to East along the Thag La ridge.
- In the final phase, 9 PUNJAB to clear the enemy from the slope between the Thag La ridge and the Namka Chu.[34]

Maj. Gen. Ashok Kalyan Verma comments:

> CO 2 RAJPUT [Lt. Col. Maha Singh Rikh] prepared and issued his orders for the operations. He could not possibly have believed that the assigned task could be carried out, yet he planned the operations across the Namka Chu. Clearly there are limits to what sub-units [infantry rifle companies] can achieve. Without worthwhile fire support it is not fair to expect troops to perform. It is a grave responsibility that command of troops carries to point out to the superiors that an impossible task was being assigned. This was perhaps the point in time when things could still have been reversed and the tragedy averted. Perhaps each one expected the other to speak up, but none did when it could have mattered.[35]

CO 2 RAJPUT's plan for the attack on 10 October was based on the personal directions given by the Corps Commander, Lt. Gen. Kaul, which were as under:

- 'C' Company to lead the advance from the Concentration Area, occupy Sinjan, and send a platoon to Karpo La II.
- 'D' Company to follow 'C' Company and occupy Tsangle and Muksar.
- In the second phase of the brigade's operation, 'A' Company to pass through 'C' Company and attack the Thag La feaure from West to East.[36]

The slope upwards on either side of the river was gentle, with ringal bamboo, rhododendron bushes and other scrub, and blue pine trees for 1000 to 3000 feet upwards on both sides, after which the slope became increasingly steep and bare with rock and low scrub close to the top of the ridge.

The Chinese defences on the steep slopes leading down to Namka Chu from the Thag La ridge were in three tiers, with the most forward on the river from Bridge I to Bridge IV within grenade-throwing distance. The second tier was a few hundred metres to the rear, up the slope. The third tier, the main defences, were on the forward slopes of the Thag La crest-line, 2000 metres (over 6000 feet) up the slope from 7 Brigade strung out in the Namka Chu valley below.[37]

Op LEGHORN began with the move of a platoon of 'D' Company 9th Punjab, to Tseng-jong (or Sinjang), a position across the Namka Chu, which had been occupied as a bridge-head for Lt. Gen. Kaul's so-called 'positional warfare' tactics to evict the Chinese. Personally taken there by the Company Commander, Maj. M.S. Chaudhary, The platoon had occupied the position at 1500 hours on 8th October 1962, and a section detached the next morning to occupy the height behind them (Karpola II). The position was reinforced the next day by a platoon of 'A' Company of the same battalion. This resulted in a major engagement on October 10, 1962, the first-ever between the armies of China and India. After a heavy bombardment by heavy mortars, this weak, barely-prepared position was attacked by a full Chinese battalion (approximately 800 men) at 0800 hours on October 10 which was repulsed after a heavy exchange of fire for about 45 minutes. A second attack came in at 0930 hours, with the Punjabis already low on ammunition, having been hastily sent out with only pouch ammunition.

The next attack came in at 1200 hours from three sides, the north, east and west, and developed into hand-to-hand fighting. Finally, realizing that the position was unable to hold on any longer, Brig. Dalvi issued orders at 1230 hours for the troops to withdraw, but the post was over-run when their ammunition ran out. To their credit, the Chinese did not resort to savagery after capturing the post, but allowed the defeated garrison to withdraw with honour, carrying their weapons and dead. The 9th Punjab troops suffered numerous casualties: 6 dead, 11 wounded, including Maj. Chaudhary who later died of his wounds, and 5 missing. Peking Radio announced the Chinese casualties as 77 dead and approximately 100 wounded.[38]

Apart from the brigade commander, the two generals above him, his divisional commander Maj. Gen. Niranjan Prasad and the corps commander Lt. Gen. Kaul, had both also had a grand-stand view of the battle. A seriously-alarmed Lt. Gen. Kaul finally agreed with what the two formation commanders on the ground, and what his predecessor as the Corps Commander responsible for NEFA, Lt. Gen. Umrao Singh, had been saying all along: that it was not possible to attack the Chinese, or to 'evict' them from the Thagla Ridge, in the present state of preparedness. He immediately sought permission from Eastern Command to go to Delhi to personally explain the position to Army Headquarters.

Lt. Col. Maha Singh Rikh, CO 2 RAJPUT, narrates his part in the events of 10 October 1962:

> At first light on the morning of 10 October the advance commenced from the concentration area with 'C' company leading. When 'C' Company arrived at a place about 500 yards short of the Temporary Bridge over the Namka Chu, heavy firing was heard from the direction of Sinjan where the

platoon of 9 PUNJAB had been located on 8 October 1962. When the visibility improved we saw a large number of Chinese attacking the platoon of the Punjabis. I was following behind 'D' Company with my 'R' Group.[39] When I reached Bridge 4, I saw the Corps Commander with his BGS, Chief Engineer and GSO1, the GOC and the Brigade Commander. I was ordered personally by the Corps Commander not to advance further, as the situation had now changed, and the enemy had reacted more violently than he had originally appreciated.

General Kaul felt that the strength of the enemy immediately opposite us was far beyond our capacity to take on with our present resources. He ordered us to go temporarily into defence, and personally told me that my unit would hold the South bank of the Namka Chu with one company each at Temporary Bridge, Bridge 4 and Bridge 3. I told the Corps Commander that these positions were dominated by the Thag La Ridge and in the event of any enemy attack would be impossible to hold. I was told that we were going into defence only temporarily and that the enemy would not attack if we remained on the South bank of the Namka Chu. I was further told that after a few days we would again carry out offensive action, in the meantime not a single inch of territory that we now held would be given up. After saying this, the Corps Commander with his staff accompanied by the GOC left. The Brigade Commande remained at Bridge 4.[40]

Thus the Namka Chu river-line became the line of Forward Defended Localities (FDLs) which were not to be given up. Lt. Col. Rikh explains his deployment:

In accordance with the orders of the Corps Commander, I deployed the Battalion with 'C' Company at the Temporary

> Bridge, 'A' Company at Bridge 3 and 'D' Company with Battalion Headquarters at Bridge 4. I requested the Brigade Commander for the reversion of 'B' Company [to] under my command. The 4 GRENADIERS which had been ordered up from Tawang started arriving on 11 October 1962 and took up positions at Bridge 1. 'B' Company was relieved on 12 October 1962 and I ordered it to take up a defended locality on the Log Bridge.[41]

Maj. Gen. Verma explains the tactical and administrative situation confronting 2nd Rajput:

> 2 RAJPUT was thus from left to right holding a frontage of over 4000 yards. The distance between the Temporary Bridge and Log Bridge was 1200 yards. That between Log Bridge and Bridge 4 was 1500 yards and between Bridge 4 and Bridge 3, 1500 yards. The left flank of the battalion was completely open. The distance between Temporary Bridge and Bridge 5 was over 9 kilometres and it took over 18 marching hours to cover. Visibility at ground and bunker level was from 30 yards to 100 yards. There was no support between companies, and in some cases even between platoons.
>
> ... the battalion was short of digging and cutting tools. There were a total of 10 dahs in the unit and only fifty per cent of the digging tools required. Men were short of all items of 'extra issue' (EI) clothing and had no snow clothing. Each man had only one blanket. In spite of all the limitations men were cheerful and happy. This was mainly due to the fact that all officers and JCOs shared the hardships with the men and remained with them throughout, eating the same food, restricting themselves to the same clothing as the men.

But the preparations of the defences and the administration were of paramount concern, as Verma amplifies:

The battalion worked day and night preparing and improving the positions. At the same time working parties had to be sent to the Tsangdhar Drop Zone to collect rations and clothing as and when it was air dropped. The journey to and from Tsangdhar took nine hours from Temporary Bridge and eight hours from Bridge 3.[42]

NOTES

1. Dalvi, *op. cit.,* p.114.
2. *Ibid.,* p. 130.
3. *History, op.cit.,* pp. 94-95, and D.K. Palit, *War in High Himalaya,* p. 196.
4. Palit, *op. cit.,* p. 195.
5. Verma, *op. cit.,* p.32.
6. Dalvi, *op. cit.,* p. 118.
7. *Ibid.,* p.175.
8. 'Pouch ammunition' is the laid-down 'on weapon' quantity of ammunition, and forms part of the 'First Line' scale of ammunition for each individual weapon in a unit. The 'First Line' scale is the quantity of ammunition for each authorized weapon of the unit, that every unit is expected to carry with them for all moves in an operational setting. The quantity is different for each type of weapon. For the bolt-action single-shot .303 Rifle No. 1 Mark III, which was the basic personal arm of the infantry, carried by most infantry soldiers, the 'pouch ammunition' was 50 rounds of ball ammunition. It came to the units packed in cloth bandoliers, in clips of 5 rounds each, with two clips in each pocket of the bandolier. The complete First Line scale of ball ammunition for the rifle was 100 rounds (of which 50 rounds were the Pouch Ammunition), and another 100 rounds was the Second Line scale.
9. Dalvi, *op. cit.,* pp. 187-188.
10. Verma, *op. cit.,* pp. 35-36.
11. Maj. Gen. Joginder Singh Dhillon, originally an Engineers officer, was Deputy CGS (DCGS) and was the officiating CGS in Lt. Gen. Kaul's absence.
12. Palit, *op. cit.,* pp. 209-210.
13. Dalvi, *op. cit.,* pp. 198-200.
14. *History, op. cit.,* p. 96.
15. Dalvi, *op. cit.,* p. 207.
16. Praval, *op. cit.,* pp. 190-191.

17. Palit, *op. cit.,* p. 209.
18. Then written as 'XXXIII Corps'.
19. Palit, *op. cit.,* p. 209.
20. Sukhwant Singh, *op. cit.,* p. 17.
21. Dalvi, *op. cit.,* p. 225.
22. *Ibid.*, p. 220.
23. Sukhwant Singh, *op. cit.,* p. 17.
24. Garver, *op. cit.,* p. 48.
25. From Johnson, Alastair Iain, and Robert S. Ross (eds.), *New Directions in the Study of China's Foreign Policy,* 2006, and Wikipedia, on the Internet at http://en.wikipedia.org/wiki/Sino-Indian_War, accessed on May 21, 2008
26. Garver, *op. cit.,* p. 52.
27. The Brigade Commander's party itself required at least 50 porters; 14 porters were required only for the Commander's Rover wireless set (the Radio Set No. 62).
28. Brig. Lakshman Singh, VSM, (Retd.), in *The Plastic Soldier* on the Internet at http://signalsingh.blogspot.in/2010/04/plastic-soldier.html.
29. The Army Chief, the Army Commander Eastern Command, the new 4 Corps Commander, the GOC 4 Infantry Division, and the author, Brig. Dalvi himself, Commander 7 Infantry Brigade.
30. Dalvi, *op. cit.,* p. 226.
31. *Ibid.*, p. 221.
32. *Ibid.*, pp. 222-223.
33. *Ibid.*, pp. 249-250.
34. Ashok Kalyan Verma, *op. cit.,* p. 41.
35. *Ibid.*
36. *Ibid.*
37. *Ibid.*, p. 50.
38. Later Chinese accounts state that 11 Chinese soldiers were killed and 22 wounded.
39. 'Reconnaissance' group: the small group of persons that normally accompany any commander on a reconnaissance ('recce'). The relevant group to whom a commander issues operational orders to is the 'Orders' group ('O' group), and the remainder of the command, the main body, is the 'Fighting' group ('F' group).
40. Verma, *op. cit.,* p. 42, from the after-action report prepared by Lt. Col. Rikh, written shortly after his release from Chinese captivity in April 1963.
41. *Ibid.*, p. 43.
42. *Ibid.*, p. 43.

6

The Battle of the Namka Chu

Marshal Liu Bocheng headed a 'strategy small group' (zhanlue xiaozhu) set up in the CMC staff, to determine the strategy for the war. On October 10, he presented his findings to Mao. Liu laid out four 'opinions' regarding the upcoming war. The crux of success was 'concentration of local superiority to achieve a swift war and swift decision.' The PLA must not disperse its forces. It must also absolutely fight well. Victory in this war was a matter directly connected to the prestige of the Chinese army and nation, he concluded. He believed that the opposing Indian troops were not local border police, but among India's best, and it was thus essential to deploy crack troops. He stated that the PLA should not be arrogant in this situation. Nor could it rely on such 'mechanistic' tactics as infiltration, isolation and encirclement. Such measures would not produce victory. The correct approach was to attack fiercely and to 'kill, wound, and capture the enemy.'[1]

Lt. Gen. Kaul reached Delhi the next day (October 11th) after the Chinese attack on 10th October, and was present at a high-powered meeting chaired by the Prime Minister and attended by the Defence Minister, the Army and Air Chiefs, the Cabinet, Foreign and Defence Secretaries, GOC-in-C Eastern Command (Lt. Gen. L.P. Sen), the Director of the Intelligence Bureau, and the Joint Secretary 'G' (Mr. H.C. Sarin) from the Defence Ministry. Explaining the seriousness of the situation

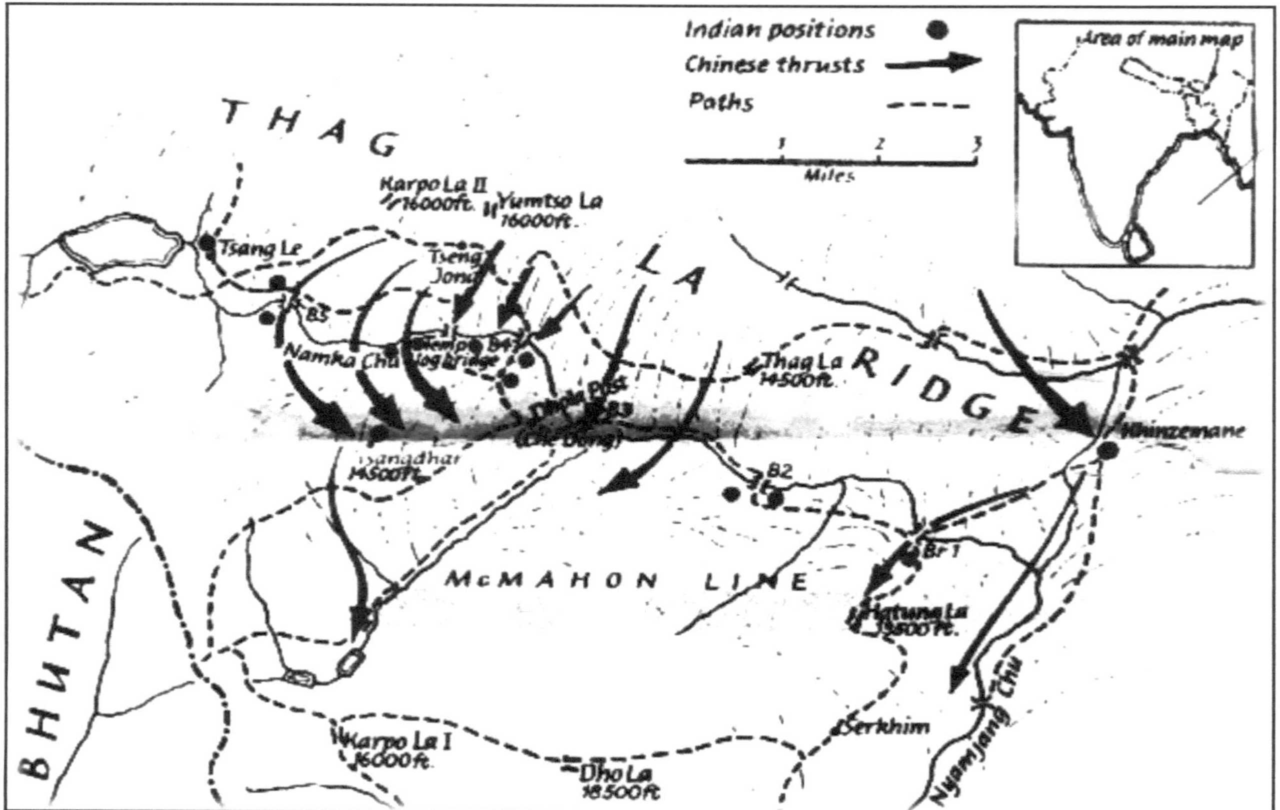
Indian positions
Chinese thrusts
Paths
1
2
3
Miles
Area of main map
THAG LA RIDGE
Karpo La II
16000ft.
Yumtso La
16000ft.
Tsang Le
Tseng Jong
B3
Namka Chu
Log Bridge
Thag La
14500ft.
Khinzemane
Tsangdhar
14500ft.
B2
Br 1
McMAHON LINE
Hatung La
Serkhim
Nyamjang Chu
Karpo La I
16000ft.
Dho La
18500ft.
BHUTAN

and the likelihood of major reverses, Lt. Gen. Kaul asked for orders to pursue one of the three alternative courses of action:

A. Continue build-up in the Kameng sector and launch an attack on the Chinese.

B. Cancel the orders for an attack, but to hold the line of the Namka Chu.

C. Hold a more advantageous position elsewhere.

Lt. Gen. Kaul seemed to indicate a preference for the last course, but his superior the Army Commander Eastern Command disagreed with him, and the Army Chief, General Thapar, concurred with the Army Commander in favour of Course 'B.' The Prime Minister readily agreed with them since it was more in line with his own thinking than withdrawing in the face of the Chinese, and thus the so-called 'present positions' became the line to be held by 7 Infantry Brigade. In spite of this, on return to his sector, with further reports of more Chinese reinforcements arriving opposite them, Lt. Gen. Kaul wavered.

On the ground, the deployment pattern ordered was non-tactical, with the battalions of the brigade strung out between Tsangle and Bridge I, along the Namka Chu, a small mountain river, instead of on the defensible high ground of the top of the high mountain ridge behind them. There were no coordinated defences as each of the locations was isolated. Instead of being asked to hold a proper brigade defended sector on tactically suitable ground, the brigade was thinly spread in small company or smaller localities across about 16 to 17 km. The localities were not fully prepared, as there was not enough time, and did not have any barbed wire or anti-personnel mines. There was not enough food, ammunition, not even proper warm clothing for the freezing weather, practically no artillery fire support, and no medical cover. There was no depth to the 'defence,' and there were no lay-back positions for a fighting withdrawal if needed. It was not a 'brigade defended sector,' that is meant to be composed of a number of 'battalion defended areas,' each comprising various 'company defended localities.' Instead it was a long thin line of company localities and even platoon localities. The only artillery fire support for the entire front was from the just two 75 mm para-droppable field guns[2] with just 421 rounds, and from only four 4.2-inch mortars[3] with a total availability of only 450 bombs. There were two platoons of .303 Vickers MMGs.[4]

The Rajputs had four 3-inch mortars with a total of only 60 bombs, and only 17 filled Light Machine Gun (LMG) magazines per .303 Bren-gun (LMG), each of 30 rounds capacity. Each man had his 'pouch ammunition' scale for his personal weapon (50 rounds of ammunition) and two grenades only. There were no reserves of ammunition. In such a situation 7 Infantry Brigade was capable of fighting for only half an hour, and of maintaining itself in that position for only about three to four days at very hard scales of rations. One of the units, 1st/9th Gorkha Rifles, which had hurriedly been made to march up from the Assam valley, was in cotton summer uniforms and had already begun to suffer casualties from the severe cold of October at those heights.

The only possible physical communication route was along a narrow foot track that ran parallel to the front, practically along it, so that when hostilities began it was immediately cut, and all the localities would have to fight in isolation for as long as they could. It was a dreadful situation. The brigade's hastily brought-together four battalions, 2nd Rajputs, (composed of Rajputs, Gujjars, and Bengalis), 1st/9th Gorkha Rifles (of *Khas* and *Thakur* Gorkhas), 9th Punjab (of Jat Sikhs and Dogra Rajputs of Punjab and Himachal Pradesh), and 4th Grenadiers (of *Kaimkhani* Muslims of Rajasthan and *Ahirs* (Yadavs) from Haryana and Rajasthan), were thus doomed from the start.

Another directive from Army Headquarters arrived on October 16 ordering aggressive patrolling, reinforcement of the forward-most position at Tsangle to a battalion, and harassing fire on enemy movement, particularly across the Thagla Pass. With the Brigade and Divisional Commanders asking for permission to withdraw, and with the Inspector-General Assam Rifles (IGAR), some of whose posts were in the forward zone, as well as his own corps headquarters staff counseling withdrawal, Lt. Gen. Kaul sent another message to Eastern Command and Army HQ saying that the Namka Chu position was untenable, and asking for withdrawing the isolated company across the Namka Chu at Tsangle back to the southern side, 'giving preference to discretion over prestige.'

On October 16, Gen. Lei Yingfu, the head of the PLA's 'war-fighting department' (*zuo zhan bu*), gave Mao his reasons for the recent Indian offensive actions in the Thag La area. The first of five suggested major Indian motives was Tibet: the persistent Chinese perception that India wanted to 'invade' Tibet and turn it into a 'colony or a protectorate of India,' to return Tibet to its pre-1949 position or to get rid of the sovereignty of the Chinese central government over Tibet, so as to create a 'buffer-zone' (*huanzhongguo*) between China and India. The final and probably most important suggested motive was India's apparent belief that China was 'bluffing' and that Nehru believed that China was weak and could be taken advantage of: that China 'barked but did not bite.'[5] Later the same day, at a CMC meeting at Xishan, on the western outskirts of Beijing, it was formally decided to 'annihilate' (*jianmie*) the Indian forces in the Thagla area. Also present were the Tibet Military District (TMD) Commander Lt. Gen. Zhang Guohua and the Sinkiang Military Region Commander Maj. Gen. He Jiachan. Two directions were given by Mao:

- First, the PLA had to secure victory and 'knock Nehru to the negotiating table,' and
- Second, the Chinese troops had to be restrained and principled.

On October 17, the CMC sent an order to the TMD, stating that PLA forces were to 'exterminate the Indian aggressor forces.'

On the same day, in the words of the Defence Ministry's *History of the Conflict with China, 1962:*

> To sort the matter out, a conference was held at Corps Headquarters in Tezpur on the morning on 17th October. V.K. Krishna Menon, B.N. Mullik, H.C. Sarin, Gen. P.N. Thapar, Maj. Gen. A.S. Guraya, [I.G.A.R.[6]], Lt. Gen. Sen, and Lt. Gen. Kaul attended it. Maj. Gen. Guraya expressed his views in favour of withdrawal. Kaul also forcefully argued in favour of immediate withdrawal. Then, at the suggestion of Mullik, the three civilians withdrew from the meeting to allow the generals themselves to take a military decision without civilian interference. After two hours of closed-door discussions, Gen. Thapar informed the Defence Minister that it was decided to hold the Namka Chu front and the Tsangle sector.[7]

It seems fantastic that the Army Commander and the Army Chief, after having heard at length the chief military proponent of the 'Forward Policy,' Lt. Gen. Kaul himself, having changed his mind after having seen the realities on the ground, and being well aware that Lt. Gen. Umrao Singh, Maj. Gen. Niranjan Prasad and Brig. Dalvi had all been against the 'forward push' from the start, should now continue to stick to it. What went on behind the closed doors is not known, but it is possible that one of two factors were behind that fateful decision:

- The two senior Generals did not have the moral courage to tell the Defence Minister, well-known for his unpleasant overbearing behaviour and his scorn for the intellectual capabilities of senior army officers, that they had changed their minds since the last meeting of 11th October.
- The Army Commander, Lt. Gen. Sen, and the Army Chief, Gen. Thapar, Kaul's two immediate seniors in the army hierarchy, who had been having to play second-fiddle to Lt. Gen. Kaul for some years because of Kaul's much greater influence with the Prime Minister and the Defence Minister, realized that Kaul was now caught in a trap of his own making, and were unwilling to let him off the hook. They saw this as an opportunity to get their own back on him, and so used their official positions as his superiors to force him to accept a decision of no withdrawal, even though they knew this was militarily the wrong decision. Perhaps they felt that the military situation would not deteriorate to the extent that it did, and that the planned defensive positions to the rear of Tawang, based on Se La, would continue to hold.

However, the official history categorically states that:

> The responsibility for continued deployment of 7 Infantry Brigade in tactically unsound positions lies squarely on the Corps Commander (*Lt. Gen. B.M. Kaul*) and the Army Commander (*Lt. Gen. L.P. Sen, nominally his immediate boss*).

After the conference of the 17th, Kaul who had been ailing, instructed GOC 4 Infantry Division that Tsangle[8] was to continue to be held, and another post was to be established on the north bank of the Namka Chu, opposite Bridge 5, to prevent the Chinese from cutting off communication with the small Tsangle locality. In the already over-strained logistics situation, and the unmilitary deployment in penny-packets, this would further compound both problems. Lt. Gen. Kaul was evacuated to Delhi the next day for treatment, suffering from pulmonary oedema resulting from his unacclimatised high-altitude privations in the Namka Chu sector.

On October 18 in Beijing, the CMC met again and approved the war plan prepared by the planning group in the CMC staff. Present at this meeting were Mao, Zhou, Liu Shaoqi, Deng Xiaoping, Lou Ruiqing, and Marshals Liu Bocheng, He Long, and Xu Xaingqian.

Later on October 18, an expanded Politbureau met and gave formal approval to the decision for a 'self-defensive counter-attack war' against India, as per the plan already approved, to be launched on October 20. Attending the meeting were Mao, Liu Shaoqi, Marshal Zhu De, Deng Xiaoping, Gen. Lou Riqing, the PLA Chief of Staff, Yang Shanghun (then Deng's assistant and in charge of organizational matters for the Central Committee of the Party), TMD Commander Lt. Gen. Zhang Guohua, Gen. Wang Shangrong, head of the Operations Department of the PLA, the diplomats Zhang Hanfu and Qiao Guanhua, and Gen. Lei Yingfu.

On the night of October 18, India's Eastern Army Commander, Lt. Gen. Sen, sent a signal from HQ 4 Corps as Corps Commander to GOC 4 Division to further build up on Tsangle. The Tsangle company was to stay put, and another company was to be sent to Bridge 5 to be located NORTH of the bridge across the Namka chu, and to dominate the area between Bridge 5 and Tsangle. Yet another company was to be located south of Bridge 5. Tsangle was four days' march away from the Dhola post. 500 men could not possibly be maintained in the Bridge 5-Tsangle area by one platoon of 30 men providing porterage on a 8-day turnaround.

The official history states:

> Kaul, commanding IV Corps from his sick-bed at his Delhi residence, ordered two more companies to strengthen Tsangle. This order would have stretched the supply effort of 7 Brigade to breaking point. Dalvi protested to Prasad against this order. Maj. Gen. Prasad had already brought this to the notice of HQ IV Corps. In reply he was told that the build-up at Tsangle would be carried out otherwise the officers defaulting in executing/implementing these orders would be removed. Niranjan Prasad passed this warning to Dalvi.

Lt. Gen. Sen had subsequently maintained that he had nothing more to do with the war in NEFA after Kaul took over the sector. Maj. Gen. Niranjan Prasad, who should have been nominated as the 'Officiating Corps Commander' in Kaul's absence was helpless and unable to take the appropriate tactical decisions. There was thus nobody in higher command in 4 Corps on the night of 19th October 1962.

A historical precedent has been applied to the explanation for Gen. Kaul's evacuation to Delhi, and subsequent return to command the corps, that of the famous German General Rommel during the battle for the North African desert. But in his case, the German Army in Africa, 'Panzerarmee Afrika' had carefully prepared battle plans known to all his subordinate commanders, and Rommel left Gen. Stumme in full command. When Stumme died of a heart attack on the battle-field, Gen Ritter von Thoma immediately took over. Thus the Germans had a commander throughout the Battle of El Alamein, and there was no confusion or paralysis due to their being no one in command.

By 19 October 2013, 7 Brigade was by and large deployed, in what was mostly an extended line, from West to East, as under:

- Bridge V: One company of 9 PUNJAB
- Temporary Bridge: 'C' Company 2 RAJPUT less a platoon, with one platoon from 'D' Company
- Log Bridge: 'B' Company 2 RAJPUT
- Bridge IV: Battalion HQ 2 RAJPUT with 'D' Company less a platoon, and a platoon of 'C' Company
- Bridge III: 'A' Company 2 RAJPUT with a platoon of Assam Rifles under command.
- To the East of 'A' Company 2 RAJPUT and about a kilometer away: HQ 7 Brigade with one company 1/9 GR
- Bridge II: 9 PUNJAB less one company
- Bridge I: 4 GRENADIERS less two companies
- Khinzemane: Tactical HQ 5 ASSAM RIFLES with three Assam Rifles platoons, and under command 'C' Company 4 GRENADIERS at Drokung Samba
- Tsangdhar: One company and Battalion HQ 1/9 GR
- Forward slopes of Tsangdhar, in depth to 'A' Company 2 RAJPUT at Bridge III: 1/9 GR less three companies (in effect only one company and the Battalion HQ)
- On the move to Bridge V: One company 1/9 GR[9]

Capt. H.S. Talwar, the troop commander of 17 Para Field Regiment, who arrived that evening in the brigade HQ, had this to say:

> That night (19 October) I had a meal in the Brigade Mess bunker in the company of six to seven officers. The gathering included the Commander, Brig. Dalvi, the Brigade Major, Rex Kharbanda, the DAA & QMG, Pereira, the IO, Capt. Tushar Gupta, the Signals Officer, Capt. Lakshman [Singh] and the OC Mortar Battery Maj. Balraj Nijjer. In the midst of this setting, the shrill ring of the Telephone Type J,

NAMKA CHU

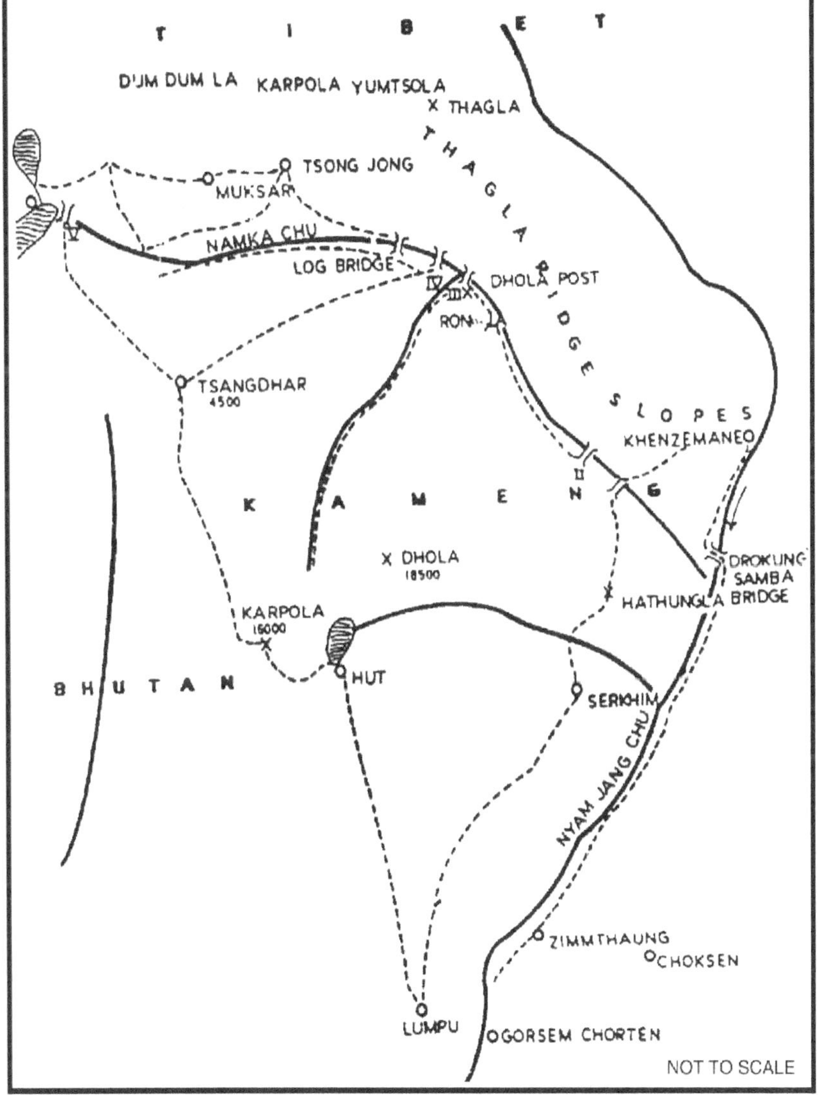
T I B E T
DUM DUM LA
KARPOLA
YUMTSOLA
X THAGLA
THAGLA RIDGE SLOPES
TSONG JONG
MUKSAR
NAMKA CHU
LOG BRIDGE
DHOLA POST
RON
TSANGDHAR
4500
KHENZEMANEO
K A M E N G
X DHOLA
18500
DROKUNG
SAMBA
BRIDGE
HATHUNGLA
KARPOLA
16000
HUT
B H U T A N
SERKHIM
NYAM JANG CHU
ZIMMTHAUNG
CHOKSEN
LUMPU
GORSEM CHORTEN
NOT TO SCALE

> interrupted the proceedings to indicate that the GOC, Niranjan Prasad, wanted to speak to the Brigade Commander, Dalvi. The GOC wanted another company strength or so to be moved to Tsangle, besides the platoon of 1/9 GR which was already on the way. Dalvi was seemingly not prepared to accept this order on the grounds that the Tsangle out-post had no tactical significance and was an additional drain on the stretched administrative resources of the Brigade. Some hot words were exchanged and in exasperation Dalvi offered to resign from the command of 7 Brigade. I was a complete outsider and witnessed the whole drama with a degree of detachment.[10]

The Chinese main defences on the Thag La ridge, with their infantry mortars and MMGs, all looked down onto the various Indian defended localities. There being no aerial reconnaissance, it was not certain, but from the amount of activity among the Chinese troops on the opposite slope for the next few days, it was apparent that the Chinese force was a division, meaning that the division's artillery and heavy mortars would in all probability be dug in on the reverse slopes of the Thag La ridgeline.

On the Chinese side, based on instructions from the highest Chinese military authority, the Central Military Commission (CMC), a forward HQ of the Tibet Military Command had been formed. This forward HQ was to command all operations in the eastern sector and was established at Lhasa on 11 June 1962. It was designated as Zang Zi 419 (Tibet Force 419). It was of a divisional size, and was tasked to prevent further Indian encroachments in the Tawang sector. It had under command 154, 155, and 157 Infantry Regiments plus combat support elements.

A separate force was tasked to prevent any Indian ingress from Sikkim through the Chumbi Valley towards Yating and Gyantse. 11 Infantry Division was initially independently tasked to prevent Indian encroachments in the eastern pant of Arunachal Pradesh, though 32 Infantry Regiment (less one battalion) and one battalion of 31 Infantry Regiment were allotted to the Tawang sector.

On 14 October 1962 the forward HQ of Tibet Military Command (HQ Force 419) moved forward to approxmately 15 km north of Khinzemane.

The Chinese plan was to attack the Indian Namka Chu positions from both flanks, while pinning them down from the front. The main thrust was to be on the Indian left (western) flank. Simultaneously, the river line positions were to be outflanked from the east to cut off their routes of withdrawal. 155 Infantry Regiment and one battalion of 157 Infantry Regiment were tasked to assault 2 RAJPUT and 1/9 GR, while the main body of 157 Infantry Regiment occupied a blocking position at Hathung La, behind the 7 Brigade's positions, to cut off the withdrawal of 9 PUNJAB and 4 GRENADIERS. The 1/9 GR positions on the Tsangdhar feature to the rear were also to be attacked by this regiment simultaneously with the assault on 2 RAJPUT on the river-line.

The 2nd Battalion of 31 Infantry Regiment (ex 11 Infantry Division) were tasked to pin down the Indian positions from the front.[11]

154 Infantry Regiment was to put in a simultaneous battalion-sized attack on the company of 4 GRENADIERS at the Drokung Samba Bridge. The reminder of the regiment was to move down the Nyamjang Chu valley to threaten the 4 Division's headquarters at Zemithang. (The presence of this Chinese force

in the Nyamjang Chu valley later made this main valley unusable by the disorganized mass of withdrawing Indian troops, who were then forced to move cross-country through Bhutan to try and get back to the plains, over the extremely difficult mountain terrain.)[12]

The Chinese plan was to attack the Indian forward positions of 2 RAJPUT from the rear and the flanks, while the Indian defensive siting was oriented towards the front, on an expected direction of attack from across the river. Thus the tactical siting was flawed, with weapon emplacements and designated arcs of fire all oriented towards a show of force towards the front.

On the nights of 17th/18th October and 18th/19th October Chinese troops had been silently infiltrated across the fordable Namka Chu to hidden locations in the little re-entrants and folds of ground on the slopes to their rear. On the day of the 19th October, the Chinese force openly carried out their obvious preparations for an attack.[13]

October in the eastern Himalaya is clear and cold, with the night temperatures dropping to minus 5 degrees Celsius, and the day temperature at those heights remaining between 5 and 8 degrees till the sun sets, after which it drops to below freezing in minutes. At the stand-to at 04:30 hours on 20th October, it was well below zero and bitterly cold, as the men stood-to in their open trenches wrapped in their blankets.

The main Chinese assault came in at 05:14 hours on 20th October. The non-tactical, 'political' deployment had ensured that there was no 'brigade defended area' and no coordination between the troops deployed to guard the two axes of ingress, i.e., Hathungla-Lumpu and Tsangdhar-Lumpu. 7 Infantry Brigade was deployed to try and hold everything at once, and as a result could hold on to nothing. Under the prevailing politically-motivated circumstances, since there were no professional plans made for an eventual withdrawal, there were no prepared layback positions, no troops earmarked for such positions, nor any detailed orders for tactical withdrawal with rearguard actions, 7 Infantry Brigade fought brief independent company-level defensive battles strung out along a thin line. While the officers and men fought gallantly and died fighting, in the best traditions of Indian warriors and of their regiments, other Chinese troops moved between these positions and moved towards the positions of the other two brigades and the divisional headquarters, far to the rear towards the plains of Assam. Brig. Dalvi and a few others were taken prisoner by the Chinese troops they accidentally bumped into on 22nd October while attempting to withdraw after the brigade's desperate short-lived defence and eventual disintegration.

Maj. Gen. Verma describes the situation in 2nd Rajput:

> In almost all the localities the realization that the attack was coming from the rear only dawned on the commanders and troops when the Chinese bugles and whistles to control their infantry closing onto the objectives became audible. The unnerving shock of this unexpected direction meant that the troops now had to get out from the shelter of the bunkers and other defences and face uphill.[14]

There was much fighting among the trees, moss-covered rocks and bushes as the assaulting Chinese infantry rushed downhill using cover from tree to tree and the firing increased in intensity. Verma describes many actions, include the following:

> Second Lieutenant Onkar Dubey, a Company Officer with 'C' Company, though located with 7 Platoon with Subedar Ram Janam Singh, had acted vigorously and taken an LMG

> [.303 Bren gun] with about 15 magazines and along with two men rushed upslope to support Roshan Singh. Dodging his way up between trees and rocks he could get to a flank to assist Roshan's despearate bid to hold the Bump. In the ensuing struggle he managed to inflict heavy casualties on the following waves of the Chinese, finally firing the last two magazines into a bunch of the enemy coming over a spur. At this stage he was severely wounded in the stomach and chest, and lost consciousness through loss of blood. He was left for dead initially by the Chinese who swept past to overrun the entire locality. The Chinese recovered him the next day on 21 October, when they were searching for their own dead. He was taken prisoner.[15]

2nd Lt. (later Lt. Col.) Bhagwan Dutt Dogra of 1/9 GR had described their experience to Lt. Col. A.K. ('Sam') Sharma, who writes:

> 1/9 GR comprised of only 400 odd men: the balloon went up for them on 29 Sep 1962. They marched back 350 km on a man-pack basis only with the barest and basic of war-like stores. On 9 Oct they were ordered on to the Namka Chu from Lumpu.
>
> On 20 October, 1/9 G R were preparing to move to Tsangle, on orders, and were caught flat-footed as the Chinese artillery barrage commenced. He had rushed around his platoon defended locality, from one trench to the other, bucking up his kanchas and rallying around for josh and stead-fastness of his lot, many of whom were down with mountain/high-altitude sickness. He manned the LMG as the No. 1 gunner rolled over dead: killed in action. When the ammo ran out, he limped back to his resting bunker, totally bushed and exhausted and all alone.

The defences were devoid of any artificial obstacle-system or protective mine-fields for the simple reason that no defence-stores, what so ever, were around! The PLA infantry had come blowing their bugles and controlling whistles. The Political Commissars were shouting *'Hindi-Chini bhai bhai'* and *'Aap yahan se chale jao'* in pidgin Hindi at the top of their voices over loud-hailers. They were saying that the Chinese had nothing against the Nepalese soldiers and that they should lay down their arms and surrender!

As he was awaiting his fate, in that dark and unlit bunker, a Chinese officer motioned to him to come out. In his angry retort, B.D. Dogra shouted back at him, to come in and get him, if he so dared to. The Chink did not dare! The PLA troops then surrounded the bunker and lobbed in White-Phosphorous (WP), stun and percussion High Explosive (HE) grenades. Dogra was wounded in the face. Three Chinese soldiers wrestled him to the ground, over-powered him, and took him prisoner.

2/Lt. B.D. Dogra's citation for MVC, in brief, reads like this:

Second Lieutenant Dogra was posted on the left flank of the battalion that guarded the track leading to the position held by the Gorkha Rifles in the Tsangdhar area in NEFA. The Chinese subjected his position to heavy shelling on the morning of 20th October, 1962, before attacking in force. The officer moved from bunker to bunker enthusing and inspiring his men. He suffered a grievous injury in the process but continued fighting. When his gunner was hit he took over the light machine gun and used it to devastating effect. Ultimately the Chinese destroyed the gun and 2/Lt Dogra was captured.[16]

Capt. (later Lt. Gen.) Ravi Eipe, commanding 'A 'Company of 2nd Rajput, narrates:

After the lifting of the artillery fire, I decided to move up to the Assam Rifles post to get a better picture of what was happening. Accordingly I moved to No. 2 Platoon (under CHM Saudagar Singh) and climbed towards the Assam Rifles post with my runner. On seeing us, heavy small arms fire started coming towards us from the Assam Rifles post which was about 70 yards away. I thought Assam Rifles men were firing at us in panic. I shouted at them to stop firing and that I was their Company Commander. They did not stop firing. Then I spotted some men in khaki and realized that the Chinese had already occupied the post and were firing at us.

... our positions were not effective to take on repeated attacks of the Chinese from uphill and we soon started losing portions of this platoon as the Chinese were able to bring down effective fire on our men who were on lower ground in only fire trenches and behind boulders.

... I saw Chinese outflanking No. 2 Platoon from the West and going towards No 1 Platoon on the river line.... At about 0700 hours the Chinese started engaging No. 1 Platoon from the rear and I could hear intense firing on both sides.... Around 0715 hours No. 3 Platoon was also attacked from the Dhola post area.... Around 0745 hours we were being attacked from both directions and we were cut off from No. 1 Platoon as the Chinese in large numbers had surrounded the platoon position and were attacking them from the rear. As the strength in No. 2 and 3 Platoons had dwindled drastically, I decided to pull out the remnants and move towards the Brigade Headquarters. No. 1 Platoon could not be contacted as the Chinese were between us and the platoon. 'A' Company had put a gallant fight in a hopeless position and had inflicted heavy casualties on the Chinese.[17]

2nd Rajputs, and 1st/9th Gorkhas had to bear the brunt of the Chinese attack. The 9th Punjabis, who were the most prepared in their defences having been moved in earliest, and the 4th Grenadiers, were mainly by-passed and could not offer the resistance they could have, because of the faulty deployment of the brigade.

Lt. Gen. Ravi Eipe (Retd.) described the situation and the action again later, in 2012:

> We were fighting in the Namkachu region, which was at an altitude of about 12,500 feet. We had to make a six-day foot march from Tawang to approach it. In the process, we had to cross the Sang Dar ridge, which is about 16,000 feet. The terrain was extremely difficult. There were some mule tracks, nothing beyond that.
>
> The roads in those days came up to Tawang. That too, it was a one-tonne-in-patches kind of track. Logistically, we were in a very difficult area where the troops had to sustain themselves on man pack. That is, you had with you whatever you carried on your back. And as far as replenishments were concerned, we were getting rations air-dropped. But because of the altitude and the closeness to the border, the aircraft were dropping at heights that tend to disperse the drops.
>
> So it was extremely difficult to collect the rations. Many of the items, even if dropped, would get caught in ravines and the troops never got what they required even if it was basic rations. Sometimes, for example, we just could not get salt. Sugar was not there. This kind of logistical problem put the troops to a lot of privation. But in spite of that, our troops displayed one great thing, and that was that they could sustain themselves on very little, and even be very cheerful with these hardships.

Secondly, because we were on man-pack basis when we had to make our defences there, we did not have the proper tools and equipment, and had to rely on very small picks and shovels that a man carries on his back, which we call tools entrenching. That's a very inefficient way of digging anything. If you wanted to cut a tree in those days, there was nothing like an electric saw, like you see in the movies now. It was only with a dha or an axe that you felled trees.

In addition to all these difficulties, the weather was hard. We did not have snow clothing, but were just sustaining ourselves at those incredible altitudes with angola shirts, that is, heavy mazari shirts with a jersey each. Every man had one blanket with him. So we used to sleep in pairs. You had a blanket and what we would call a ground sheet each, that's all. Even an officer had to sleep with someone else. That way, each pair of soldiers had two blankets over them.

But the main reason why we got into this kind of situation was because of the overall assessment, which somehow was extremely faulty. Our perception of China was that it was a very benign country. It was an era of 'Hindi-Chini bhai bhai.' The political thought process in the country precluded the possibility of China as a real threat.

Consequently, the preparations to undertake such an operation were very tardy. There was a mismatch between our perception of the enemy and what the enemy actually did. That is the reason why we got into so many problems. Otherwise, we would have gone into this war with better preparations: built roads and so on. That is the reason we were caught on the wrong foot.

At a national level, we did not read the enemy's intentions properly.

The other thing is that we were deployed in a fashion that could be criticised severely, from a military point of view. Our principle always is that you must occupy heights so that the enemy who wants to attack you climbs up to you, and then you have the advantage of height when you want to deal with him. But here, we were deployed along a nullah or river, so that our attackers got the advantage over us. He could come behind us and on top of us.

This happened because of the belief that the line we occupied was not a defensive line; it was just a political line temporarily to establish our claim to what we are holding. So, there again, we were not very realistic. When our battalion was attacked, we were not only on low ground, but also facing the enemy here with the attack coming from behind.

I had 95 men under me; I was a Captain. The whole battalion had 513 men of all ranks in the Namkachu area. Of these, 282 were killed. Of my 95, only 14, including I, survived! All this on just one day! The enemy captured another 171.

The battle on that day went thus: we woke up and occupied our defences at 5.15 AM, just before first light. Fifteen minutes later, the enemy started heavy artillery shelling. They could see our positions clearly. Their fire was very effective, as the distance was short. In some cases, they could even use guns for direct firing. They could hit our bunkers, and some of our bunkers just blew up into smithereens.

In the meantime, in the darkness, unknown to us, the Chinese had crossed further up North and were coming behind our positions. This shelling carried on for about 45 minutes. Then we heard a bugle, and the shelling stopped. Instead, firing began from behind. When we realised that this attack was coming from behind us, we organised ourselves to turn behind and keep firing. But the advantage was to the Chinese, who were on top.

In spite of the fact that we were in an unfavourable position, we continued fighting. We could hold on for nearly another 45 minutes, by which time we had suffered extensive casualties.

I was not in communication with the battalion commander or anyone else. So I took whatever men I could to the Bde HQ. The Brigade Commander was there, and heard the firing. All the companies of the 2nd Rajput had been attacked simultaneously in the same manner, and that is why we suffered such losses.[18]

Maj. Gen. Verma describes the attack on the 2nd Rajput's Bridge IV position:

The Chinese had from their positions on the Thag La slopes realized that the Bridge 4 position had the unit's headquarters located in it. The 3-inch mortar positions and the sigmal bunker were singled out for early destruction.... Gurdial [*Maj. Gurdial Singh, the Battalion 2IC*] realized that the attack was coming from uphill and behind.... As the mortar shelling stopped for the deadly pause before the Chinese attack commenced, all doubts of the direction of attack were dispelled as the sound of bugles and whistles and even the chattering of the enemy could be heard in the cover uphill. The need was to get the men out of the bunkers to face uphill. Meanwhile Lieutenant Bhup [Singh] had rushed up to join the CO in the Battalion Command Post further up the hill.

The full force of the Chinese attack struck the Bengali 12 Platoon under Jemadar[19] Biswas, the Battalion Command Post in the centre and Subedar Ram Chander's 'C' Company platoon towards the East. The bunched-up Chinese pouring down were being cut down by the volley of rifle and LMG fire from the hastily-readjusted defences. Lieutenant Colonel Rikh, Captain Gurcharan Singh (the Adjutant) and Lieutenant Bhup Singh had resorted to using the Command Post's rear entrance as a fighting position ... unaware of what was happening below, the CO in his Command Post and the two flanking platoons could barely fight off the first two waves of the Chinese attack. The enormous advantage of automatic fire from AK-47 carbines, Chinese automatic rifles (with folded bayonets) and light machine guns fired mainly from the hip as they moved from tree to tree and from rock to rock began to tell. In spite of suffering casualties the Chinese kept pouring down and soon started getting past the still-resisting bunkers.... A third attack was launched by the Chinese from the South and South-West. This attack was mounted against the now depleted 'C' Company platoon and remnants of the Battalion Headquarters. It was a desperate one-sided struggle and the defenders were swamped. Almost the last resistance continued from the Battalion Command Post.[20]

Lt. Col. Rikh narrates in his own words:

When the enemy had overrun the upper 'D' Company platoon they commenced firing into the blind side of my bunker with a heavy machine gun trying to make a hole in the bunker. Captain Bhatia and I continued to engage the enemy from the doorway of the bunker ... to see what had happened. As I stepped out of the bunker, a Chinese soldier who had crawled up to the side of the bunker threw a grenade at me. This grenade hit my rifle and exploded. My left jaw was broken and my lip cut open. I fell down.... I got up with the help of Bhup Singh and leaning against the door started firing at the enemy closing in on the bunker. An enemy LMG burst fired into the doorway killed my Adjutant, Captain Bhatia, and broke the top of my left shoulder. I had the pleasure of killing the Chinese who had shot my Adjutant. Finally an enemy bullet hit my left elbow and broke it. Due to the loss of blood I fell down with my left leg outside the bunker. A Chinese fired a burst into it and broke my leg below the knee. Lieutenant Bhup Singh pulled me in and covered me with a blanket.

The Chinese were now closing in on the bunker from all sides. Lieutenant Bhup Singh [*along with one jawan*] manned the doorway and single-handed kept the Chinese at bay. By this time all firing outside had ceased. This was the last bunker holding out. Our ammunition finally finished. The Chinese, seeing that all firing from the bunker had ceased, rushed into it and overpowered Bhup Singh. We were taken outside and I was put on a stretcher and my wounds bandaged later by a Chinese nursing orderly.[21]

Verma sums up the gallant 2nd Rajput resistance:

Of the effective strength of 513 all ranks of 2 RAJPUT, 282 were killed including 4 officers and 6 JCOs. Wounded and captured were 81 including 2 officers and 3 JCOs. Those who were captured unwounded were 90, including 3 officers and 2 JCOs. Only a total of 60 all ranks got away. These last were mainy from the rear and administrative elements of 'D' Company on Bridge 4 and some from 'A' Company.[22]

Capt. Lakshman Singh, the Brigade Signals Officer, was at the Brigade HQ at Rongla, less than a kilometre from the Chinese positions in the Namka Chu valley. He describes the last moments of their functioning at the 7 Brigade HQ:

> When the Indian radios fell silent, it had been taken to mean that they had been overrun. There was no brigade left to command after three hours.... A young Lieutenant[23] with a few soldiers, and [thereafter] the company commander protecting the Brigade HQ walked in soon after, dazed, still pointing his revolver. He informed Brigadier Dalvi that the Chinese were just 200 metres behind, and in hot pursuit. The order to abandon the Brigade HQ was sounded.

Brig. Dalvi and his officers left to regroup at Tsangdhar.... His signals sub-unit stayed behind and were instructed to leave after shutting down the radio. 'Everybody has gone,' Capt. Lakshman Singh said in his last message over the wireless set. 'I am closing down the post.' He then led his signals group of 40 men away from the shattered brigade headquarters.[24]

7 Brigade's overall story is best told by its own commander:

> At exactly 5 on the morning of 20th October 1962, the Chinese opposite Bridge III fired two Verey lights. This signal was followed by a cannonade of over 150 guns and heavy mortars, exposed on the forward slopes of Thagla.... The Chinese used 76 mm guns which were fed and fired automatically, and 120 mm mortars.... This was the moment of truth. As the first salvoes crashed overhead there were a few minutes of petrifying shock. The contrast with the tranquility that had obtained hitherto made it doubly impressive.... It had started. This was the end of years of miscalculations: months of suspense; days of hope, and the end of a confused, nightmare week. The cataclysm broke on the dawn of a day which India will never forget. The Battle of the Namka Chu must surely achieve the black prominence of the Battles of Panipat and Plassey.

The bombardment lasted an hour and soon after massive infantry assaults followed, substantiating Nelson's famous dictum: 'Only numbers can annihilate.' The fate of India was now in the hands of three weak companies of the Rajput Regiment and two unbalanced companies of the 9th Gorkhas. At that time India had an Army of over 400,000 men but due to our stubborn refusal to think in strategic terms, only 600 men were engaged in the initial battle. This flimsy barrier was pierced with consummate ease by the powerful force which the Chinese had mustered, to teach India a lasting lesson.

At all events, within a few minutes of the Chinese attack, 7 Brigade lost its cohesion. There was no hope of reinforcement or influencing the battle in any way. I had no reserves and very soon no communication with my battalions as the lines were cut.... Events took place with such bewildering swiftness that it is difficult to piece together an accurate account of the tactical battle. The Namka Chu battlefield soon became a mosaic of sprawling humans locked in mortal combat. The men fought in small sub-units under their officers and JCO's and continued to resist even when isolated and encircled. A random sample of group and individual heroism will best throw into relief the pattern of fighting.

The Chinese had encircled us with one large and two small pincer movements. Before mounting frontal attacks against the Rajputs they had infiltrated one battalion behind them, and cut off the Gorkhas from the Rajputs. The Rajputs were attacked from two directions at the same time. They had no hope. They were trapped.... The Rajputs and the Gorkhas put up a spirited fight against overwhelmimg odds for over three hours despite the demoralising lack of artillery defensive fire support.[25]

9th Punjab had not been subjected to the heavy shelling of the 20th morning. At around 11:00 hours, Brig. Dalvi ordered them to withdraw towards Hathung La. When the battalion was beginning to pull back, they were shelled and fired upon, followed by a Chinese assault. After heavy fighting the battalion mangaged to break contact and withdraw. However, the Chinese had already occupied Hathungla before they reached there, where they were again engaged. They fought hard and well in every action. Eventually they withdrew through Bhutan, including the isolated company at Tsangle.

4th Grenadiers had been deployed partly along the Namka Chu (Bridge I) under 7 Brigade, and partly backwards along the Nyamjang Chu under 4 Div HQ. 'D' Company was directly under the Div HQ with a platoon at Serkhim and a platoon at Hathungla. 'C' Company was at the Drokung Samba bridge, about a kilometer short of Khinzemane. It was attacked by about a battalion of Chinese on the 20th October morning. The Chinese had blown up the bridge on the Nyamjang Chu, and thus this company were cut off and not in a position to fall back to rejoin the rest of the battalion. Fighting witih their backs to the wall under their commander, Second Lt. G.V.P. Rao, they fought hard as long as they could, with him and a number of his men being killed, some wounded and captured.[26]

Brig. Dalvi describes his brigade's battle:

Major B.K. Pant's leadership and indomitable courage is a true epic ... [His] company held fast against three waves of Chinese attacks and suffered heavy casualties. The enemy called for heavier artillery concentrations before launching the fourth attack. Pant was wounded in the stomach and both legs. Despite his agony he continued to inspire his men, who seeing the indomitable will of this man, rose to superhuman heights and broke the fourth attack. Pant losing blood rapidly was nearing his end but would not cry 'enough....' His last words were: *'Men of the Rajput Regiment, you were born to die for your country. God has selected this small river for which you must die. Stand up and fight as true Rajputs.'*[27]

The Punjabis who had fought the Chinese to a standstill (in the initial engagements) were out-flanked and suffered all their casualties while withdrawing over Hathungla Pass and the Dhola Massif. The same fate befell the Grenadiers. These two famous units were sacrificed without a fight due to our faulty dispositions.[28]

Brig. Dalvi continues:

The full story of the ill-fated Thagla Battle, if the massacre can be dignified by such a title, may never be known as many of those who took part were killed in action.... Undersupplied and ill-prepared, these men fought a lonely mountain battle and few in the rest of the country, or indeed the Army knew of their ordeal and their squandered heroism, unredeemed by the faintest trace of success.

The Gorkhas, the Rajputs, the Sikhs, the Dogras, the Bengalis, the Mussulmans of the Grenadiers, the *Ahirs*, the South Indian signalers and all the others from the four corners of India had nothing to sustain them but their regimental pride and traditions They had done what they had done because they were soldiers. For no man can do more than give his life for his Country.

The story of gallantry beyond the call of duty was reenacted in many platoons and companies. At 'Temporary

> Bridge,' Naik Roshan Singh's section clung doggedly to its position till every man was killed. The 'Bridge Four' garrison repulsed two waves of Chinese attackers. The third attack wiped out a whole platoon of Bengalis, commanded by Jemadar Biswas, who was killed leading a gallant, but hopeless bayonet charge. Subedar Dasrath Singh's platoon was reduced to seven men and had exhausted its ammunition in repulsing three Chinese attacks. Undeterred, the gallant men, led by Dasrath, got ready to show the Chinese what the Rajputs were made of. They charged the fourth attacking wave with the bayonet. In the ensuing hand-to-hand fighting, four more men were killed. The three survivors, seriously wounded, were captured. Jemadar Bose's platoon was left with only ten men after halting three Chinese attacks. He too charged with the bayonet and gave his life – as did most of his platoon.
>
> The heavy casualties suffered by 7 Brigade speak for themselves. The Rajputs who had 513 all ranks in the Namka Chu had the following casualties: (a) Killed – 282 including 4 Officers and 6 JCO's (b) Wounded and captured 81, including 2 Officers and 3 JCO's (c) Captured unwounded 90, including 3 Officers and 2 JCO's. Only 60 all ranks or about 9 per cent got away and these were mainly from rear and administrative parties left behind at Tsangdhar, Lumpu and Towang.[29]

All the units of 7 Infantry Brigade fought back as best they could, given their circumstances, but being deployed on indefensible ground could offer only fleeting and token resistance. 7 Brigade had a total of 493 killed on the morning of 20th October 1962, and by mid-day had ceased to exist.

The Tac HQ of 4 Division at Zemithang was soon under threat from the advancing Chinese, who had sent a force forwards along the Nymanjang Chu valley towards Lumpu and Tawang. It managed to withdraw on October 21st morning, along with a company of 4th Garhwal Rifles which had been deployed to protect it. On October 21st, as the Divisional Commander, Maj. Gen. Niranjan Prasad, was walking back towards Tawang, he received a message appointing him the Officiating Corps Commander. Maj. Praval comments:

> Had he been given the appointment four days earlier, he might have authorized 7 Brigade to move back to more defensible positions.[30]

NOTES

1. John W. Garver, *China's Decision for War with India in 1962, op.cit.,* pp. 54-55.
2. Of 'F' Troop, of 52 Para Field Battery of 17 Parachute Field Regiment.
3. One troop of 34 (Maratha) Heavy Mortar Battery.
4. Both of 'C' Company, 6th Mahar Machine Gun Battalion; No. 9 Platoon with 1/9 G.R., and No. 8 Platoon with 2 RAJPUT at Bridge 4.
5. Garver, *op. cit.*, p. 56.
6. Inspector-General Assam Rifles; the officer who was the administrative head of the Assam Rifles in those days. The post was later upgraded to that of Director-General Assam Rifles (DGAR).
7. *History, op. cit.*, p. 102.
8. Tsangle was a small, isolated and tactically untenable locality occupied on the orders of Lt. Gen. Sen before the arrival of Lt. Gen. Kaul as Corps Commander. It was across the Namka Chu and had no military tactical value.
9. Verma, *op. cit.*, p. 46, and *History, op. cit.*, pp. 116-118.
10. Quoted by Brig. Lakshman Singh, VSM, (Retd.), *Op. cit.*
11. Verma, *op. cit.*, p. 58-59.
12. *Ibid.,* p. 59.
13. *Ibid.,* pp. 50-53.
14. *Ibid.,* p. 62.
15. *Ibid.,* p. 63.
16. Lt. Col A.K. ('Sam') Sharma, pers. comn., 2013.
17. Verma, *op. cit.*, pp. 71-73.

18. Interview to South Asian Institute for Strategic Affiars, 18 Sep 2012, on the Internet at www.southasian idea.com.
19. This Junior Commissioned Officer (JCO) rank is now known as 'Naib-Subedar.'.
20. Verma, *op. cit.*, pp. 67-68.
21. *Ibid.,* pp. 68-69.
22. *Ibid.,* p. 74.
23. Actually, an understandably 'shaken' Capt. Eipe. Brig. Lakshman Singh, VSM (Retd.), pers. commn., June 19, 2013.
24. As told to Sandeep Unnithan of India TODAY, by Brig. Lakshman Singh, VSM (Retd.), published in the online version on October 18, 2012.
25. Dalvi, *op. cit.*, p. 319.
26. Palsokar, Col. R.D., *The Grenadiers: A Tradition of Valour* (Jabalpur, Grenadiers Regimental Centre, 1980), pp. 309-310.
27. Dalvi, *op. cit.*, p. 321.
28. *Ibid.,* p. 322.
29. *Ibid.,* pp. 322-323.
30. Praval, *op.cit.,* p. 205.

7

The Battle of Bumla (Tawang)

Tawang is 345 km from Tezpur in the plains of Assam, which was then the location of the 4 Infantry Divisional Headquarters. Tawang itself consists of a well spread-out collection of settlements, including the famous monastery, occupying nearly 6 sq km on a slope and a spur extending southwards from the Himalayan watershed which forms the Tibetan border at Bumla, only 37 km away at the edge of the Tibetan plateau. It had been nominated the Division's 'Vital Ground.' Tawang itself, ie, the area of the town and the monastery, is not a tactically suitable location for defence, having been inhabited on ground best suited for agriculture and living comfort, near the monastery whose site had been revealed to the 6th Dalai Lama[1] by a white horse in a dream, but it does require a fairly extensive local perimeter defence. Therefore the Tawang defences were sited at the nominated 'Vital Ground' which was a nexus of minor ridges above the Tawang township, about 15 to 18 km to the north, between Pankentong and Milaktongla, on the route to Bumla.

Distances from Tawang to the Sino-Indian border at Bumla are as under:

Tawang – Pankengtong Tso (4030 m)	13 km	
Pankengtong Tso – Mila (4200 m)	19 km	
Mila – Klemta (4230 m)	07 km	
Klemta – Bumla (4580 m)	08 km	(Sino-Indian border)
Total distance Tawang to Bumla:	37 km	

7 Infantry Brigade had originally been tasked for the defence of Tawang. It was planned to have been held by the brigade less

one battalion (i.e., two battalions plus supporting elements, six platoons of 5th Assam Rifles, and the brigade headquarters) in well-prepared defences, including the local perimeter defence of the township, where the brigade HQ was located.

However, the Government of India's insistence that a show of force had to be made against the Chinese in the area of the Thagla Ridge area, five to six days of hard foot-marching (the only possible mode of movement) away, over steep bridle-paths and foot-tracks for about 135 km, had thrown this planning into total disarray. Brig. Dalvi, Commander 7 Infantry Brigade was originally the man responsible. He explains his predicament:

> From the very outset there was a divided aim, i.e., to defend Towang as well as to challenge the Chinese intrusion into the Thagla area. In the event we were weak everywhere. There was 'a certain woolliness of thought and indecision of purpose.' Despite the mounting tension there was no strategic plan or dispositions throughout the September crisis.[2]

If both these tasks had to be simultaneously carried out, then 4 Infantry Div would require a minimum of a brigade each for the Thagla Ridge-Namka Chu area and one for the defence of Tawang. In any case, under the prevailing circumstances it was neither possible to move forward another brigade in time, nor would it have been possible to maintain and stock a force of two brigades either for an impending battle or even to remain in the area through the oncoming winter. Even to attempt both requirements would have meant having to divert the entire supply-dropping resources of the air force to this one sector alone, foregoing supply drops to the air-maintained positions in Ladakh and in the Walong sector of eastern Arunachal Pradesh, and even then it was doubtful.

As it was, one of 7 Brigade's original battalions, 1st Sikh, were left behind in the Tawang area, with a company deployed forward in the covering role from the Bumla border, where there was an old Assam Rifles post of 5th Assam Rifles, down to the main defences between Pankentong and Milaktongla. 4th Garhwal Rifles had already been moved into Tawang a fortnight earlier.

In the period of panic after the disintegration of the brigade at Namka Chu, in which there was no effective nominated Corps Commander available in the battle zone, the importance of Tawang got overlooked, and with the decision to build up on Se La taken at higher levels, Tawang was left with only one battalion (1st Sikhs), two companies of 4th Garhwal Rifles, and five platoons of Assam Rifles to hold it, the sixth Assam Rifles platoon having been sent off to establish the Dhola post in June.

The first infantry unit to be moved forward as the Thagla drama unfolded was 13th Dogras from 11 Infantry Brigade (committed around Manipur in a counter-insurgency role since soon after its arrival in the eastern theatre), which arrived at Tawang on 21st October.

1st Sikhs were already holding the main defenses at Milaktongla, 6 km south of Bumla, with one company and the Battalion HQ. Two companies held features dominating the tracks that led to Tawang. There was an Assam Rifles platoon post at Bumla itself, with one Sikh company located between the two positions, which had one platoon further forward on the IB Ridge a km short of the Bumla border post of the Assam Rifles. 4th Garhwal Rifles had its Battalion HQ and one company at Tawang, a company on the Bumla-Jang Track at Landa, and a third company at Pankentong, north of Tawang. The two companies of 13th Dogras were therefore deployed to hold the western approaches to Tawang.

Tawang itself, which was to have had a battalion for its perimeter defence, instead had one company of 4th Garhwal two km to its north, and two platoons of Assam Rifles, the artillery field regiment, and the brigade headquarters without its commander and others who had gone westwards to establish the brigade's tactical headquarters for the Namka Chu operations. Of the remaining two Assam Rifles platoons one was at Sametso covering an approach from Tsaksen, and the other at Lumla. The second company of 4th Garhwal was at Chaksang on the Jang ridge to block the track from Bumla that by-passed Tawang and went to the bridge on the river behind.

Fire support was to be provided by 97 Field Battery with eight guns, deployed a short distance from Tawang on the Bumla road approach. Two mountain batteries, 2 (Derajat) and 7 (Bengal) were deployed in support of the two infantry battalions, with a troop of heavy mortars deployed west of Milaktongla. However, the border pass of Bumla itself was out of range of the deployed artillery.

This was the situation at Tawang on 20th October 1962, with the two Garhwali companies still preparing their defences, and no brigade commander or any other adequately senior officer in overall command. Since Tawang had been identified as the politically most important locality in the Kameng area, this state of affairs should have been prevented by the Army Commander, Lt. Gen. Sen, who was the senior-most commander who should have had knowledge of the situation.

On 22nd October the Army Commander, Lt. Gen L.P. Sen, arrived in Tawang. The GOC 4 Div, Maj. Gen. Niranjan Prasad, reached Tawang around 1800 hours the same day, after a hard day's march from his earlier Tac HQ at Zemithang, which had come under threat from the advancing Chinese.

The Chinese advance on Tawang was in three main prongs. The first was on the Bumla-Tongpengla approach. The second by-passed Tawang and went from Bumla to Jang, on the line of communication. The third prong was a part of the force which had advanced into the Nyamjang Chu valley from Khinzemane. It moved towards Tawang via Sametso.

The Chinese force moving via Tongpengla attacked the Assam Rifles platoon at Bumla which was defended in a professional and determined manner, and the Chinese were unable to break through easily. They were able to overrun this post only at 04:30 hours on 23rd October. The 1st Sikh platoon under Subedar Joginder Singh at the IB Ridge were attacked next. The platoon of the 5th Assam Rifles and the 1st Sikhs gave a very good account of themselves, giving the Chinese leading elements a bloody nose before eventually getting overwhelmed and falling back in professional fashion. By 07:30 hours the Chinese reached the 1st Sikh company's delaying position at Tongpengla. Here again they were resisted fiercely till 11:00 hours.

The evacuation of Tawang was decided upon by the Army Commander, Lt. Gen. L. P. Sen, on October 23rd, after the battle at Bumla. A great deal of confusion was caused by his vaccilation before this final decision to evacuate was given. He was probably influenced by the swift advance of the Chinese forces on 23rd October and the fact that the 4 GARHWAL company at Jang had been engaged by the enemy, who was evidently making an effort to cut off the Tawang garrison. Since Tawang had not been prepared for evacuation, the sudden withdrawal led to avoidable chaos, with all guns, mortars, ammunition, supplies and clothing built up so painstakingly having to be abandoned.

On 24th October, Maj. Gen. Niranjan Prasad was relieved of command, while he was preparing to fight the second phase of the battle at Se La.

NOTES

1. The 6th Dalai Lama, Tsangyang Gyatso, was a Monpa by ethnicity, and was born in 1682 at the Urgelling monastery, 5 km from Tawang.
2. Dalvi, *op. cit.,* p. 201.

8

The Sela and Bomdila Debacle

Maj. Praval explains the confusion caused by orders and counter-orders:

> Sen's orders, which he issued before flying back from Towang, were that the forward troops should break contact; thereafter they, together with the garrison in Towang, should fall laterally back on Jang. In case Jang was already in enemy hands, the troops were to make for Bomdi La, where he intended to position 65 Infantry Brigade. This formation, under Brig. Sayeed, was then on the move from Secunderabad.
>
> These orders were, however, changed that night. The changed orders, issued by 4 Corps, required 62 Brigade, [*which had arrived from Ramgarh*], to hold Se La.... The decision to hold Se La had a profound effect on the campaign.[1]

In the hasty and frantic buildup of Op LEGHORN since early October, 4 Infantry Division now found itself commanding none of its original brigades (7, 5 and 11), but instead had four new ones: an *ad hoc* brigade at Tawang, 48, 62 and 65.

On October 23rd, the Army Chief, Gen. P.N. Thapar accompanied by his DMO, Brig. D.K. Palit, visited HQ 4 Corps in Tezpur, and took the decision to hold the Sela position firmly. The new orders issued by HQ 4 Corps: Jang was to be held by

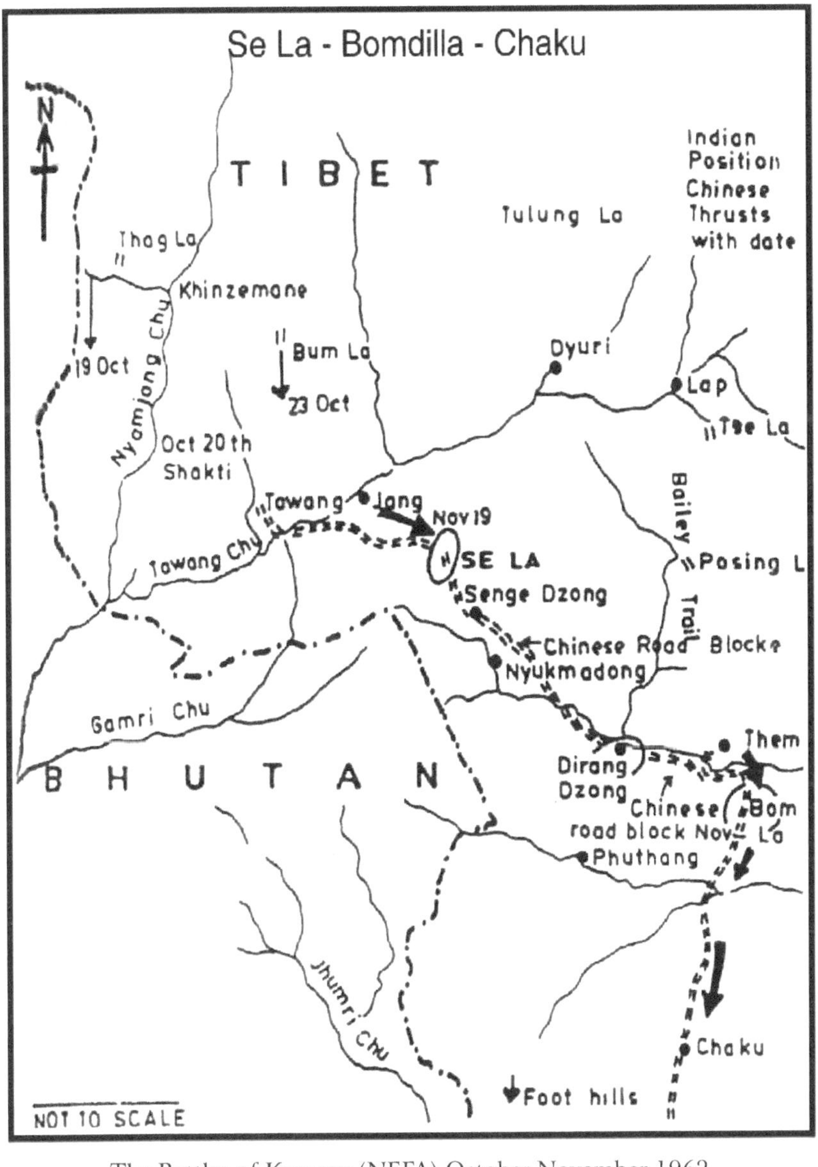

The Battles of Kameng (NEFA) October-November 1962.

HQ 4 Artillery Brigade with some Engineers troops which were already there, and 4th Garhwal Rifles. Sela was to be held by 62 Infantry Brigade with 1 SIKH and 4 SIKH LI (of 48 Infantry Brigade). The latter battalion was being flown in from the Punjab.

Maj. Praval comments:

> Holding Se La was tempting in many ways. 'Holding it would mean loss of less territory; an important consideration politically.... ' Many people thought Se La was impregnable due to its height, 4,180 metres. There was a steep climb to the pass from the Towang Chu valley and the road was dominated by the pass and the peaks on its flanks. All these factors made Se La a strong position. But it was not impregnable and there were tracks that bypassed it. The Chinese were not road-bound like the Indian Army and could isolate Se La. They had already proved that their speed of movement in organized fighting bodies upto regimental strength was remarkable. The main disadvantage of holding it, except as a delaying position, was its distance from Indian bases. Its very height was another disadvantage; its garrison would have to operate at high altitudes. Also, the long line of communication from Bomdila would need protection.[2]

By 24th October, 4 GARHWAL had deployed a company on the bridge at Jang, and the rest of the battalion was occupying positions on the Jang-Sela axis. Tac HQ of 4 Div had been established at Dirang Dzong, 64 kilometres south-east of Sela. On the evening of 24th October the advancing Chinese troops began to engage the bridge position, which was then blown up, and the battalion withdrew and took up a screen position ahead of Sela.

On October 24th, while the Chinese advanced through the mountains towards Assam, there was a sudden and wholesale change of commanders, on the eve of what everyone who mattered in Delhi now realized was an impending battle. These unnecessary and ill-advised (for this stage in the ongoing operations) command changes were ordered by the Army Chief Gen. Thapar on one basis only: the 'valour factor.' Each of the new commanders suddenly appointed was a gallantry award winner form earlier in his service.

Maj. Gen. Harbaksh Singh, the Chief of Staff at HQ Western Command at Shimla (Himachal Pradesh) was rushed by air on promotion to replace Lt .Gen. B.M. Kaul, who had fallen ill and been evacuated to Delhi on 18th October, as GOC 4 Corps. Maj. Gen. Niranjan Prasad was replaced as GOC 4 Infantry Division by Maj. Gen. Anant Singh Pathania, Brig. N.K. 'Nandi' Lal, Commander 62 Brigade, was replaced by Brig. Hoshiar Singh, Brig. G.M. Sayeed of 65 Brigade was replaced by Brig. A.S. Cheema, and Brig. Kalyan Singh, who was preparing for an imminent battle at Tawang, suddenly found himself replaced by Brig. G.S. Gill. The only brigade commander who was not changed was Brig. Gurbux Singh commanding 48 Brigade.

None of these new commanders were familiar with the terrain, the state of affairs, or knew the officers and units under their command. The apparent logic behind these changes was that battle-hardened formation commanders with actual war-fighting experience, as evidenced by the gallantry awards they had won in battle, would prove better than those without. These awards had actually been won during the Second World War when the officers concerned were much younger. Whether gallantry awards won over twenty years previously in fighting at company level gave a brigade commander or divisional commander the mental capability to conduct a formation battle, which is more of a mind-game and requires formation-handling experience as well as moral fibre of a high order, rather than raw physical courage, is a moot point.

Maj. Gen. Niranjan Prasad's only mistake so far had been not resigning in protest when one of his brigades (7 Infantry Brigade at the Namka Chu) was given a militarily impossible task. Some of the formation commanders chosen so suddenly were clearly not suited to their sudden new responsibilities. Maj. Gen. A.S. Pathania, for example, was suddenly pulled out from the relaxed appointment of Director-General National Cadet Corps in Delhi, and was certainly not in the kind of physical shape required to suddenly command a divisional battle in a high-altitude area, more so without any acclimatization at all. Though a highly-decorated officer, having been awarded the Military Cross in WW-II and the Mahaveer Chakra in the J&K operations in 1948, he was visibly unhappy to be suddenly thrown into a battle situation purely because of his gallantry awards.[3] He had been despondent from the time of his arrival to take over the division from Maj.Gen. Niranjan Prasad. The appropriately chosen Div Tac HQ location was the Senge Spur of the Sela complex, but Maj. Gen A.S. Pathania immediately started suffering from severe headache there, a common symptom experienced if no acclimatization is carried out.

Brig. Hoshiar Singh, who had won the gallantry awards of IOM, IDSM, and the French *Croix de Guerre* as a Subedar of the Rajputana Rifles in the Second World War, and was in charge of administration at the National Defence Academy at Khadakvasla in Poona, was suddenly pitch-forked into a live battle situation with a collection of infantry battalions which had themselves been pulled in helter-skelter from various parts of India.

Lt. Gen. Harbaksh Singh as Corps Commander, with the full support of Army Headquarters, began to prepare Sela for a defensive battle as the new Main Defensive Position, with stocking by both road and air put in full swing. As noted, however, the new divisional and brigade commanders knew neither the terrain, nor the battalions and other supporting units, nor even the staff of their own HQ. To their credit, most of them tried their best, though Maj. Gen. A.S. Pathania's mental and physical unpreparedness, and his resultant tactical re-deployment of his Div Tac HQ and the infantry deployments at Sela, was to eventually have disastrous consequences for the nation.

The changes were an unnecessary panic reaction, and contributed to the confusion. To make matters worse, Lt. Gen. B.M. Kaul was suddenly re-instated, after six days, as 4 Corps Commander on 30th October, on the insistence of the Prime Minister and the Defence Minister Krishna Menon, in order to salvage his military reputation.

Capt. Pran Pahwa of 135 Heavy Mortar Battery had arrived with his unit, affiliated to 48 Infantry Brigade of 17 Infantry Division, at New Misamari from the division's permanent station Ambala. They were tasked to move up to Bomdila. While still in New Misamari his unit received a signal that Lt. Gen. Kaul had once again taken over from Lt. Gen. Harbaksh Singh. He writes:

> The signal specifically stated that the message must be read out to all ranks at roll call. I still remember an all-round feeling of dejection caused by this announcement.[4]

As it happened, there was a lull in the fighting from 24th October onwards, which probably contributed to this decision to re-instate Gen. Kaul. This lasted until 16th November, but the emphasis on battle somehow changed after the return of Lt. Gen. Kaul, from preparations for fighting the Chinese to primarily administrative preparations to deal with the severity of the winter, whose grip at those heights was already fearsome.

Maj. Gen. Sukhwant Singh comments:

> As Harbaksh Singh was getting down to the task, Kaul staged a comeback with the tacit consent of Nehru. Along with him came some highly decorated fresh blood in Pathania to command the division and Hoshiar Singh to take charge of the Sela brigade. He asked for Korla[5] also, but he could not be made available readily. Kaul felt that these great fighters would do better than educated and articulate officers like Dalvi (commander of the ill-fated brigade at the Namka Chu position) with whom he had difficulties earlier. Little did he realize at that time that these gentlemen had won decorations as company and battalion commanders, but higher command needed leaders of different arbor and mettle....
>
> Meanwhile, the Chinese pushed their Tibetan road system to link up with our roadhead at Tawang....[6]

On assuming command of 4 Div, Maj. Gen. Pathania made an estimate of his requirements for the defence of the Sela-Dirang Dzong-Bomdila axis and informed HQ 4 Corps that he needed 17 infantry battalions for the task. The Corps Commander asked Eastern Command and Army Headqurters for two more infantry divisions.[7]

The rapid changes in the command structures during the month of October 1962, with battle impending, had a profound implications on the military conduct of affairs in the Kameng sector, and need to be re-stated to underscore their impact, and the in-built potential for confusion:

- On 4th October 1962, with the outbreak of war imminent, not merely the Corps Commander, but the entire Corps Headquarters, including all operational and logistics staff were, were changed, with 33 Corps being replaced by 4 Corps.
- A new Corps Commander was appointed simultaneously along with the change of operational responsibilities and the creation of a new 4 Corps Headquarters.
- Within the next two weeks, all three of 4 Infantry Division's original brigades (5, 7 and 11) had disappeared from its 'Order of Battle' and been replaced by new brigades. Even 7 Brigade, while it still existed up to 20th October, had received new battalions and was virtually a new brigade, in reality also having shed one battalion which was left to defend Tawang independently.
- All the brigade commanders of the new brigades being inducted were replaced as these brigades entered the war zone, and new commanders appointed, who neither knew their own battalions and their officers, nor did they know their own headquarters staff.
- On 24th October the Divisional Commander of 4 Infantry Division and the Corps Commander of 4 Corps were changed simultaneously.
- On 30th October the recently-arrived new Corps Commander was again replaced by the former Corps Commander.

On the diplomatic front there was communication with the Chinese government during the entire war. On 24th October 1962, Chinese Premier Zhou En-lai sent Nehru a letter, proposing:

1. A negotiated settlement of the boundary

2. That both sides disengage and withdraw twenty kilometers from present lines of actual control

3. A Chinese withdrawal north in NEFA

4. That China and India not cross lines of present control in Aksai Chin.

Nehru's October 27 reply expressed interest in the restoration of peace and friendly relations and suggested a return to the 'boundary prior to 8 September 1962.' He was categorically concerned about a mutual twenty kilometer withdrawal after "40 or 60 kilometers of blatant military aggression." He wanted the creation of a larger immediate buffer zone and thus resist the possibility of a repeat offensive. Zhou responded on 4th November to Nehru's query of 24th October about what the Chinese meant by their offer to return to the 'line of actual control.' Zhou's November 4th reply repeated his 1959 offer to return to the McMahon Line in NEFA and the Chinese traditionally claimed MacDonald Line in Aksai Chin. The Chinese PM clarified that they meant the line or 'position as on 7th November 1959,' and not the one where their forces were at that moment. On 11th November 1962, the Indian Parliament announced a national emergency and passed a resolution which stated their intent to "drive out the aggressors from the sacred soil of India." On 14th November Nehru rejected the Chinese offer of a cease-fire, questioning the Chinese interpretation of the 7th November 1959 line to mean the line it had claimed as the boundary since 1960.

OPERATION OLYMPUS

Lt. Gen. Kaul and Maj. Gen. Pathania decided to fight the divisional battle on the heights along the main axis Tawang-Tezpur. 62 Infantry Brigade, with five battalions, was to occupy a compact defended area on Se La, with the pass itself at 13,700 ft and its shoulders up to around 16,000 ft.[8] Of these five battalions, 4th Garhwal Rifles remained deployed forward, in the covering troops role at Nuranang. The artillery support was to be from three field batteries, a Heavy Mortar Battery and another troop of another Heavy Mortar Battery.[9] There was also a machine-gun platoon, placed under command of one of the infantry battalions.[10]

Strangely, 4 Divison's headquarters and 65 Brigade with two of its battalions were to deploy at Dirang Dzong down in the valley at 6,000 ft, surrounded by the high mountain features which dominated the valley. HQ 65 Brigade was at Ewang, a short distance to the north of HQ 4 Infantry Division at Dirang Dzong.

By 6th November the Se La defences were well-prepared with bunkers, barbed wire and mines. The brigade was stocked with three first-line scales of ammunition and fifteen days' rations. The position was well-supported by artillery and heavy mortars.

48 Brigade was to be deployed at Bomdila at 10,000 ft. One of 62 Brigade's battalions was deployed to cover the Poshingla approach, which by-passed Se La and arrived directly at Bomdila.

On the ground, none of the newly arriving battalions knew each other, nor did they know the new brigade HQ under whom they were suddenly placed. Unrelated and confusing tasks were given to the arriving units. For example, 1st Sikh LI, on arrival at Misamari from Ambala on 25th October along with the 'R' Group of HQ 48 Infantry Brigade, was ordered to send one of its companies, 'B' Company under Maj. Janardhan Lal ('Guru') Sharma, for a recce in strength as a special patrol towards the Bhutan border, an area for which they were eventually not tasked.[11]

48 Brigade was tasked on October 28 for the defence of Bomdila sector, and 1st Sikh LI less its 'B' Company made a forced march of three days from Foothills to reach Bomdila on November 11. The brigade, which became actually became one only when it received two other battalions from elsewhere (5th Guards and 1st Madras) was poorly prepared for the defence of Bomdila on November 14, with only one first line of small arms ammunition (SAA), half a first line of artillery ammunition, which was later built up to one full first line by November 17, and rations for 15 days. By 1000 hrs on November 16, 1st Sikh LI managed to occupy it defensive position, after digging its positions ever since its arrival. All weapon pits, fire trenches, and bunkers were ready, except for overhead cover in some cases. But apart from one first line of SAA, it had only 280 bombs for its 3-in mortars, and no defence stores such as barbed wire or mines.

Similarly, 2nd Sikh LI, a sister battalion of the same regiment, was at their peace-station in Chennai (Madras) when they were pulled out in end-1961 for the liberation of Goa, leaving their heavier baggge and families in Chennai. They remained there in Goa under 'operational' conditions for almost a year till suddenly pulled out and rushed off to Tezpur, for induction into NEFA. They were then detached from 65 Infantry Brigade and given to 62 Infantry Brigade at Sela. They moved from the hot tropical coast right up to freezing alpine heights with no preparation.

The inductions of most of the other battalions were stories of a similar nature. These rapid changes in the command and fighting formation structures during the month of October 1962, with battle impending, had a profound effect on the military conduct of affairs in the Kameng sector.

Bomdila was held by 48 Infantry Brigade with three infantry battalions, with a platoon of machine-guns. It was supported by a field battery, a mountain battery and two Stuart tanks.[12]

The next Chinese attack came on 16th November on the 4th Garhwal, who stood firm and beat off four attacks. They were then ordered to disengage and withdraw, and to fall back on their brigade's main position on Se La. They performed this difficult operation successfully as well, and their Commanding Officer, Lt. Col. B.M. Bhattacharjea, was awarded a Mahaveer Chakra (MVC) for his gallant conduct and command of the battalion in this battle, with the battalion later being granted the battle honour 'Nuranang.' The collapse of the 4 Divisional sector happened the next night and the following day. The Chinese infiltration tactics, and their use of ambushes and harassing tasks with the aim of undermining morale, had begun to work on the divisional and corps commanders' minds.

Maj. Gen. A.S. Pathania, the GOC 4 Infantry Division, seemed to have got affected by the general pessimism that permeated the entire 4 Corps since Gen. Kaul's return.[13] At 2230 hrs on 17th November he telephoned the corps headquarters asking for permission to withdraw 62 Brigade from Se La, since reports had come in of Chinese infiltration and he feared the enemy were out-flanking the brigade position with a view to isolating it and capturing it later. This brigade position was well dug-in with adequate supplies and artillery cover, and the commander, Brig. Hoshiar Singh, protested very strongly. He was confident that he was quite capable of holding on, even if isolated, and had been repulsing the Chinese who were already probing his defences all day. One of the battalions, 4th Garhwal, had broken up a Chinese assault on its forward companies, killing 200 Chinese while its own casualties were only two dead and eight wounded. However he was over-ruled, and ordered to fall back on Dirang Dzong in the valley behind him. Maj. Gen. Pathania's plan for 62 Brigade was that it should join 65 Brigade and Divisional HQ, and the combined force would then fight its way to Bomdila.[14]

The BM of the brigade, Maj. Jaidev Singh Datta, has recorded the detailed briefing given by the Brigade Commander's at about 18:30 hours on November 17th in his book *Recollections of the Se La Bomdila Debacle 1962* (2013). The stated intention was to 'withdraw from Se la to Dirang Dzong with a view to take up defences in the Divisional Defended Sector at Bomdila.' A detailed method with timings was given, as per the standard procedure. Some changes were ordered at about 22:00 hours. 2 SIKH LI (less one company) were ordered to withdraw from the Kye La position and their Battalion HQ area and to take up a delaying position at Nyukmadong. The plan and the subsequent changes were informed to the COs of the infantry battalions on the telephone, as well as to the Divisional Commander. The Brigade Commander's intention was to give the detailed orders to the COs personally the next day, 18th November.[15]

Early next morning (18th November) Brig. Hoshiar Singh left the Brigade HQ at about 04:00 hours, to watch the progress of the withdrawal of 2 SIKH LI and of 4 GARHWAL. Maj. Gen. J.S. Datta (Retd.), then-BM of the brigade, writes:

> The Brigade Commander met the commanding officers of 1 Sikh, 2 Sikh Light infantry and 4 Garhwal Rifles on his way to Se La. The Commanding Officer of 1 Sikh informed Brigadier Hoshiar Singh that his Battalion had to withdraw from its defences due to enemy pressure; he tried to stabilize his area but was not successful.[16]

The withdrawal ran into a Chinese block at Nyukmadong and turned into a rout, with the brigade commander himself later being caught in an ambush and killed.[17] The details of the withdrawal are in an entire chapter in Maj. Gen. Datta's book.[18]

The collapse of the Kameng sector of NEFA began with Lt. Gen. Kaul's ambiguous order to Maj. Gen. Pathania for withdrawal in a situation where 62 Infantry Brigade, under Brigadier Hoshiar Singh, comprising 1st Sikh, 2nd Sikh Light Infantry,[19] 4th Garhwal Rifles, 4th Sikh Light Infantry,[20] 13th Dogra, and supporting arms[21] were dug in and prepared, and ready to fight. Demoralisation actually set in AFTER they were given orders to withdraw. Nevertheless they withdrew in military fashion, with the rear-parties of both 4th Garhwal Rifles and of 4th Sikh Light Infantry giving a very good account of themselves against determined Chinese attacks. The withdrawal orders were precise, but unavoidably incomplete, because there were neither detailed orders from Corps HQ to Divisional HQ, nor from Divisional HQ to the brigade.

The brigade's withdrawal lost cohesion after coming under fire from positions established by the Chinese on Nyukmadong ridge. This location was actually the designated 'Intermediate Defensive Position' behind Se La, overlooking the Se La-Dirang Dzong road, and which 2nd Sikh Light Infantry (2 SIKH LI) had been tasked to occupy, to cover the brigade's withdrawal to the 'New Main Defensive Position' at Bomdila. The Chinese managed to reach it before 2 SIKH LI could. This disintegration that began at about 1100 hrs, while the brigade's Rear Guard, 13th Dogras, was engaged with the enemy at Se La, led to the situation where Lt. Col. A.R. Irani, CO 2 SIKH LI, was forced to admit to the Brigade Commander, that he was unable to get hold of his own command.

Fortunately, the Chinese road-blocks, which consisted of small ambush positions, were successfully cleared by a Rear Party of 1st Sikh, consisting of the battalion's Sniper Section and the Battalion HQ Platoon, commanded by the 2nd-in-Command (2IC) of the battalion, Major Gurdip Singh Kler. The aggressive and successful removal of the Chinese ambush positions on the road enabled the brigade's main body and those vehicles which had not been caught in Chinese fire further forward to push through down to Dirang Dzong.

ANALYSIS OF THE FALL OF SELA AND THE DISINTEGRATION OF THE DIRANG VALLEY POSITIONS

To understand the disraveling of the Sela defences it is necessary to look back at 17th November and 2 SIKH LI. After having received the orders at 2200 hrs on 17th November, 2 SIKH LI had been permitted to withdraw from their Sela defences (the Kye La localities) on night 17th/18th November itself. Had they managed to perform their given task, dislodging the Chinese who had arrived at Nyukmadong the very same night, and thus could not have been very well dug-in and prepared, the story of the withdrawal of 62 Brigade could have well turned out entirely different.

The battalion may have got affected by low morale once the withdrawal began. Perhaps through sheer bad luck, they already had a few reverses during the earlier period in the Se La defences, when the Chinese had begun probing, suffering casualties in early November when one of their small reconnaissance patrols along the Mago Chu was ambushed. They then lost one officer (*2ndLt. M.S. Khaira*) and 30 men on night 15th/16th November when a two company-strong raiding patrol under the battalion's 2IC, Major Surender Singh Jaspal, was itself attacked by about a battalion-strength of Chinese shortly after midnight while taking up a night harbour near Luguthang. This patrol, ordered by the Brigade HQ, had an additional company and a platoon of 1st Sikh in support, with one platoon providing a firm base for the patrol to fall back to, and the rest as fighting porters carrying 3-inch mortar ammunition, which the men had very reluctantly been made to do. They had an artillery FOO (*Forward Observation Officer*), and were self-contained for four days. The platoon of 1st Sikh providing the firm base was also attacked simultaneously and thrown back, while the artillery FOO was unable to communicate with the control wireless set at the command post established at Kye La, and thus unable to bring down artillery fire, even though the column was within the range of the field guns at Se La, and the fire-fight continued for two hours. This failed operation had been a setback for the brigade.

By contrast, 4th Garhwal Rifles had been getting the better of the enemy in this phase of aggressive patrolling by both sides, actually even managing to take a Chinese prisoner.

When the divisional headquarters and 65 Brigade down in Dirang Dzong came under small-arms fire for the first time that morning, Maj. Gen. Pathania panicked and ordered the divisional headquarters and 65 Brigade to evacuate Dirang Dzong. This panic evacuation was not done in the appropriate military manner, after some deliberation, planning and orders from the GOC to the Commander 65 Brigade, and from him in turn to his two battalion commanders (*of 4th Rajput and 19th Maratha Light Infantry*) and other elements of brigade troops. The move should have been executed as a tactical withdrawal, with a vanguard as part of an advanced guard, a rear guard, designated layback positions, and all other tactical precautions. The GOC had apparently hoped to reach Bomdila and there to join 48 Brigade. Whilst they were heading in that direction, rumours spread that Bomdila had fallen, though in fact it was not evacuated until 1600 hrs that afternoon. Without establishing the true situation, the whole force headed by the GOC, turned and made for the plains. Maj. J.R. Saigal, the logistics staff officer (DAA & QMG) of 65 Infantry Brigade, is highly critical of the way in which the 65 Brigade Commander, Brig. A.S. Cheema, abandoned the brigade's senior operations staff officer [the Brigade Major (BM)], Maj. Wadke, in his hurry to depart, and of the GOC, who had been twice decorated for personal gallantry in action, for losing the battle in his mind and panicking. He accuses the GOC of driving away in a jeep driven by Maj. Narinder Singh, the GSO2 (Operations) of the Divisional HQ, deserting his command of over 15,000 troops, which was thus paralysed, and of abdicating his responsibility of defending 20,000 sq. kms of territory. He believes that the battle was thus lost UNFOUGHT in a matter of minutes at about 0600 hrs on 18th November 1962.

BOMDILA

The next defensive position, Bomdila, the responsibility of 48 Infantry Brigade under Brig. Gurbux Singh, fell equally ignominiously. In this case it fell without the brigade being allowed to put up a proper fight, greatly due to the impractical orders and counter-orders from the Corps HQ, which left it prematurely vacated. The Chinese, having swiftly advanced right up to Bomdila and beyond, and occupied Bomdila without much resistance, swept on to their claim line and then declared a unilateral cease-fire on November 20. They had achieved their military objective. Why the defence of Bomdila disintegrated is given below.

By mid-morning of the 18th, the only remaining formation in a defensive position was 48 Brigade at Bomdila, with two of its battalions deployed at that location. The Corps Commander, Lt. Gen. Kaul, rang up the Brigade Commander, Brig. Gurbaksh Singh, and ordered him to send a strong force to reinforce the Dirang Dzong position, evidently unaware that the position had already been vacated. In spite of the brigadier's protest that he had no force to spare, and any elements sent forward would weaken his position, which was just about adequate to fight it out where they were, he was ordered to comply immediately. Two precious companies of infantry, a troop of Stuart light tanks from the squadron of 7th Light Cavalry, and a section of mountain guns were sent forward, leaving the cooks and clerks of the brigade to hurriedly try and plug the gap thus created in the brigade defences. The relief column from Bomdila for Dirang Dzong fell into a Chinese ambush an hour's move out of Bomdila, and was forced to withdraw, but reaching their old positions at Bomdila, found them occupied by the Chinese.

In the meantime, the Chinese had attacked the 5th Guards' position at Thembang which was blocking the Poshingla approach, who put up a gallant fight, but were ambushed during their withdrawal towards Bomdila, and again the withdrawal turned into a rout, with the battalion disintegrating as a force, making their way back through the thick jungle in small groups to the plains.

Brig. Gurbaksh Singh, left with only four infantry companies holding Bomdila, decided to fall back some 12 kms to Rupa, where he was expecting to meet two more infantry battalions which were still being moved forward. He began the withdrawal from Bomdila at 1600 hours. Having collected the arriving battalions during the night, the brigade began feverishly preparing a new position to meet the attack which they were sure would come in the morning. During the night however, in the early hours of the 19th, Lt. Gen. Kaul spoke personally to Brig. Gurbaksh Singh and ordered him to withdraw to Chaku, in the foothills. The military historian Capt. Amarinder Singh[22] writes:

> The brigade duly withdrew as ordered. Two hours later, the brigadier was told by Kaul to return to Rupa. 48 Brigade turned about once more, retracing its steps only to find that Rupa and the adjoining heights were in the hands of the Chinese.[23]

The last hastily-deployed Indian defensive position was at Chaku, a high point on the Bomdila-Tezpur road, occupied by the withdrawing elements of 3rd Sikh Light Infantry, 3rd J&K Rifles, and 6/8th Gorkha Rifles. At 0300 hours on 20th November, this was over-run by the Chinese, and no defences were left between the Chinese and the Corps HQ at Tezpur.

中印反?戰中，印軍第七旅被全殲並俘虜第七旅旅長達爾維準將

On 20th November, with his 4 Corps no longer in effective existence, Lt. Gen. Kaul and 4 Corps headquarters had withdrawn 160 kms from Tezpur to Guwahati (Gauhati). The Chinese, having reached their 'Claim Line' declared their unilateral ceasefire at midnight on 20th November.

The troops of 4 Infantry Division, through poor leadership at the higher levels, were no longer effective, and found their way in small groups back to the plains and finally to the Divisional Concentration Point at Ramgarh in Jharkhand. Only 4th Rajput withdrew to the plains in textbook manner as a formed unit, in spite of suffering a serious set-back. The battalion had been deployed on the Nyukmadong Ridge as part of the Sela defences, from which it was withdrawing. It was involved in the last battle of the war, on 21st November, at Lagheya Gompa on the Mandala ridge, west of Bomdila, where it fell into a massive ambush. Here they counter-attacked the well dug-in Chinese blocking position, losing 7 officers and 168 men killed in the ambush and their counter-attack, including their gallant CO, Lt. Col. Brahmanand Avasthy, Maj. Yogesh Tandon and Capt. Chhatrapati Singh.[24]

NOTES

1. Praval, *op.cit.* p. 208.
2. *Ibid.*
3. D.K. Palit, *op. cit.,* p. 259.
4. Pahwa, Lt. Gen. Pran, 'The Attack on Bomdi-La: A Personal Experience,' in *USI Journal,* Vol. CXLII, No. 590, October-December 2012, p. 590.
5. Brig. Korla, another WW II gallantry award winner.
6. Sukhwant Singh, *op. cit.,* p. 18.
7. Praval, *op. cit.,* p. 209.
8. 1 SIKH, 2 SIKH LI, and 4 SIKH LI were holding positions on the features around the pass. 4 GARHWAL held the screen position North-West of Sela, and 13 DOGRA was South of Sela Pass at Senge, guarding the Dropping Zone.
9. Two field batteries from 5 Field Regiment, one from 6 Field Regiment, 2 (Derajat) Mountain Battery, 116 Heavy Mortar Battery and a troop of 34 Heavy Mortar Battery.

10. 2 SIKH LI.
11. Ministry of Defence, *History, op. cit.*, pp. 167-168 and p.177.
12. From 7th Light Cavalry. The regiment less a squadron was moved from Varanasi in end-October. The tanks had reached Bomdila with difficulty, and were unable to climb from Dirang Dzong to Sela.
13. The officers of the divisional headquarters are said to have exclaimed, when they first heard of Gen. Kaul's return to the command of 4 Corps: *'He has come back? Now God save us'.*
14. Praval, *op. cit.* p. 215.
15. Datta, Maj. Gen. J.S., *Recollections of the Se La Bomdila Debacle 1962,* 2013 pp. 33-40.
16. *Ibid.,* p. 40.
17. As per Chinese accounts it appears that Brig. Hoshiar Singh, Commander 62 Brigade, was killed in an encounter with Chinese troops of 154 Infantry Regiment near Phudung.
18. Datta, *op. cit.,* pp. 41-48.
19. ex 65 Brigade.
20. ex 48 Brigade.
21. Artillery batteries of 5th Field Regiment, 6th Field Regiment, 22 Mountain Regiment and 36th (Maratha) Light Regiment, a platoon of MMG's from 7th Mahar (MG), and 19 Field Company Engineers.
22. Formerly the Chief Minister of Punjab.
23. Amarinder Singh, *Lest We Forget, 1999,* p. 211.
24. *Ibid.*, p. 212.

9

The Deployment in Sikkim

In this emerging scenario of panic during end-October-early November 1962, it was realized that Sikkim had to be defended. The nearest point of the Tibet border to the plains was in Sikkim, which had become a protectorate of British India in 1861. The southern tip of Tibet's Chumbi Valley and the two main passes there, Nathu La and Jelep La, were approaches that had to be guarded. 17 Infantry Division was already located in the plains of north Bengal, tasked primarily to protect the narrow strip of plains that connected Assam to West Bengal and the India-East Pakistan border, with its headquarters in Binaguri. 20 Infantry Division, with its headquarters in Ranchi, and its brigades and battalions separately located from Barrackpore near Kolkata in the south, to one battalion[1] at Lebong, Darjeeling, in the north, was mobilized to deploy in Sikkim.

Lt. Gen. Harbaksh Singh, who had been side-stepped after being displaced in 4 Corps by Lt. Gen. Kaul, to 33 Corps which had moved its headquarters from Shillong to Siliguri, gave his orders to 20 Infantry Division on 15th November at Bourdong[2] in Sikkim, at the temporary location of HQ 20 Division, on the Siliguri-Gangtok road. He ordered the division to deploy in 'box' fashion, and briefed the officers of the division in the presence of their Divisional Commander. He told the officers that they were to hold on, even if the Chinese by-passed them and carried on down to Siliguri.

Maj. Gen. Kamta Prasad, GOC 20 Division, ordered the deployment of 202 Infantry Brigade in the Tukla area,* facing Jelep La, on the traditional trade route from Lhasa to Kalimpong, the same route as was used by Colonel Younghusband in his 1903-04 expedition against Tibet, with its headquarters to be located in Nathang. 165 Infantry Brigade was deployed as the Chhangu (Tsomgo) 'Box' in the Chhangu-Mile 17 area, with its HQ in Karponang, covering the approach from Nathu La to Gangtok, and 66 Infantry Brigade, the third brigade, was to occupy a 'box' with two battalions in the Mile 8 area near Gangtok. Divisional HQ was to be in Gangtok.

This deployment and build-up had to be carried out on the poor road system then existing: a proper road existed only up to Gangtok; ahead of Gangtok there was only a jeepable road which could take a maximum of a jeep and a trailer. The deployment to Kupup-Nathang had to be carried out via Chhangu, in other words, across the enemy's front. All defence stores, ammunition, equipment, and rations went either by jeep-&-trailer, man-packed, or pony-packed, whether it was the equipment of the Advanced Dressing Stations of the two forward brigades, signal communications equipment or anything else.

Lt. Gen. Harbaksh's briefing, even at that time when the shameful abandonment of Sela, Dirang Dzong and Bomdila had not yet taken place, indicates that the Indian Army was capable of deploying correctly, and fighting an appropriate form of defensive battle against the infiltration tactics of the Chinese forces. All it needed was correct leadership, no undermining of the authority of intermediate formation commanders by giving impractical direct orders from the Corps headquarters to brigades, and no impractical, politically-motivated deployments and deadlines imposed by Army Headquarters. Even the official

History acknowledges that it is widely believed that had Lt. Gen. Harbaksh Singh not been replaced by Lt. Gen. Kaul as GOC 4 Corps after just six days in command, there might have been no rout of 4 Division at Sela-Bomdila.[3]

***Note:**

1. 202 Infantry Brigade was composed of 4th Guards, 15th Punjab, and 14th Dogras, 165 Infantry Brigade deployed with 16th Madras ex 66 Brigade, 1st Dogras ex 66 Brigade, 3rd Jats, and 5/11 Gorkha Rifles, 66 Infantry Brigade wase left with two battalions: 1st Maratha and 3rd/9th Gorkha Rifles.
2. The Tukla dispositions were:

   Tukla Left: 4th Guards (1st Rajput[4]), under Lt. Col. V.A.G. Pinto.

   Tukla Right: 15th Punjab (1st Patiala[5]), under Lt. Col. J.S. Mandher.

   Lungthu-Nathang: 14th Dogras, under Lt. Col. Behl.

NOTES

1. 14th Dogras.
2. Between Rangpo and the Singtam bridge.
3. *History of the Conflict with China,* 1962, *op. cit.,* p. 421.
4. Earlier title of this unit, for some years written in brackets after its current title for ease of identification.
5. Earlier title of this unit, for some years written in brackets after its current title for ease of identification.

10

Analysis of the Debacle in Kameng

It can be surmised, as some observers such as Allen Whiting have done, that the three-week lull after October 24th was probably intended to provide an opportunity for India to rethink its approach and abandon its 'Forward Policy.'[1]

It is also true, though, that a pause after any initial major operational move by the Chinese has been a standard policy in classical Chinese warfare strategy, in order to see how the enemy reacts, and to adjust one's policy or tactics accordingly. It is believed that the decisions of October 6 and October 16 were for a multi-stage war: Indian forces would first be given a sharp and bloody warning, after which Chinese troops would halt and re-organize for the next offensive.

In the second week of November 2008, the Chinese Ministry of Foreign Affairs declassified almost 70 percent of its diplomatic archives dating from 1960 to 1965. Among the 41,097 items revealed was one that gave the reasons behind China's sudden call for a truce in its border war with India in late 1962. It revealed that it was a political pause, with practical advantage for the military campaign. If India did not re-orient its frontier policy, then the next stage would be a massive assault to the southern fringe of the Himalayas. It is thus possible that had Nehru agreed to boundary talks after the Zhou proposal of October 24, the next phase of the Chinese offensive may never have taken place. The Indian attack in the Walong sector, and the November 14 letter gave the Chinese the feeling that India did not want negotiations, and the Chinese military offensive was re-continued from November 16 onwards.

The debacle in the Kameng Frontier Division has been the subject of much debate and of numerous books, and is known for the ignominy earned by the Indian Army for the non-battles of Sela and Bomdila. The reasons are:

- The decision by Lt. Gen. B.M. Kaul to allow Maj. Gen. A.S. Pathania to pull the Div Tac HQ down to the Dirang valley from its originally correctly-selected site on the Senge spur. This was aggravated by the fact that A.S. Pathania brought down a brigade HQ and two of its battalions with it, as local protection for the Div Tac HQ. This greatly negated the truly Herculean effort put in by the 'Q' branches at all levels, from Army HQ down to Corps and 4 Div, and by the Air Force, in stocking Se La to turn it into a fortress which at best the Chinese could only by-pass but not capture. The additional two battalions and the presence of the Div Commander would also have had their own stabilizing effect.
- The ambiguously worded permission given by Lt. Gen. Kaul to Maj. Gen. A.S. Pathania on 17th November evening, allowing him to withdraw from the Sela complex at his discretion. Maj. Gen. Pathania then ordered Brig. Hoshiar Singh to withdraw that very night (night 17/18 November), which Brig. Hoshiar Singh protested against, saying that he was organized and prepared to fight, even if bypassed. On the Div Commander's insistence, he said that he could only organize a withdrawal for the next night (night 18/19 November), as it was not possible to do so at such short notice. Brig. Hoshiar Singh's consequent orders created uneasiness among the troops at Sela.

- The low morale in much of 4 Div's troops, caused by the confusion, and by the tales brought back by the survivors of the Namka Chu battle and the troops who had retreated from Tawang. This was greatly added to by the entire officer cadre's low morale due to their lack of confidence in Lt. Gen. Kaul's command and leadership qualities. This resulted in the unordered and premature abandonment of its defensive positions by 1st Sikh, which occurred on night 17/18 November when 2nd Sikh LI was being pulled back through them that night, from Kye La into the Se La main defenses. Once this happened, control over both units by their own officers became difficult. This was the precise beginning of the debacle at Se La. But there were other players who had contributed, other than the Chinese who had been getting the better of 2nd Sikh LI before their withdrawal into the Se La main defences. 1st Sikh had been ordered to abandon the Se La defences the last of all on night 18/19 November, as per the brigade commander's orders, but Lt. Col. B.N. ('Baij') Mehta, C.O. 1st Sikh, had on his own given orders to his 2 I/C, Adjutant, and QM for the withdrawal of the battalion on 2330 hors on 17th November. This undoubtedly added to the confusion and jitteriness of his troops. In the event, this unplanned abandonment totally compromised the planned withdrawals of the other battalions, 4th Garhwal Rifles, which had been putting up a good fight and getting the better of the Chinese on every occasion, 13th Dogra, and 4th Sikh LI, as well as of 62 Brigade HQ and the smaller elements of the fighting and supporting arms.
- Brig. A.S. Cheema, Commander 65 Brigade's, shameful abandonment of his brigade (physically comprising only two battalions—4th Rajput and 19th Maratha LI: the third battalion was 2nd Sikh LI which had been given to the Se La

brigade) down in the Dirang valley, on 18th November. This made a difficult situation much worse, by adding further confusion to the rout that took place on 18th November.

- The Div Tac HQ' known intentions of pulling out of the Dirang valley without permission from the Corps HQ, to the Tenga valley south of Bomdila, and its abandonment of its Tac HQ location without properly controlling and coordinating to the extent possible, also contributed to the 'withdrawal-turned-into-rout.'

As noted earlier, even the *History of the Conflict with China, 1962* acknowledges that it is widely believed that had Lt. Gen. Harbaksh Singh not been replaced by Lt. Gen. Kaul as GOC 4 Corps after just six days in command, there might have been no rout of 4 Division at Sela-Bomdila.[2] However, there were other contributory factors too, in addition to the officer cadre's lack of confidence in the Corps Commander. The official *History* specifically mentions a few in its own analysis:

> There had been persistent rumours that some senior officers favoured retreat from Se La also, and wanted 4 Div to make a stand at Bomdila. This was true, and those favouring Bomdila included Brig K.K. Singh, (BGS, HQ IV Corps), Maj. Gen. A.S. Pathania himself, and Lt. Col. Manohar Singh, GSO 1 in HQ IV Corps.[3]

To this number can be added the Army Commander, Lt. Gen. L.P. Sen.

Regarding the disgraceful Se La fiasco, the *History* comments:

> In such a climate of retreat and demoralization, the wildest rumours were believed, and any tactical withdrawal could turn into a rout. And this is what happened at Se La.

The Se La position was exceedingly strong, well-stocked and held by a brigade of five battalions. Troops were first told that Se La would be held even if its L of C was cut. Then on 17th evening they learnt that withdrawal would again start the next night. But within few hours they saw 2nd Sikh LI being pulled back: their confusion and demoralization was complete and the rout began.[4]

The authors of the *History* analyse the causes of defeat in the Kameng sector as under:

> An enemy Division of about four brigades, thus defeated and destroyed 4 Inf Div of three brigades in defensive positions when normally a successful attack required a numerical superiority of 3:1. The enemy, moreover, had no artillery support, and had been able to carry only mortars and MGs with him over the difficult mountain tracks. Though most of the Indian troops were hurriedly inducted from the plains and thrown into battle without proper acclimatization or winter equipment, the basic causes of the defeat lay in the areas of leadership and morale.[5]
>
> There was no question of or thought of recapturing Tawang but only of holding up the Chinese advance at Se La, or even at Bomdi La. The all-important initiative, therefore, always remained with the enemy, and he could choose the time and place for his next blow.[6]

Thapar and Sen refused to give any orders on Pathania's request for permission to withdraw, leaving the decision to Kaul even though he was not present. Kaul, with his severely limited experience of actual fighting, issued orders for moving even Companies and Platoons, and thought that tanks could operate successfully against road blocks in the mountains. On the vital question of withdrawal of 4 Div from Dirang Dzong, Kaul totally failed to impose his will and control events, or even his subordinate Commanders. By the night of 17-18 November, the Commanders were as badly demoralized as the troops. And battles are lost or won basically in the minds of the Commanders. The debacles at Se La and Bomdi La will remain classic examples of this classic dictum.[7]

Lt. Gen. S.H.F.J. Manekshaw, MC, who succeeded Lt. Gen. Kaul in the command of 4 Corps soon thereafter said: *'The troops were demoralised because of their commanders.'*[8]

Brig. H.S. Sodhi comments:

It is pertinent to examine the scenario if Se La had been held, with the Division HQ and 65 Infantry Brigade based at Senge, and the Chinese had been forced to put in an attack. Se La is a formidable position. It could be defended well seeing the battle of 4 Garhwal in the screen position. To attack the position the Chinese would have had to bring forward their 11 and also (their) 55 Divisions. This would have taken time. Snow would have put a damper on the operations and Chinese build up. If Se La had lasted even 10 days, the Chinese Unit 419 would have run out of its self-contained administration and would have either had to be replenished or withdrawn. The whole course of the war would have turned. There is no doubt the number of casualties would have been far less than that actually suffered during the debacle.[9]

Maj. Gen. Sukhwant Singh agrees with this assessment:

Analysing our conduct with hindsight, I can say that there was nothing really wrong with the concept of holding bottlenecks in depth along the line of communications in strength, so long as a hard-hitting mobile force was available to operate off the roads, using these defended areas as pivots to destroy the enemy in contact.

The main flaw in Kaul's handling of the situation was that he did not have a mobile force, and so when the necessity arose he started denuding his depth firm-base. Moreover, the the formation commanders were over-sensitive to roadblocks. Instead of fighting from prepared positions they upstuck, ending in a disorganized race for the rear areas through successive ambushes, more so when the Indian Army remained roadbound.

Above all, the leadership, as also the soldiery, had no heart in the fight.[10]

Brig. Sodhi also adds:

Given even 7 to 10 days delay by this means, not only the entire brigade at Se La would have been saved, but the arrival of 5 Infantry Division by then would have changed the situation in our favour. Bomdi La may not have fallen. And above all, the country and the Army would not have been disgraced.[11]

Maj. Praval has this to add:

On 19 November, 5 Infantry Division had begun to arrive at Foot Hills from Punjab. But it was, by then, too late to retrieve the situation. Had this division arrived a week earlier, or had General Pathania held on to Se La till its arrival, the story in Kameng might have been different. The delay in pulling out 5 Division from Punjab was due to the fact that India was not sure of Pakistan's intentions during the early stages of the hostilities.[12]

Maj. Gen. Kuldeep Singh Bajwa, however, is not convinced that the deployment plan of 4 Infantry Division to fight the Chinese attack on Kameng was the right one. He believes the division should have fought the Chinese at Bomdila. He comments:

> By 17 November 4 Div, made up to its full complement of arms and services, could have established a formidable defence at Bomdila. Unfortunately it was spread out in three groups: 62 Bde [brigade] Gp [group] (five battalions) was at Se La; 48 Bde Gp (three battalions) at Bomdi La, and HQ 4 Div with 65 Bde (two battalions) in between at Dirang Dzong, with hardly any prepared defences. This posture anticipated a Chinese advance astride the road axis, but the Se La massif could be out-flanked using existing tracks, and the Chinese could cut off the road to Bomdi La by coming down the Tembang spur overlooking Dirang Dzong valley. There were thus serious inherent weaknesses in the defensive posture of 4 Div....
>
> More seriously, a clear concept of how the battle would be fought under different contingencies of enemy action had not been evolved. . . . A concept of battle if the Se La complex was cut off should have been worked out. On 17 November Se La complex had one week's supplies and was not equipped to fight as an impregnable defensive box. Defences at Dirang Dzong were inadequate and the road to Bomdi La had not been secured.
>
> Adding to the already deep spread of the Division Pathania was resorting to further ad hoc deployments by rushing off platoons and companies from Bomdi La to block likely outflanking routes as subsequently visualized.... With this Bomdi La was left with one and a half battalion that was one third of the strength for adequate defence.[13]

Maj. Gen. Bajwa also comments tellingly on Lt. Gen. Kaul's style of command:

> Pathania, now realizing the imminent threat to the Div HQ from the Thembang spur, and the dangerous potential of the two-pronged threat to the Se la complex from the north as well as the south, sought permission from Corps HQ to withdraw from both locations and set up a consolidated divisional defence at Bomdi La. Since Corps HQ could not consult Kaul, who was still floating around in a helicopter near Walong, this was not agreed to.
>
> This episode clearly showed up Kaul's frustrating conduct of battle by first over-centralizing authority, and then remaining out of touch with the critical area of battle. It is obvious that he had not determined relative priorities of criticality of battle in different sectors of his command. The Se La-Bomdi La sector was the most critical and Kaul should have positioned himself from where he could intervene quickly in this sector if needed. Chinese advance down the Lohit valley was not a major threat, and the defence of Walong should have been left to Commander 11 Bde. The best place for Kaul to have been was at his Corps HQ.[14]

The official *History* highlights some of the causes of the debacle in the Kameng sector:

- Tawang had been declared the Divisional Vital Ground, but there were not sufficient troops to defend it. It was perforce abandoned. Thereafter differences cropped up as to where the main defenses of 4 Infantry Div. should be located, at Se La or Bomdila. This controversy was allowed to rage openly with all its adverse implications.

- Decisions were taken on an *ad hoc* basis. The result was confusion all around. Formations were ordered to move out practically without any notice to destinations not known to them. Under the circumstances, chopping and pruning of units was freely resorted to. Unplanned induction of troops and the consequent breaking of original formations ruined the cohesiveness and compactness of fighting formations. Affiliations between formations and units were broken. Esprit-de-corps, so very essential for a fighting formation, was lost in the process, thereby impairing the fighting ability of troops.
- There was frequent interference by senior commanders in the sphere of commanders below, to the extent of issuing orders about minor tactical details. Orders were issued as to how battalions, even companies, were to be deployed, or which place was to be occupied, and so on. Such orders tied down the hands of local commanders completely. By taking away the independence of action of local commanders, it seriously hampered the efforts put in for the attainment of a given objective.
- Another factor which hampered the smooth conduct of operations was the large-scale change of commanders during the course of the operations. And such changes were often effected because of likes or dislikes of the decision makers.[15]

NOTES

1. Allen S. Whiting, *The Chinese Calculus of Deterrrence. India and Indochina,* 1975.
2. *History of the Conflict with China, 1962,* p. 421.
3. *Ibid.,* p. 217.
4. *Ibid.*
5. *Ibid.*
6. *Ibid.,* p. 218.

7. *Ibid.*
8. Praval, *op. cit.,* p. 238.
9. H.S. Sodhi, *Significant Battles Since Independence,* 2007, p. 158-159.
10. Sukhwant Singh, *op. cit.,* p. 19.
11. H.S. Sodhi, *Top Brass,* p. 44.
12. Praval, *op. cit.,* p. 223.
13. Bajwa, *op. cit.,* pp. 157-158.
14. *Ibid.*, p. 159.
15. *History, op. cit.,* pp. 217-218.

11

The Western Sector: The Ladakh Battle

As per a Chinese account, Chinese troops counterattacked simultaneously on 20th October 1962 on the western sector of the border, where by October 'the Indian Army had deployed about 6,000 troops, including the 114th Brigade with six battalions.' Of these forces, about 1,300 Indian troops had been stationed in some 40 strongholds or outposts placed in what China viewed as its own territory. In response, China had deployed about 6,300 troops, including two infantry regiments, some independent battalions, and supporting artillery units, forces that operated under the command of the Kangxiwa Headquarters of the Xinjiang Military Region.[1]

The Chinese attacked on October 20, as in NEFA, but the effects were not as disastrous as in NEFA, mainly because the forward zone was being thinned out anyway due to the difficulties of maintenance in winter. The post of 14 J&K Militia at Chip Chap River in the north was forced to withdraw to Daulat Beg Oldi, and finally to Thoise. The two posts of a company of 1/8 Gorkha Rifles at Sirijap, commanded by Maj. Dhan Singh Thapa, held off two Chinese attacks, taking many casualties, and the only seven remnants fell back. A new divisional HQ, 3 Infantry Division, was raised during the lull after October 20-November 1962 for coordinating the defence of Ladakh. 114 Brigade's responsibility was reduced to the

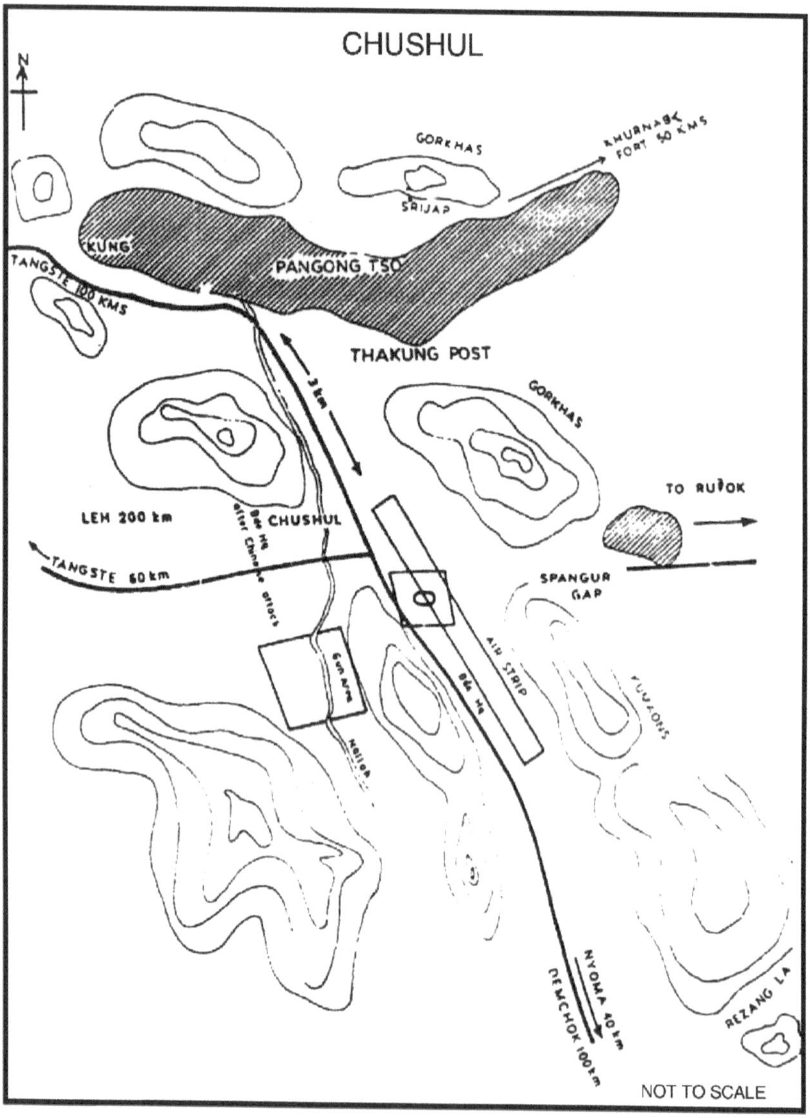
CHUSHUL
N
GORKHAS
SRIJAP
KUNG
PANGONG TSO
TANGSTE 100 KMS
THAKUNG POST
3 km
GORKHAS
TO RUTOK
LEH 200 km
CHUSHUL
TANGSTE 60 km
SPANGUR GAP
AIR STRIP
NYOMA 40 km
DEMCHOK 100 km
REZANG LA
NOT TO SCALE

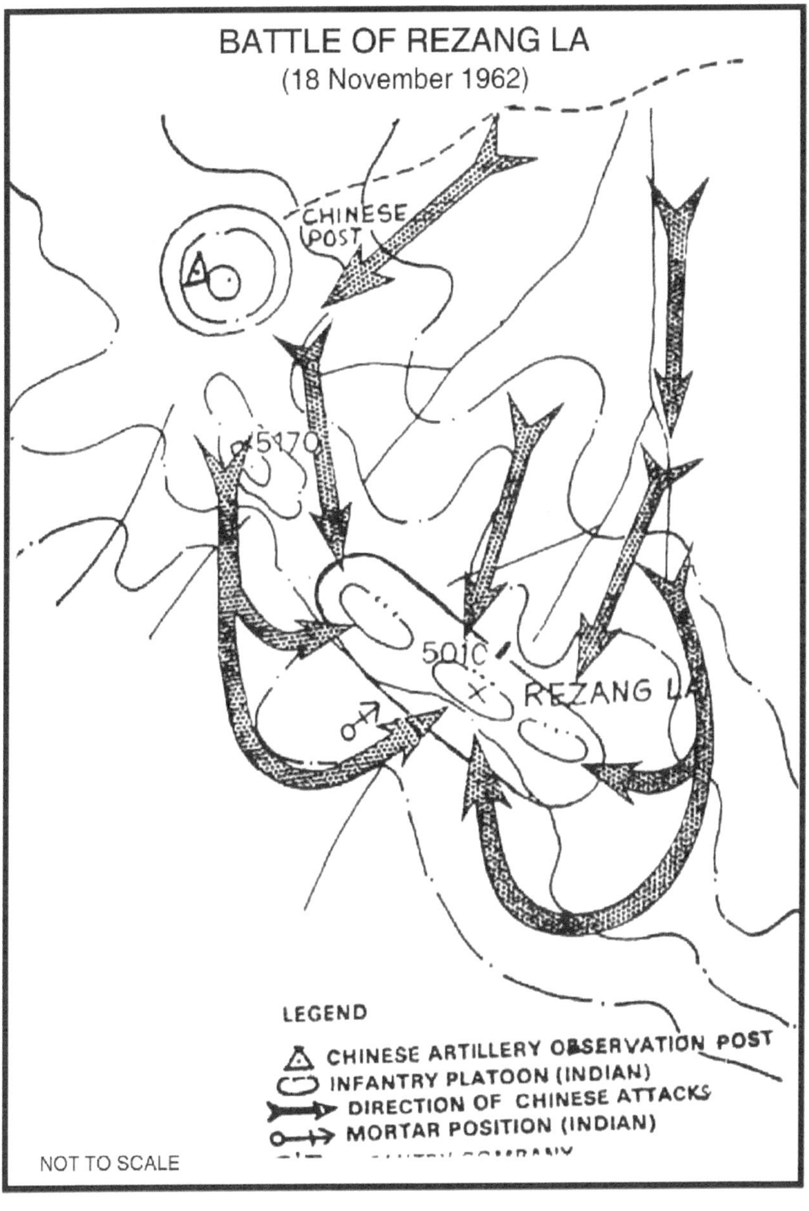
BATTLE OF REZANG LA
(18 November 1962)
CHINESE POST
5170
5010
REZANG LA
LEGEND
CHINESE ARTILLERY OBSERVATION POST
INFANTRY PLATOON (INDIAN)
DIRECTION OF CHINESE ATTACKS
MORTAR POSITION (INDIAN)
NOT TO SCALE

defence of Chushul, the newly-inducted 70 Brigade was given the southern sector, while 163 Brigade was located at Leh.

The Battle of Chushul, from November 18th to 21st, 1962, actually took place after most of the disastrous events of the eastern sector had already happened. When the Chinese attack was renewed in November, 114 Infantry Brigade under Brigadier T.N. ('Tappy') Raina,[2] gave a very good account of itself. He had deployed his brigade tactically, the two forward battalions which faced the Chinese attack fought with professional skill and bravery, the infantry rifle companies actually engaged by the Chinese losing most of their officers and men, but not giving up. 'C' Company of 13th Kumaon, entirely composed of Ahirs (Yadavs) under Maj. Shaitan Singh, at Rezangla, and two companies of 1st/8th Gorkha Rifles, of Magar and Gurung Gorkhas, in the 'Gurung Hill' area, made the Chinese pay heavily for their capture of the area up to their Claim Line in the Chushul area, by making epic 'last man-last round' stands. However, out of all the Indian troops deployed by November 18th, only these three companies of two battalions of one brigade had actually been engaged by the Chinese. The other two brigades had not been involved in the fighting at all.

NOTES

1. Wortzel, Larry M., 'Concentrating Forces and Audacious Action: PLA Lessons from the Sino-Indian War,' in Laurie Burkilt, Andrew Scobell, Larry M. Wortzel, (Eds.), *The Chinese People's Liberation Army at 75,* (Carlisle, Penn., USA, US Army War College, Strategic Studies Institute, 2003), p. 340.
2. Of the Kumaon Regiment, and later to become Chief of Army Staff.

12

The Walong Battle and the End of the War

4 Infantry Division on induction had been given the responsibility for the entire NEFA front of about 500 km, a totally impractical assignment. The Walong sector, at the eastern end of NEFA, which was the operational responsibility of 5 Brigade of 4 Div from end-1959, was too far away for HQ 4 Infantry Division to coordinate or command from Kameng or even from Tezpur, in western Assam. There was initially just an Assam Rifles platoon in the entire Walong sector. On the arrival of 4 Infantry Division a battalion was located in the Walong sector. 2nd Rajput had been located here till June 1962, and were relieved by 6th Kumaon. When 62 Infantry Brigade from Ramgarh arrived in NEFA in September 1962, two of its three battalions, viz., 4th Sikh and 2/8 Gorkha Rifles, were sent directly to Jorhat and put under 5 Brigade.

The Walong sector, named after a village about 32 km from the McMahon Line, lies mostly in the deep valley of the Lohit River. The river flows in the valley at about 1,300 metres above mean sea level, but the heights of the features on either side are from about 2,500 metres to 3,500 metres. The river is deep and has an extremely strong current; it is thus not fordable and not navigable. Walong itself had an airstrip suitable for light aircraft, such as the Otters and the Caribous, which were the only means of rapid re-supply to this sector, the road-head in 1962 being

WALONG

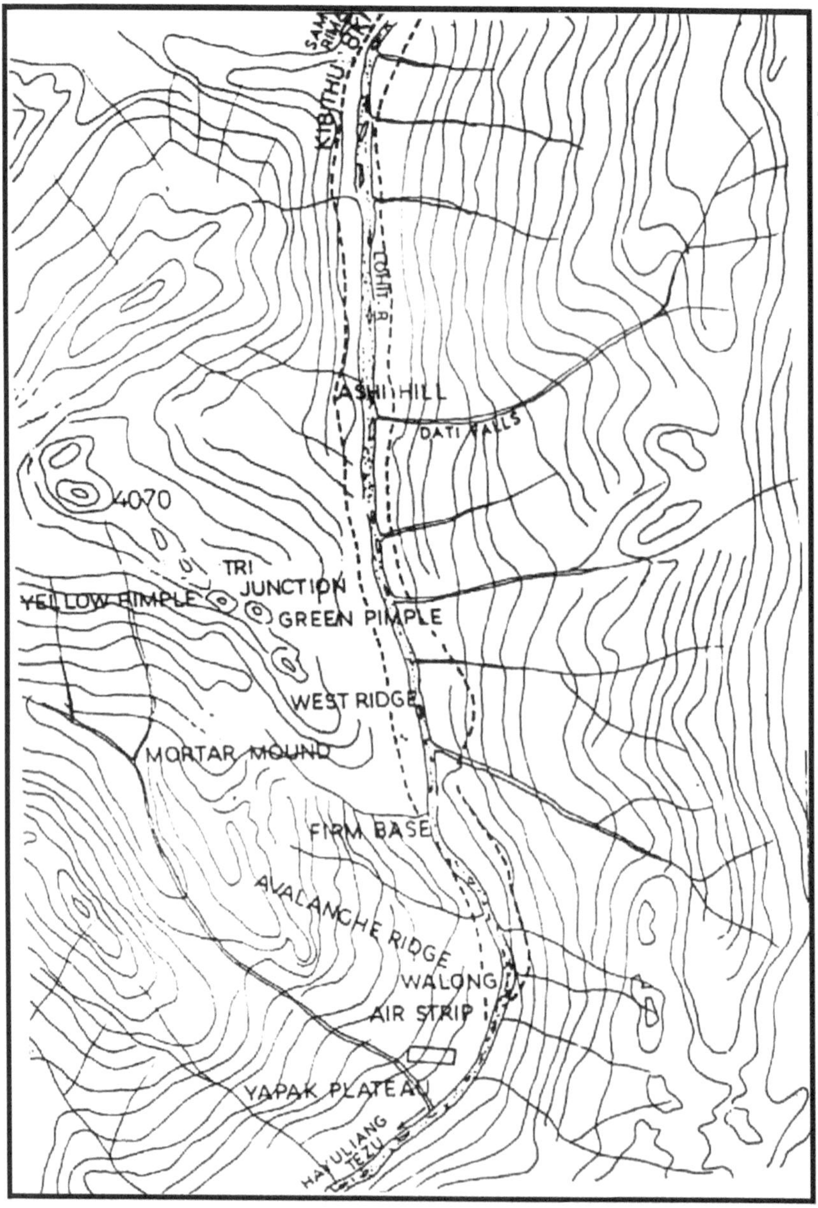

NOT TO SCALE

further back at Teju. Assam Rifles platoons and one infantry battalion were the only military presence in this area since the arrival of 4 Infantry Division. Due to increased Chinese activity across the McMahon Line in this area since August 1962, 6th Kumaon, the lone battalion in this area was augmented in October by 4th Sikh.

On June 30th 1962, a platoon post of 2nd Assam Rifles had been established on a feature called Mohan Ridge, to the east of the Lohit River, towards the border tri-junction of India, Tibet and Myanmar. On October 19th, due to reported Chinese activity across the McMahon Line, 'A' Coy of 6th Kumaon[1] had been sent forward to Dichu, while another battalion, 4th Sikh, was in the process of being inducted into the sector. A platoon from the Kumaoni company was moved further forward to Kibithoo before October 20th, while another Kumaoni platoon had been sent forward to reinforce the Mohan Ridge post. Both these forward platoons were pushed back by the Chinese when they attacked them on night October 21-22. Troops at Dichu and at Mohan Ridge were ordered to fall back on Kibithoo. With increasing Chinese pressure, the Kumaoni forward elements had all been pulled back into the main Walong defences by 25th. October.

With two battalions, 4th Sikh and 6th Kumaon, now in Walong, there arose problems of coordination in this isolated sector. It was thus decided that operations in this sector would be handled by an independent infantry brigade. On October 25, for this purpose, 181 Infantry Brigade was made responsible for the Walong area. Brig. J.C. Hartley, Military Cross, of the Sikh Regiment, Commander 181 Brigade, took over command of this active sector from 5 Brigade on October 27. By lucky coincidence, 4th Sikh, now under his brigade command, was his own battalion, and this battalion at least would have taken great heart from the fact.

In the lull after the first phase of the Chinese attack from October 20th-24th, a new divisional HQ was set up, named 2 Infantry Division (2 Div), to take over operational responsibility in the Subansiri, Siang and Lohit Frontier Divisions of NEFA. Maj. Gen. Mohinder Singh Pathania,[2] who was GOC 23 Infantry Division at the time, was given command of the new 2 Div. He arrived at Walong on October 26. 181 Brigade was accordingly placed under his 2 Div. But Maj. Gen. Pathania preferred to have Brig. N.C. Rawlley, Military Cross, and his 11 Infantry Brigade placed under his command. 11 Brigade, one of 4 Div's original brigades, had after 4 Division's arrival in Assam, been re-located in Nagaland. The 11 Brigade Commander arrived at Walong on October 31 (FN), with his brigade following. The command hierarchy for the sector at this stage thus became: 11 Infantry Brigade responsible for the sector, under 2 Infantry Division which was under Lt. Gen. Kaul's 4 Corps.

As Brig. Sodhi comments:

> This meant that, in just a period of ten days, there were three changes of command which left its mark on the preparations for the coming battle.[3]

To add to the confusion, 2/8 Gorkha Rifles, which were in the process of induction and already had two companies located in the sector on October 31, were ordered back to 5 Brigade which had been made responsible for the Siang Frontier Division, and 3/3 Gorkha Rifles (3/3 G.R.) were flown in, which could concentrate at Walong only in the first week of November. This resulted in its being deployed with two companies on either bank of the unfordable Lohit River, two of them going under command of 4th Sikh, while one of the 4th Sikh companies came under command 3/3 G.R.

The Indian defences were not rationally organized, and companies of the three different battalions (4 SIKH, 6 KUMAON and 3/3 GR) were intermingled, and companies of one battalion were placed under command another battalion. Two of the battalions held positions on both sides of the river. The arrangements were not good for command and control. In addition, the brigade's dispositions were linear with little or no depth.

The Chinese had managed to occupy two features, named Green Pimple and Yellow Pimple, facing the Kumaoni positions in the west of the brigade defensive layout. The Brigade Commander, Brig, Rawlley, ordered 6th Kumaon to capture Green Pimple, but the assault launched on 6th November did not succeed.

On November 14, 'D' Coy 4th Sikh and two companies of 6th Kumaon were launched into an attack to dislodge the Chinese from the two tactically important features Green Pimple and Yellow Pimple. The attacks failed; the Kumaonis being beaten back just 50 m from the crest of the Yellow Pimple feature. The assaulting Kumaoni companies were ordered to stand firm in their present position, but they were unable to resist the Chinese counter-attack at midnight the next night, and fell back to the Trijunction feature which had been the base for this operation. A second Chinese counter-attack on 15th November on Trijunction was repulsed. In the meantime, 4th Dogras had begun to arrive in Walong, and a Dogra company plus Kumaoni troops from the other localities which the Dogras had relieved were rushed to reinforce Trijunction. The reinforced Trijunction position repulsed two more Chinese attacks.

The Chinese counter-offensive which began at 03:00 hours on November 16th on both sides of the Lohit River forced the brigade to retreat from Walong in some disorder through very difficult terrain. Not organized for a withdrawal, neither tactically nor logistically, the troops of 11 Brigade, after heavy fighting and a spirited defence by all four battalions, Kumaonis, Sikhs, Gorkhas and Dogras, were forced to withdraw in small parties down the Lohit valley to the Assam plain, suffering casualties from Chinese action and the combined effects of lack of food and the terrain. Maj. Gen. Bajwa attributes the unnecessary loss of life and the suffering to Lt. Gen. Kaul and Maj. Gen. M.S. Pathania, caused by their forcing an unprepared brigade to attack a superior Chinese force, as was initially attempted with 7 Brigade at Thagla.[4]

The official History is critical of the *'over-eagerness to execute an "offensive defense" plan' that 'led to the collapse of the front.'* It adds:

> ... the offensive was started on 14 November without knowing correctly the strength of the enemy and without the concentration of his own troops on the launching pad to the required level of strength. It is surmised that undue haste in launching this assault, without making a firm base and without catering for the likely reaction by the enemy, was made in order to complete it on 14th November, so as to make it a gift to Prime Minister Nehru on his birthday. The assault so launched not only failed but it boomeranged.[5]

Nevertheless, it must be noted that this was the only sector in which an offensive action was undertaken.

THE END OF THE WAR

As noted in the chapter on the events of Sela and Bomdila in the Kameng sector of NEFA, the Chinese, having reached their 'Claim Line' declared their unilateral ceasefire at midnight on 20th November 1962. They announced that beginning from midday on 21st November, the Chinese 'frontier guards' would cease fire along the entire Sino-Indian border, and that beginning from 1st December they would begin to withdraw to positions 20 kilometres behind the 'line of actual control' which had existed between China and India on 7th November 1959.

The Chinese government spelt out that although the Chinese 'frontier guards' had been fighting on Chinese territory north of the 'traditional boundary line' along the foothills, they would withdraw north of the line of actual control along the 'illegal McMahon Line' in the eastern sector and also in the middle and western sectors. They expected India to similarly keep its armed forces 20 kilometres away from the 'line of actual control,' failing which they reserved the right to strike back.

Pandit Nehru made a radio broadcast to the nation on 20th November, in which he practically bid farewell to the people of Assam, and there was a complete sense of panic in the government.[6] The Home Ministry ordered the civil administration to evacuate Tezpur, and it has been claimed that Indian Army Headquarters was thinking of pulling its forces out of Assam. There were rumours that the Chinese were about to take over Tezpur, and that Lt. Gen. Kaul had been captured. Of this rumour President Radhakrishnan is reported to have remarked, *'It is, unfortunately, untrue.'* Nehru broke his non-alignment policy and appealed to the American Government for help, through their embassy in Delhi, asking for fifteen squadrons of American aircraft, both fighters and bombers, though this was denied later. However, the American government did not accede to this request, but instead sent a military mission and a squadron of C-130 Hercules transport aircraft to India.

On the diplomatic front there had been communication with the Chinese government during the entire war, with Chinese Premier Zhou En-lai responding on 4th November to Nehru's query of 24th October about what the Chinese meant by their offer to return to the 'line of actual control.' The Chinese PM clarified that they meant the line or 'position as on 7th November 1959,' and not the one where their forces were at that moment. On 11th November 1962, the Indian Parliament had resolved 'to drive the aggressor out,' and on 14th November Nehru had rejected the Chinese offer of a cease-fire, questioning the Chinese interpretation of the 7th November 1959 line to mean the line it had claimed as the boundary since 1960. The 14th November letter had given the Chinese the feeling that India did not want negotiations, and as seen above, the Chinese military offensive was re-continued from 16th November onwards. In the eastern-most part of Arunachal Pradesh, Walong was captured by the Chinese, and the Chinese moves and attacks in Kameng have been already narrated.

After the cease-fire, it was also later clarified by China that she would strike back if India attempted to resume the 'forward policy' in the western sector, or if India moved troops back into the area of the Thagla Ridge. It allowed for both governments establishing civilian police posts on their own sides of the 'line of actual control.'

The COAS, Gen. P.N. Thapar had resigned on 19 November 1962, even before the war had ended. The Eastern Army Commander, Lt. Gen. L.P. Sen resigned a few days later, and Lt. Gen. B.M. Kaul resigned on 11 December 1962. But before Kaul resigned, Prime Minister Nehru had suggested that Kaul be promoted to General and made the Chief of Army Staff, a suggestion that was immediately turned down as ridiculous by President Radhakrishnan.

The Chinese began withdrawing from the areas they had captured on 1st December 1962. All the Indian weapons, vehicles and other equipment captured by them were handed back in well-maintained condition to Indian civil administrative parties. It is now known that they withdrew as per their own plan. Their restoration of the *status quo ante* on India's northern border prevented them from being censured by the international community for territorial acquisition by force.[7]

NOTES

1. The battalion which had recently relieved 2nd Rajput in the Walong sector.
2. A cousin of Maj. Gen. A.S. Pathania's.
3. H.S. Sodhi, *Top Brass, op. cit.,* p. 32.
4. Bajwa, *op.cit.,* p. 157.
5. *History of the Conflict with China, 1962, op. cit.,* p. 424.
6. This so-called 'farewell' broadcast' to Assam has caused much resentment amongst the educated people of Assam, but it has generally not been fully quoted. Nehru's 'farewell to Assam' was taken out of context by the media. His exact words in his address to the nation on All India Radio on November 20, 1962, were: 'Huge Chinese armies have been marching in the northern part of NEFA. We have had reverses at Walong, Se La and today Bomdila, a small town in NEFA, has also fallen. We shall not rest till the invader goes out of India or is pushed out. I want to make that clear to all of you, and, especially our countrymen in Assam, to whom our heart goes out at this moment.'
7. Bajwa, *op. cit.,* p. 173.

PART III

REFLECTION

13

Analysis and Lessons

Though popularly known as the '1962 War' or the '1962 War with China' the armed clash was really a serious border conflict rather a war. The 1962 conflict involved only a small fraction of the Indian Army (two plus divisions) and of the Chinese Peoples' Liberation Army (four plus divisions). The air forces of both the countries were not used for offensive operations against each other. If it is understood that the armed clash of 1962 was an extension of, or the result of an extension of, the 'forward policies' of both China and of India in the period from 1959 onwards, then the whole operation was aimed at 'conveying a message' about each country's position on the border issue. It was therefore a border clash on a somewhat large scale.

Chen Feng and Larry Wortzel (2003) have collaborated on an analysis of the Sino-Indian war of 1962 in which, primarily using Chinese accounts of the war, they demonstrate China was successful largely because of careful, long-term PLA preparation. As per them, the PLA is quite proud of its record in the war, especially since it suffered such heavy losses in combat in the Korean War. It believes that:

> China's overwhelming victory can be attributed to strong political leadership and proper use of military strategy, or campaign art (*zhanyi zhudong quan*).

Larry Wortzel states:

> In what it characterizes for itself as the 'Counterattack for Self-Defence on the China-India Border' the PLA destroyed the fighting strength and captured personnel of three brigades of the Indian Army. The Indian 7th Brigade, including its commander Brigadier Dalvi, the 62nd Brigade and the 4th Artillery Brigade were all rendered ineffective. In addition, the PLA seriously mauled five other Indian brigades (the 11th, 48th, 65th, 67th, and 114th).
>
> China's military historians have attributed this success to a combination of audacious action on the battlefield, good leadership, taking advantage of the terrain, good logistics and strong ideological preparation. By 'audacious action' PLA leaders mean the use of inititative and a vigorous offense. On the whole, China's victory was characterized as an example of good strategy and strong initiative in campaign art (*zhanyi zhudong quan*). PLA theorists and historians point to Mao Zedong's discussion of the need to 'create local superiority in the campaign' by concentrating strengths at decisive points as the inspiration for the conduct of the campaign against India.[1]

Any analysis of the 1962 Sino-Indian border war needs to examine two different sets of factors, the political and the military.

POLITICAL FACTORS

The critical political factors which led to the war, and which also dictated certain military decisions that contributed to the debacle in Arunchal Pradesh, are given below.

- India's refusal to negotiate and arrive at a territory and border agreement with China regarding their respective claims in Aksai Chin and the Kameng Frontier Division of NEFA.

- China's belief that India had hegemonistic designs on Tibet.
- The Indian belief that China would not actually go to war over the Indian 'Forward Policy' deployments of small military posts in disputed areas in the border zone.
- The Indian decision to occupy the Thag La ridge, which was shown on Indian maps as within Tibet, by establishing an Indian post across the Namka Chu mountain stream.

  The decision in September 1962 to 'evict' the Chinese troops deployed on the Thag La ridge was a strategic error of incalculable proportions. (It was also, of course, a military operational-level as well as a tactical-level error).
- The decision to appoint a politically-desirable, rather than a professionally more competent general, Lt. Gen. B.M. Kaul, to head the eviction attempt. More so when the senior command echelons on the site, the Brigade Commander, the Divisional Commander, and the Corps Commander, had all advised against precipitate action in deploying forward and in attempting to attack without adequate logistical preparation.
- The decision to carry out the eviction attempt in October 1962 before the winter set in, rather than to wait till the next spring when the logistical buildup necessary might have been completed.
- The decision to deploy 7 Infantry Brigade in an extended line of platoon and company-sized localities along the line of the Namka Chu, instead of in a tactical brigade deployment in more defensible positions with adequate depth on high ground to the immediate rear, as suggested by Brig. Dalvi, Commander 7 Infantry Brigade.
- The decision to occupy Sela as 4 Infantry Division's main defensive position after the withdrawal from Tawang, so as to

give away less territory to the Chinese, rather than occupying a stronger defensive position based on Bomdila, further to the rear and close to the Assam plains. (It must be noted, however, that this decision was also taken as a military decision necessary at that time (23rd-24th October), by the Divsional Commander, Maj. Gen. Niranjan Prasad, as necessary to prevent a panicked withdrawal, rather than a retreat to the next fighting position. His not attempting this would have led to total loss of command and control in the existing conditions of confusion and panic. It is extremely doubtful whether the disorganized and panicky mass of soldiery could have been brought under adequate control for them to be used for the new main defensive position sought to be created at Bomdila.)

- The decision to re-appoint Lt. Gen. B.M. Kaul as the GOC 4 Corps, when a new Corps Commander, Lt. Gen. Harbaksh Singh, had already taken over and was re-organising the defences of the Kameng sector.

MILITARY FACTORS

Poor intelligence has been a perennial weakness of the Indian state. There was the most glaring error in appreciating the Chinese intentions. The Intelligence Bureau had adequate information on the Chinese strength on India's northern borders, down to the location and movements of the infantry divisions and brigades. The assessments that would convert this information into intelligence were wrong, as events have proved. The Chinese divisions opposite the Kameng sector were the 11th Infantry Division, the 419th Tibet Force, and the last to be brought in was the 55th Infantry Division. This was originally located at Xining, and was moved in, reaching Tawang in mid-November 1962, travelling about 2100 km in eight days.

It is worthwhile to examine the Chinese account of the operations before analyzing the war from the Indian point of view. In the eastern theatre of war in NEFA, in the Namka Chu-Khinzemane sector, Wortzel, based on Chinese accounts, states:

> The Chinese assembled a smaller force of about 10,000 troops on the eastern sector, under the command of the Tibetan Military Region and consisting of five infantry regiments and some artillery units. In contrast to the Indian forces, however, PLA troops were acclimated to the terrain and had better roads and supply lines approaching the border. On October 20 the PLA began its counterattack against the Indian troops, focusing on Kejielang north of the McMahon Line. At 7:30 am, Chinese artillery began 15 minutes of preparatory shelling, destroying Indian artillery positions and parts of Indian fortifications. Chinese infantry then broke through the Indian fortifications. Within 1 day, the PLA wiped out the Indian Seventh Brigade and captured its commander Brigadier Dalvi. One day later, the PLA forces again crossed the McMahon Line, recovering the area around Zimithang.[2]

The Chinese accounts state that by mid-November 1962 India had moved a total of 50,000 troops to the Sino-Indian border, with 22,000 of these being in the eastern sector. These were under the 4 Corps and comprised three Indian divisions consisting of 14 brigades in total. 4 Division with five brigades had 15 battalions on the Tawang-Tezpur axis. Wortzel adds:

> To counter the Indian deployments, the PLA General Staff Department (GSD) sent two more divisions into Tibet. According to the noted historian of the PLA, William Whitson, both of these divisions came from the 46th Corps (or Army, since a PLA army at that time was equivalent to an

Indian corps). The GSD-directed deployment increased Chinese troop strength on the eastern sector of the border to five somewhat understrength divisions—in total, about 25,000 soldiers. With these deployments complete, the CMC on November 12, 1962, ratified the PLA second phase plan of operation. Chinese troops were to begin an offensive designed to wipe out three to four Indian brigades, including the brigades in the Tawang Tract and the single brigade in Walong, also in the eastern sector near Burma. In the western sector, the operations plan called for the PLA to eliminate the invading Indian troops in strongholds in the area of Pangong Lake.[3]

The Chinese attack in the Kameng sector was controlled by the Tibet Military District, which had the following forces:

(a) 419 Tibet Force, comprising 154, 155, and 157 Infantry Regiments (the equivalent of Indian brigades)

(b) 11 Infantry Division, for the operations consisting of 32 and 33 Infantry Regiments, and possibly a battalion of 31 Infantry Regiment.

(c) 55 Infantry Division, comprising 163, 164 and 165 Infantry Regiments.

(d) 306, 308 and 540 Artillery Regiments.

(e) 136 Engineer Regiment.

(f) Four additional infantry companies from the Shannan Military Sub-District.

(g) Additional service elements.

(h) Total strength: About 22,000, of which the infantry component was eight regiments plus.[4]

A second major intelligence failure in appreciating the enemy's intentions occurred after the fall of Tawang. It was felt that the Chinese would not advance further and there would be no more fighting, seemingly forgetting that the Chinese claim line lay in the Himalayan foothills. Accordingly, there was not enough urgency in building up troops and logistic support at the next defensive positions, which should have been done. The Corps Commander apparently was more concerned about the troops being able to face the winter than the Chinese.

China's broad strategy for the 'counter-attack in self-defence' was that the main attack would be in the eastern sector, while the Chinese forces in the western sector would coordinate with the eastern sector. The operational plan was to be aimed at expelling Indian troops north of the Chinese claim line at the southern foothills of the Himalayas, which they called the 'traditional and customary' boundary.

After the break-in phase at the Namka Chu and Bumla-Tawang, the Chinese advance in Kameng was planned and executed along multiple axes. Four different routes were used:

(a) 55 Infantry Division astride the road axis Tawang-Sela.

(b) 419 Tibet Force moved west of the road axis through the narrow strip between Sela and the Bhutan border, on two different routes, with strict instructions not to enter Bhutan.

(c) 11 Infantry Division carried out a wide eastern outflanking move to cut off the Sela-Dirang Dzong road.[5]

The tactical plan called for concerted attack by converging columns. By this method, the Indian positions were to be split into numerous segments and then destroyed piecemeal. Marshal Liu Bocheng, head of the core group of the CMC, gave an analogy for the plan of attack against the assessed Indian dispositions: 'smashing the head (Sela), cutting off the tail (Bomdila), snapping the waist (Road Sela-Dirang Dzong), and dissecting the belly (Dirang Dzong).'[6]

The primarily military factors that influenced the outcome of the 1962 war with China are of two types, one organizational, and the other operational or tactical. They are briefly listed together, in chronological order, below:

- The militarily unsound 'Forward Policy' deployments under Op ONKAR, whereby non-tactically sited sub-units as small as platoons were deployed in disputed areas where they could neither be easily administratively sustained, nor provided appropriate fire support by airpower or artillery, or even re-inforced quickly.
- The decision to hurriedly deploy 7 Infantry Brigade forward and concentrate it at Tawang, as part of Op ONKAR, even before the logistical arrangements for administrative sustenance of an entire brigade could be made.
- The decision to re-deploy 7 Brigade about a 100 km away to the west, in the Thagla-Namka Chu area before logistical arrangements could be made for its maintenance in that area.
- The decision to use 7 Brigade, at that time a hastily-scraped together collecetion of units which were neither administratively nor physically in a properly equipped and clothed, properly acclimatized, and properly trained state, to mount an attack against well-prepared and entrenched Chinese positions.
- The decision to 'create' a nominal 4 Corps, without any more troops than those already available to the existing 33 Corps responsible for the defence of the area, which amounted to the existing two brigades of 4 Infantry Division.
- The decision to use 7 Brigade in its existing state to attack the Chinese Thag La positions by or on 10th October 1962, rather than to build up a larger force with adequate logistical capabilities and attempt the 'eviction' the following summer.
- The vacillation by the Army Commander, Lt. Gen. L.P. Sen, in the decision to hold Tawang, initially designated 4

Infantry Division's 'Vital Ground,' in the face of Chinese attacks and advances towards Tawang from 20th to 23rd October 1962.

- The initial lack of a decision, and the delay in the decision, to appoint Maj. Gen. Niranjan Prasad, GOC 4 Infanry Division, as 'Officiating GOC 4 Corps' (officiating Corps Commander) as soon as Lt. Gen. Kaul was taken ill on his trip to Delhi.
- Tactically, the errors of judgment on the part of the Army Chief and the Army Commander Eastern Command, Gen. P.N. Thapar and Lt. Gen. L.P. Sen respectively, on their insisting on the line of the Namka Chu being held. This insistence left 7 Brigade no time to re-deploy from the untenable positions initially ordered by the Corps Commander Lt. Gen. B.M. Kaul, as requested up to the last possible minute by the Brigade Commander, Brig. Dalvi.
- The vacillation at the highest levels (Army Headqurters, Eastern Command, and 4 Corps) while troops were withdrawing under enemy pressure, on whether Se La or Bomdila should be the next main defensive position after the evacuation of Tawang.
- The change of almost all the Divisional and Brigade Commanders in the Kameng region of NEFA in the period 24th October to 16th November 1962.
- The impractical and whimsical organizational changes and tactical deployments, including deployment of sub-units of battalions on both sides of the uncrossable Lohit River, in the Walong sector prior to 14th November 1962.
- The unrealistic expectations of the decision to counter-attack the intruding Chinese in the Walong sector, with the existing availability of troops and their organisationally faulty deployment, for what was apparently an entirely non-military reason (the Prime Minister's birthday on 14th November).

- The lack of any planning and troop resources for a withdrawal (a proper fighting retreat) from the forward positions in the Walong sector down the Lohit valley.
- The decision to change the Se La dispositions from the 'Harbaksh Singh-Palit plan' in order to suit the new 4 Divisional Commander, Maj. Gen. A.S. Pathania, and allowing a brigade and the Div HQ to be removed from the planning for the Se La defences, and be brought down and sited in the Dirang valley.
- The wrong decisions on the part of the 4 Div Commander, Maj. Gen. A.S. Pathania, to move sub-units away from the Se La defences for tactically less-important operational tasks, at a time when the Se La defences had already been contacted by the advancing Chinese forces.
- The lack of a strong directive on the 17th November evening, for the Se La defences to stand firm and fight, from either the Army Commander, Lt. Gen. Sen, or from the Army Chief, Gen. Thapar, to the 4 Div Commander, Maj. Gen. A.S. Pathania, when the Div Commander was asking for permission to withdraw from Se La, at a time when their subordinate, the 4 Corps Commander, Lt. Gen. Kaul, was not available to give the decision. (The two senior Generals were at the time both present in the 4 Corps Operations Room, while Lt. Gen. Kaul was in a helicopter above the Walong sector, and out of communication).
- The interference in the organized defence of Bomdila by the 4 Corps Commander, Lt. Gen. Kaul, at a time when enemy contact with the defences was imminent, by withdrawing units and sub-units for less-important tactical tasks.

There were perhaps errors of tactical judgment by the Army Chief and the DMO at Army Headquarters, Brig. D.K. Palit,[7] in their decision to change 4 Infantry Division's revised Vital Ground at that point of time from Bomdila to Sela, a decision which seems debatable in hindsight. Nevertheless, the decision by Maj. Gen. Niranjan Prasad to halt the troops retreating in concision and panic, and to start organizing a fighting position at Se La, has to be accepted as the right decision and correct action at the time. Whether Se La should have continued as a Delaying Position, or the new Main Defensive Position, is the only issue that can be debated, given the distances involved from Tawang to the Assam plains, over 300 kilometres.

There were errors on the part of Maj. Gen. A.S. Pathania as GOC 4 Infantry Division, in his being too sensitive to outflanking moves by the Chinese. Instead of waiting for the enemy attacks on prepared positions, he wasted troops by sending them out in insufficient strength to clear road-blocks, thereby weakening the defensive position itself, and not achieving the task of clearing the Chinese from the road either. This led to the 'withdrawal mentality' wherein Indian positions which appeared as if about to be cut off were withdrawn. This added to the confusion created by other reasons, and led to the rout, wherein just one Chinese division and an additional brigade were able to overrun an Indian division of equal size in a defensive role in mountain terrain. The troops were not given a proper chance to stand and fight it out. Where this was done, the troops gave a good account of themselves.

There was a further major error on the part of the Corps Commander, Lt. Gen. Kaul, in giving an ambiguously worded withdrawal order to the Divisional Commander of 4 Infantry Division.

The decision to make Se La the main defensive position of 4 Infantry Division, at a stage in the operations when battle had already been joined, may perhaps have been unwise, but the decisions and orders that led to its abandonment on night 17th/18th October were suicidal, and caused the whole division to come undone. It turned what could have been a check to the Chinese advance into a rout, and opened the way for them to thereafter roll onwards down to the Assam plains.

Failure to anticipate Chinese move on unprepared tracks for outflanking moves

There was a conspicuous failure to anticipate the Chinese use of rough and narrow, unprepared tracks for outflanking movements. In addition, their speed of advance on such tracks was not anticipated. This failure, coupled to an unnecessary fear of being outflanked, had serious repercussions, as it unfortunately made some commanders at brigade and above irresolute in a defensive campaign. The Chinese 11 Infantry Division, with its 33 Infantry Regiment leading, carried out a wide outflanking move from the east of the Sela-Dirang Dzong-Bomdila axis, by way of Tse La, Poshing La, and Thembang, to cut off the Dirang Dzong-Bomdila Road. This division moved on man-pack basis, with each soldier carrying about 30 kg of provisions in addition to his weapon and its ammunition. They were also provided 1000 porters recruited locally in Tibet. The division marched 160 km in six days and nights, capturing Poshingla on November 15th, and securing Thembang at last light on Nov 17th. On the night November 17th/18th they captured a bridge on the Dirang Dzong –Bomdila road, thereby cutting off HQ 4 Infantry Division from the south.[8]

Gen. Slim's counter to such outflanking manoeuvres by the Japanese Army in the Burma campaign had been to stand fast in one's own defensive positions and to patrol aggressively to cut the advancing enemy's lines of communication. This was not done to any appreciable extent in the Kameng sector of Arunachal Pradesh.

TACTICAL-LEVEL DEPLOYMENT ERRORS

Indian tactical deployments were unsuited to the defensive requirement in the case of 7 Infantry Brigade at the Namka Chu, at both the brigade and battalion level and at the company and platoon defended locality level. Since the brigade and even battalion deployments had been dictated by the Corps Commander himself, the Brigade Commander and the Battalion Commanders cannot be faulted for the lack of depth in the extended linear layout and the lack of mutual support between the defended localities. This allowed the Chinese to penetrate between the localities and get behind them one or even two mights before the assault was mounted.

A serious error was committed at the level of the company and platoon defended localities of 2nd Rajput and perhaps in other battalions of the forward linear deployment. These localities were neither sited for all-round defence nor even organized for all-round defence, but had all their fire trenches and weapon emplacements oriented towards the front, facing the entranced Chinese positions across the Namka Chu. Since their was no mutual support between the defended localities, and the attacking Chinese troops had already penetrated the defensive layout and positioned themselves behind the Indian localities, these were assaulted from the rear, towards which none of the firing positions were oriented. The prominently-visible bunkers, which were attacked by 75mm recoilless rifle fire, had firing ports only towards the front, and were blind behind and to some extent to the flanks.

By contrast, a Chinese defensive position prepared by a Chinese battalion, deployed to dominate the Jang defile behind Tawang, was sited for all-round defence. It was connected by a communication trench in two concentric approximately circular layouts, utilizing the existing contours of the slope of a ridge. The two concentric circles utilized the available false crests in the sloping ground to maximum effect. There were living and shelter bunkers connected to these trenches, and trenches to listening positions reached outwards to these foxholes.[9]

DEFENSIVE AND OFFENSIVE COMBAT

Infantry sub-units displayed courage, determination and fighting skill, particularly where entire companies were employed together under their Company Commanders. Above the company level, the effectiveness of the troops was determined by the overall situation obtaining in the particular brigade sector at any given point of time. Since the panicky withdrawal in the Kameng sector has received the most attention from all historians and analysts, it is worth examining the Chinese view of the reasons for their success in advance and attack.

Larry Wortzel states, from Chinese sources, that:

> PLA tactics emphasized the rapid concentration of force at decisive points to surround enemy forces and defeat them in detail (*Jizhong youshi bingli*)....
>
> PLA histories also emphasize that the superior knowledge of the terrain and the region by Chinese border troops and reinforcing main forces gave them the ability to take advantage of difficult terrain. For example, the PLA was able to operate more effectively in deep valleys and densely forested areas, in darkness, or when cloud or mist obscured visibility....
>
> One way that the PLA adapted quickly to the challenges posed by the terrain was to advance on parallel routes to one point of attack.

The establishment and decisive use of a relatively strong reserve by battalion and regimental-sized units was also a significant lesson the PLA took from the war. The use of reserves at the proper time contributed to the ability to mass combat power quickly and decisively at important points on the battlefield. As a general rule, 'PLA border forces were able to mass three and one-half to four times the combat power of Indian forces at the decisive point of combat.'

Massing fire effectively was also a critical factor in combat. At one point cited in the PLA history, an Indian platoon surrendered to a seven-man squad that concentrated its fire at the decisive place and time. At another point, five platoons of the PLA concentrated at the right point forced the surrender of an Indian infantry battalion.[10]

COMMAND AND CONTROL

Major problems were caused in the long run by the following:

(a) Breaking of the chain of command, with orders being issued direct from Army HQ to brigades and units.

(b) No detailed written orders being issued to the Army for action against the Chinese: all instructions to the Army from the Government had been verbal, till the note on the subject from the Government of India. This was a brief note signed by H.C. Sarin, a mere Joint Secretary in the Ministry, which had been grudgingly produced on demand. The higher echelons of the Army, the Army Headquarters and the Eastern Command HQ at Lucknow, had perhaps deliberately not been committing themselves to writing till this very late stage in the buildup to war against the Chinese. A few lines on paper by a relatively junior official sent a nation to war with permanent external relations and national security implications, not to mention the lives of thousands of its soldiers and citizens, and a vast expenditure. It was an inexcusably casual way to embark upon an undertaking as serious as war. What is even more amazing; this peremptory note was accepted as an order by an Army Chief.

(c) Not issuing of clear orders to the key members in the chain of command, and not delegating authority to take care of the absence of any senior commander, as was the case during Lt. Gen. Kaul's illness and consequent absence from his headquarters on 18th, 19th and 20th October. In this instance, the Army Chief and the Defence Minister should immediately have appointed another commander the moment Gen. Kaul was evacuated. Failing the above happening, the Army Commander, Lt. Gen. Sen, who had regularly been flying to Tezpur, and was fully alive to the situation, should have assumed command of 4 Corps in addition to his own responsibilities as the Army Commander, instead of nominating Maj. Gen. Niranjan Prasad, GOC 4 Division as 'Officiating Corps Commander' at a critical juncture AFTER the Chinese had attacked and over-run 7 Brigade. Niranjan Prasad was at the time located at his Tactical HQ in Zemithang, 95 km ahead of Tawang, and barely in touch with the Corps HQ. His location was in a remote salient at the western end of the Corps Zone, while the responsibility included operations taking place in the Walong sector, far to the east at the north-eastern tip of Arunachal Pradesh. The problem with this solution was though it would have put the responsibility on Sen's shoulders, he himself did not know the ground, a critical error for a senior military commander, since he had flown over the Nyamjang Chu - Namka Chu sector in a helicopter for the first time only after the Chinese attack on 21st October, and had set foot on the ground at Tawang only at that time.

(d) Lt. Gen. Sen as Army Commander, though correctly basing himself at Tezpur, issued orders from the Corps HQ for re-deployment at Bomdila, much further to the rear, ignoring the great defensive potential of the enormous Se La massif, and ignoring the Army Headquarters' plans. His counter-orders to Niranjan Prasad's orders to the withdrawing Tawang garrison and other troops of 4 Infantry Division for deployment at Se La, created great confusion and near-panic. This hastily arrived-at decision of his was contrary to both the Army Headquarters' plan to re-deploy at Se La, and to established practical battle protocol.

(e) At the brigade level, in the Walong sector, the rifle companies of the three different battalions were deployed in a non-contiguous manner, with companies of one battalion having to be placed under other battalions. This was a result of their piecemeal deployment, but the resultant command and control arrangements were totally unsatisfactory.

In Ladakh, only three companies of one of the three brigades of 3 Infantry Division were actually involved. Thus only three out of the eight infantry rifle companies of the two regular infantry battalions of 114 Infantry Brigade were actually engaged, though undoubtedly in very severe fighting in which they fought well and gallantly. (The third regular battalion of the brigade had actually arrived in the sector only on 2nd October). The two other brigades of the division, 70 Infantry Brigade and 163 Infantry Brigade, were not engaged. At a divisional level therefore, only three out of the division's thirty-six regular infantry companies (of the nine battalions of infantry) were actually engaged, though it would not have been possible for the entire force to be immediately brought to bear upon the attacking Chinese for practical reasons of distance and lack of readiness. Nevertheless, in spite of 114 Brigade's orderly and pre-planned withdrawal to its new defences near Chushul village, Brig. Sodhi believes that the withdrawal *'could be viewed as premature.'*[11]

CASUALTIES SUSTAINED

The operations were not really large-scale in the sense of numbers of formations and troops actually employed on both sides in both the western and the eastern sectors, about two-and-a-half division's worth of troops on India's side and four to five divisions of Chinese troops, but there was far too much confusion on the Indian side. The actual fighting took place only over 13 days. Relative to the size of the Indian Army, only a small number were engaged.

Xu Yan gives Chinese casualties for the war to be 2,400.[12] In the Kameng sector, Chinese casualties were given by Chinese sources to be 225 killed (27 officers and 198 men) and 477 wounded (46 officers and 431 men).[13] The total Indian casualties as per Maj. Praval, were 9,743; of which 1,423 were killed, 3,078 wounded, 1,655 missing believed killed, and 3,587 taken prisoner.[14] James Calvin's 1984 study gave Indian casualty figures to be 1,383 killed and 1,636 missing.[15] It is believed that 2,420 out of the total killed and missing casualties occurred in NEFA. However, as per the official *History,* the total casualties were 2,616, including killed and seriously wounded; out of these 875 were directly attributable to enemy action. The rest were due to other causes including weather and accidents. This figure evidently does not include those taken prisoner.

According to PLA records from Chinese archives, Indian casualties during the war were 4,897 killed or wounded and

3,968 captured. As perry Wortzel, the Indian Defence Ministry in 1965 showed 1,383 Indian soldiers killed, 1,696 missing in action, 3,968 soldiers captured, and 1,047 soldiers wounded. In comparison, PLA casualties in the war were quite small, with 722 Chinese soldiers killed and 1,697 wounded. In addition, no soldier of the PLA was captured during the war, a rarity in the history of warfare.[16]

On December 26, 1962, the Chinese Red Cross had informed their Indian counterpart that the PRC was holding 3,895 prisoners.[17] The difference between the Chinese figures of 3,968 captured, and 3,895 prisoners held as on 26th December 1962 is probably the number of wounded Indian prisoners who died in Chinese captivity.

As per the *History* the Indian Army had not taken any Chinese prisoner.[18] However, this author had himself seen two Chinese prisoners in the prisoners' enclosure attached to the quarter-guard of the Rajputana Rifles Regimental Centre in Delhi Cantonment, in the winter of 1963-64.[19]

RETREAT AND WITHDRAWAL

Field Marshal Sir William Slim,[20] who had been forced to retreat from Burma when the Japanese attacked in 1942, had explained:

> In war it is all-important to gain and retain the initiative, to make the enemy conform to your action, to dance to your tune. When you are advancing, this normally follows; if you withdraw, it is neither so obvious nor so easy. Yet it is possible. There are three reasons for retreat: self-preservation, to save your force from destruction; pressure elsewhere which makes you accept loss of territory in one place to enable you to transfer troops to a more vital front;

> and, lastly, to draw the enemy into a situation so unfavourable to him that the initiative must pass to you.
>
> Here was the contrast between the forced retreat of 1942, whose object became merely the preservation of our troops as an intact force, and that of 1944, which was carefully calculated to lead inevitably to our regaining the initiative.... Yet so many scrambles to escape have been described as 'withdrawals according to plan' ... it was possible to fight defensively and even to retreat, yet keep the initiative.'[21]

But even Field Marshal Slim concedes that from the point of view of morale, a withdrawal is not the best opening for a decisive battle.[22] But then, as explained by Brig. Dalvi, as was evident in this case:

> Since we decided to sit on the McMahon Line, we could only manoeuvre backward, unless we were prepared to invade Tibet....[23]
>
> The strategic deployment and dispositions of regular troops is dictated solely by the ground and administrative factors. To put it simply, it was necessary to move *[forward]* from firm base to firm base, and not backward from the political boundaries of the country. Political and military boundaries seldom coincide.[24]

In spite of the fact that so many of the Indian Army senior officers had experience of the Burma war, including many who had been in the initial fighting retreat, one of the world's longest at about 1,500 km, and a considerable feat of arms in itself, it is clear that what actually happened was not as described by Field Marshal Slim.

Brig. Sodhi's comments are relevant:

Withdrawal is an operation of war. Having to resort to this is part of the imponderables of war and no dishonour is involved – if this is conducted as an operation of war.

He opined that the disgrace comes when events take the shape of the events of 1962 in the Kameng and Walong sectors of NEFA, where *'the withdrawal turned into a retreat and soon into a rout.'*

He squarely lays the blame on the senior officers:

The first to break were the senior officers who panicked and left the scene without even making sure that all the units had been informed and that the withdrawal was according to plan. The panic gradually spread to the units who tried to keep together but were so dispersed into smaller and smaller groups till all semblance of control was lost.[25]

The *History* comments:

After the battle of Namka Chu and the withdrawal from Tawang, defeatist miasma seems to have overpowered the officers and men in NEFA. It almost became a rule that whenever any formation position was threatened or attacked by the Chinese they were to withdraw.'[26]

THE LT. GEN. KAUL FACTOR

Regarding Lt. Gen. Kaul's influence, and as to why neither the Eastern Army Commander nor the Army Chief gave any firm decision to Maj. Gen. A.S. Pathania on the crucial evening of November 17, 1962 at Tezpur, or even before, Gen. Manekshaw's anecdotal information is telling. When taking over 4 Corps after the discredited Bijji Kaul, Lt.Gen. Manekshaw had asked Lt. Gen. Bogey Sen, the Army

Commander: *'Bogey, why didn't you come as Army Commander, sack the Corps Commander and take over yourself?'* Sen's reply was:

> It is all very well for you to say this, Sam, but do you know what his stature was then? He never talked to me; he would just pick up the phone and talk to the Prime Minister. He never even consulted the COAS. I would have got no support from anyone. Krishna Menon and Bijji Kaul were running the armed forces of the country.[27]

LACK OF MODERN WEAPONS

After the war the lack of more modern personal weapons for the infantry was brought up as the one of the reasons for the humiliating Indian failure. Brig. Sodhi disclaims this:

> This had nothing to do with the .303 rifles. Wherever the troops made a stand, these same rifles gave an excellent account of themselves. This is not to suggest that better rifles were not needed, but that the bad performance of the senior officers cannot be blamed on these rifles. The failure was NOT of the troops, the units, the rifles, but of the senior officers.[28]

Capt. Pran Pahwa was the 2IC of 135 Heavy Mortar Battery (two troops of 4 x 4.2 inch mortars each) of 30 Heavy Mortar Regiment and was very actively involved in the war, including a do-or-die one-to-one encounter with a Chinese soldier at Bomdila. He comments on the issue of the supposedly outdated arms and equipment with the Indian forces:

> It is popularly believed that one of the reasons we lost the 1962 War was because of our outdated equipment. This may be true for other areas but not for the Bomdi-La, Dirang and Se-La Axis because there never was any set-piece battle here

> (except perhaps at Thembang to some extent) and even our existing weapons were hardly used ... the result would have been no different even if we had the latest equipment.[29]

A major strategic mistake was not using the air force in the ground attack role against the Chinese, especially in Ladakh, where the Chinese forces were most exposed during the day time, to relieve the pressure on the ground troops. Interdiction missions against Chinese logistical convoys moving forward after hostilities were joined, and offensive missions against the enemy airfields and logistical assets on the Tibetan plateau were all possible, but no effective coordination between the Army and the Air Force on this aspect took place, in spite of the Air Force's gallant efforts to keep the troops supplied with all the necessities of operations, particularly in NEFA.

The Indian Air Force (IAF) had more modern, or at the very least equivalent, aircraft compared to the Chinese PLA Air Force (PLAAF), and in a better state of maintenance and organisation. The IAF was in a position to drop 336 tonnes of bombs per day on Chinese roads and airbases in Tibet using its Canberra bombers and Hawker Hunter fighter/ground attack aircraft.

By contrast, the Chinese Ilyushin-28 light bombers and MiG-19 fighters could have dropped only 45 tonnes of bombs per day on cities in Assam (*See map*). The IAF'S aircraft and its operational bases at Srinagar, Ambala, Bagdogra (Siliguri), Tezpur, Jorhat and Chhabua (Dibrugarh) had all the geographical advantages which the Chinese did not, in complete contrast to the Army which had all the disadvantages as compared to the Chinese PLA. The IAF's near sea-level bases allowed the fighter aircraft to take off with a much greater bomb load or total ordnance load than the less capable PLAAF, which had to operate from high-altitude bases on the Tibetan plateau

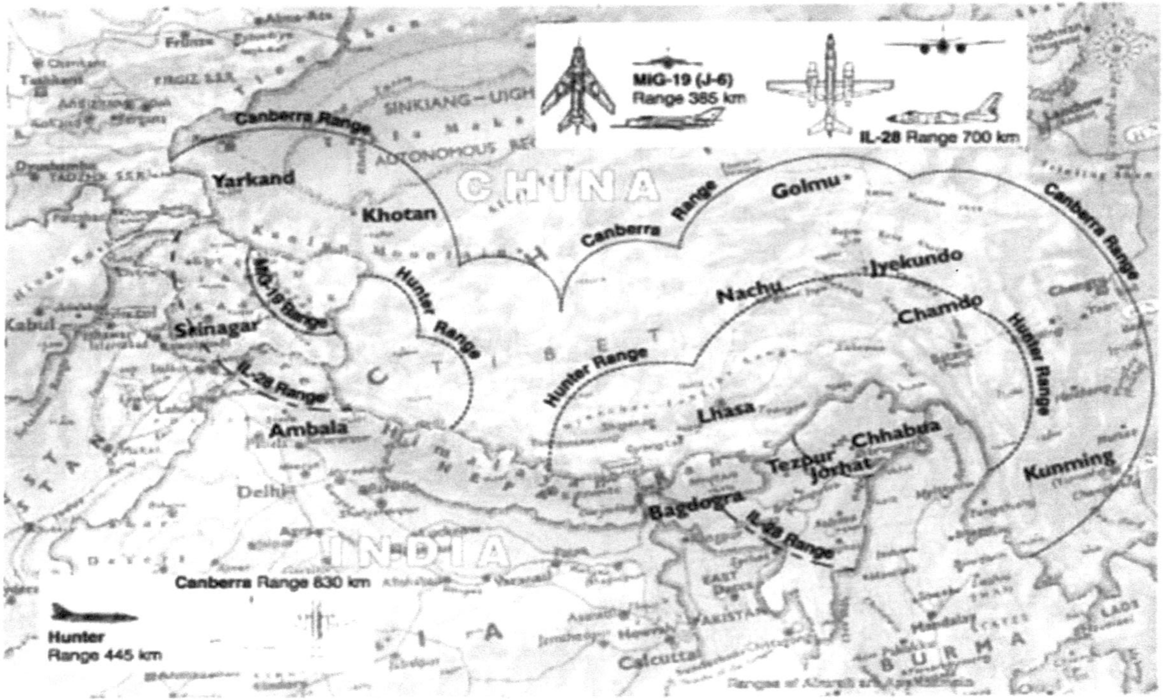

Operational Ranges of Indian and Chinese Aircraft in 1962.

with its thin air. Thus most of the PLAAF's airbases, including nearby ones not in Tibet proper, such as Kunming in the east and Khotan in the north, were all accessible to IAF aircraft, whereas the PLAAF could only plan on a very limited number of Indian targets. But though the IAF in Assam did get put on to 'standby' when the reverses in NEFA began, the Army did not eventually ask the Government for this support, nor did the government on its own think of using it.

The reasons were that there was a belief in Air HQ that the steep, jungle-clad terrain in NEFA did not present worthwhile targets for effective engagement, while Army HQ believed that the use of offensive air support would invite retaliation against the IAF'S transport aircraft on which the Army's maintenance depended. The Government on its part seemed to have got taken in by the American Ambassador's belief that the Chinese PLAAF was more capable than the IAF, and that escalation of the conflict into the aerial dimension would have invited massive Chinese retaliation with bombing of Indian cities. With the attention of the world actually riveted to the simultaneously–happening Cuban missile crisis between the USA and the Soviet Union, perhaps it feared that India might not get any international sympathy. At any rate, India did not use its most modern and capable force, which held all the advantages vis-a-vis Chinese air-power, and which could have easily been used. This was a major error of omission.

It is, however, equally a fact that Indian combat air-power could be practically used only in the interdiction role on the Tibetan plateau, and not for close air support (CAS) in the mountains of Arunchal Pradesh. There would also have been a problem of adequate combat range for Indian fighter aircraft to be used in the Ladakh sector, which is the only sector where CAS may have been feasible, since the fighters were based in the plains of the Punjab. The Canberra light bomber was perhaps the only combat aircraft with the range for combat missions against ground targets on the Ladakh front.

Lt. Gen. Pran Pahwa (Retd.), a participant in the 1962 war at Bomdila in the Kameng Sector as earlier noted, also holds strong views on the use of air-power in the 1962 war. He states:

> There is a view that the result of the war would have been different if we had used our Air Force as we enjoyed a clear advantage over the Chinese in this area. I do not agree.... No amount of air support, no matter how effective it was could have possibly have made up for the poor leadership and lack of professionalism that was on display in these places *[Bomdila, Dirang and Se-La]*. Even at the technical level it is questionable whether aircraft fitted with the avionics of that era would have been very effective in the hilly terrain and the thick undergrowth of that area.[30]

The real reason why CAS was not feasible against suitable targets in the mountains of NEFA was not any limitation of the aircraft themselves, but of the Indian military organization and its preparations for war. The Indian organizational structure prevented effective coordination between the Army and the Air Force, except for supply-dropping by air. The other reason was a complete lack of training in mountain flying.

Gp. Capt. A.G. Bewoor (Retd.) believes that the Air Force was not fully prepared to provide Close Air Support over the battlefields of the 1962 war:

THE TERRITORY AND OUR AIRCRAFT IN 1962

The battles were fought at Walong where the Lohit flows Westward. In NEFA, the battle was along the Tawang-Bomdi La-

Se La axis heading for Tezpur. In Ladakh it was in the area of Chip Chap, Pangong Tso, Demchok, and territories beyond Darbuk & Chushul. Heights at Walong were close to 8000 feet, higher in NEFA and much higher in Ladakh. What we had were, De Havilland Vampires, Dassault Ouragans (Toofanis), Dassault Mysteres, Hawker Hunters, Folland Gnats, English Electric Canberra and B-24 Liberators.

TRAINING IN HILL FLYING

Back in 1962, hill flying was very restricted, because neither the Govt nor the IAF expected to fight the Chinese in the mountains, and with Pakistan, it was to be in Punjab/Rajasthan. No one had ever tried out bombing, rocket or front gun attacks in the hills/mountains. No SOPs existed about heights to fly, dive angles, weapon release heights, escape routes, weather impact in afternoon operations, range/endurance versus weapon loads, search/rescue, helicopter support etc.

If at all any training was done it was a one off. The type of training that is truly required for quality CAS in the mountains was not even thought of in July 1962. Quality cooperation with the Army was nonexistent. They made their plans, we made our Counter Air Op plans. TACs were for namesake. Very few IAF officers studied Army ops of war, the Army expected CAS as and when demanded, very much like Arty support, and wanted it to be on call, and under command. The IAF believed in centralised control, and the necessity of exploiting range and flexibility of air power. Truly then, in 1962 we were far from a cohesive Joint operations military machine. Our pilots had not mastered the art of transposing Grid Ref points from a One Inch map onto a million-map.

The Vampires, Toofanis and Gnats just did not have the juice and training to go into Ladakh. In NEFA they had the range, but no training at all. Indeed the Hunter and possibly the Mystere could have done some offensive activity, but again, where was the training? Only the Canberra could have put in attacks in Ladakh where it was all in the open. For NEFA their crew were untrained for Jungle / Hills combination.

Who would have guided the aircraft to the correct target? We had no FACs[31] trained in the mountains?

The Army was in retreat, front lines were unknown, maps were poor, hill/valley flying along the Towang-Bomdi La-Sela axis had never been done by fighter pilots. Even Dak crew were uncertain of where to go, who would be there, and who will actually receive the drop. Recollect the loss of a helicopter with S/L Sehgal, in that sector. Where would the "four aircraft formation" have gone? Let's forget about whether the PLAAF would have intervened. Let's ask what the IAF would have done with its fighters.

The Army's Eastern Command was in Lucknow, ours was in Calcutta. Kalinga Airways still flew in Transport Support Role for the Army. Of course there were fighters in the "East," but they did not do range practice in NEFA, or Sikkim, they did it at Dudhkundi or Dulanmukh ranges both in the plains. Hill flying is done to give pilots exposure in handling the ac in valleys. Knowledge of every valley, entry/exit points, how to distinguish the "third ridge" from the 'fifth' was never taught to fighter pilots. This was the job of the Dak and Otter pilots.

We made many "Blue on Blue" attacks in 1965 as well as in 1971. What would we have done in 1962? Would the enemy be identifiable in the melee that was going on? Had any fighter pilot even flown to the battle area in say June/July 1962 for familiarisation? If it can be said today that the IAF would have taken part if permitted by Govt, what actually did the IAF do as realistic training in preparation when things were hotting up for months before the Chinese attacked? The truth is that we did nothing. We cannot blame the Govt for not gearing up. It was up to the field commanders, and policy framers and operational staff in Air HQs to visualise what may happen in case of a battle in NEFA or Ladakh. The Chinese had clearly indicated what they wanted. The possible battle zones were quite easily understood in Air HQ. After all the Army had taken a "forward posture" and it was known where they were deployed. Did we limber up for the possibility of engaging ground troops in valleys at heights above 9,000 feet? We did not. We were still training for aerial combat, and CAS in the plains, with our very own private Counter Air Operations (CAO). The irony is that there were no CAO targets in Tibet or China.

By Oct 1962 no fighter had even landed in Srinagar, forget about Leh. We just did not have the wherewithal to wage an air war against the Chinese in Oct 62.[32]

THE OVERALL ANALYSIS

'Of the three widely separated sectors where the fighting took place, the Army performance was very bad, amounting to a rout, in one; it was bad enough in the second; and quite creditable in the third one,' wrote Brig Sodhi, analyzing the war.[33]

Brig. H.S. Sodhi believes that:

> The war with China was winnable given: better appreciation of the then Chinese military situation and development; patience for another about six months; better professional leadership especially in NEFA and a stronger COAS; combat air support. The outcome, militarily and politically, could have been vastly different.[34]

The Government of India's *History of the Conflict with China, 1962* sums up the war by saying:

> In the ultimate analysis, it was the superior leadership and higher morale of the Chinese army that tilted the balance heavily in favour of the China. As against that, the Army top brass in India did not possess the either the vision to see the military operation in its right perspective, or they lacked guts to express their objective assessment of the situation to the Government with all the firmness at their command. And, when an armed conflict between India and China became inevitable, the field commanders did not give that inspiring leadership which would have enabled the troops to perform creditably.[35]

LESSONS

Politically-sponsored Generals: The lesson about politically-sponsored generals, is worth repeating. In Brig. Dalvi's words:

> In the political sphere, the lesson is that the selection, appointment and replacement of commanders must be made objectively. Mr. Menon and Gen. Thapar knew of Kaul's illness and his evacuation to Delhi on 18th October. The failure to appoint a commander during Kaul's illness was a blunder of incalculable dimensions on the part of the Defence Mnister and the Army Chief. The crux of the matter is that the whole affair was handled in a typically subjective manner, by the political bosses ... the troops have a right to be led by generals who are 100 per cent fit and in whom they have professional confidence.... There is no doubt that any other general who had fallen ill would have been replaced at once. An ordinary general would not have been permitted to retain a lien on his appointment. There would have been no extraneous factors introduced into a straightforward matter. There would have been no thought given to the

repercussions on the General's reputation, and what others might think. In fact the change would probably have gone unnoticed by the Public. Herein lies another lesson. Generals of the Indian Army should never become controversial figures. They should serve in anonymity and should have no outside sponsorship.[36]

Lack of Moral Courage: The lack of moral courage at higher levels in the Army has been brought out in the official History itself, saying that after General K.S. Thimayya, Lt. Gen. S.D. Verma and Lt. Gen. S.P.P. Thorat, the Army was dominated by senior officers who either agreed with the Government's assessment of the Chinese intentions, or were too weak to stand up to the aggressive Defence Minister Krishna Menon, who was always supported by Prime Minister Nehru. As a consequence the actual ground-level conditions, as represented by Lt. Gen. Umrao Singh, Maj. Gen. Niranjan Prasad and Brig. Dalvi, were either ignored or not allowed to reach the top political leadership. At the stage when the decision to appoint Lt. Gen. Kaul as the Corps Commander of a new '4 Corps,' was being taken, the Army Chief, Gen. Thapar, should have explained the realities to the Defence Minister, and if need be, the Prime Minister. They should have been apprised that a new corps cannot be conjured up overnight, or even in a few days. The new, so-called 4 Corps had only a single division under command, instead of two or three, and none of the necessary corps logistics infarastructure. 4 Infantry Division itself had only two brigades available in NEFA, instead of a division's usual three, and both these were already committed, hundreds of kilometers apart. In effect, Lt. Gen. Kaul as Corps Commander had only two infantry brigades, 5 Brigade and 7 Brigade, instead of a normal corps' usual complement of six (for a two-division corps) to nine infantry brigades (for a three-division corps).

Avoidance of Personality-oriented Operational Decisions: The official *History* is critical of the 'over-eagerness to execute an "offensive defense plan" that led to the collapse of the front.' It adds, 'It is surmised that undue haste in launching this assault, without making a firm base and without catering for the likely reaction by the enemy, was made in order to complete it on 14th November, so as to make it a gift to Prime Minister Nehru on his birthday.'

Weapons and Equipment: That weapons and equipment need to be up to date is a lesson that has not been too well-learned. The Chinese infantry mortars at the 'battle' of the Namka Chu, if such a gallant but one-sided massacre can be called a battle, out-ranged the pitiful artillery support available to 7 Brigade. Technological innovations threaten to make the weapons and equipment of the army, navy and the air force ineffective as and when they are introduced into the armed forces of potential adversaries. Instead of grudging and belated responses, India needs to switch to being pro-active in introducing whatever is needed.

After-action Lessons Learnt: The lesson of the necessity of transparency, after the period of secrecy and military necessity is actually over, so that the nation can introspect, has not yet been learned. The Henderson Brooks Report on the 1962 disaster has not yet been released either to the Parliament or to the public.

Survival Rations: Many lives were lost due to privation during the panic retreats in NEFA, partly or wholly due to starvation, because of the lack of anything to eat for days. Unlike during the Second World War, when all troops were issued with chocolate-based survival rations in sealed packs, no emergency rations had been issued as these had not been catered for prior to this conflict. Even during earlier wars and campaigns, such as the North-West Frontier campaigns and the First World War, Indian troops had carried parched gram and jaggery (*'gur'*) as emergency rations.

Night withdrawal: While in contact with an attacking enemy, the forward troops should not have been withdrawn through troops holding depth areas, as happened at Sela, when 2 SIKH LI troops were withdrawn through the positions of 1 SIKH.[37]

CONCLUSION

The Sino-Indian War of 1962 was a sorry tale of political misjudgement, incorrect intelligence appreciation, and military mismanagement of the highest order.

The 4 Infantry Division that fought, or did not fight, in the Kameng Sector in October-November 1962 was not the same division that it was when it was sent from Ambala east to Assam and Arunachal Pradesh (then NEFA). The once-famous division of the Second World War, and India's showpiece division since Independence, was broken up. Its integral brigades, 5 Brigade, 7 Brigade, and 11 Brigade, and thus most of the original battalions which had once been together, were not used together. Only the original 7 Brigade was sent to the Kameng sector of NEFA, and that too could only maintain one battalion of this brigade forward, at Tawang, supposedly the Divisional Vital Ground, since the administrative infrastructure did not exist. Under-strength, under-prepared and ill-equipped infantry battalions, from wherever they were in the plains, were rushed up to be placed under this Brigade Headquarters to carry out an impossible military task. A logistical support system for 7 Brigade either to attack or to fight a defensive battle had not yet been set up. 5 Brigade was responsible for the rest of the Sino-Indian border in NEFA, including the Walong sector, nearly 500 km away to the east. The third brigade of the division, 11 Brigade, had been sent initially to Sikkim, thereafter earmarked for the defence of Sela and Bomdila, and then diverted to Nagaland.

The *ad hoc* nature of the arrangements can be judged from the fact that, in response to the Chinese reaction to the setting up of the Dhola post, the one battalion at Tawang (9th Punjab) was hurried off a 100 kilometres to the west, while even more *ad hoc* arrangements were made for the defence of Tawang. The Commander Artillery 4 Division was flown up to take command of the 'Tawang Sector,' though he had not been adequately briefed as to what exactly he was in charge of, against what, and with what. He had been chosen for the task because, apparently, there was no task for the Commander Artillery in the forthcoming operations. The Divisional Machine-Gun Battalion Commander had been placed in charge of the Line of Communication from Foothills (near Tezpur in the Assam plains) all the way up to Tawang.

Brig. Dalvi tellingly comments:

> 4 Division never fought as a Division and thus did not sully its international fame. It had only two brigades stretched over 300 miles.... The Division had no depth, no reserves, and was unbalanced. It was never able to deploy its fire-power or administrative cover. The troops in NEFA could more adequately have been named 'Border Guards.'
>
> Perhaps the most ironic fact of all is that 4th Division had been commanded by Generals Thapar, Sen, and Kaul – the three Generals who led the Division to 'these series of reverses.'[38]

To make matters worse, the 7 Brigade Commander was ordered to shed his brigade staff in Tawang to assist the new Sector Commander in the arrangements for troop movement.

This would have put the 7 Brigade Commander in the position of having to conduct a forthcoming brigade battle without a staff. This was an unforgivable breach of military organization and working procedures.

Brig. Dalvi comments on the organizational problems:

> These *ad hoc* measures stemmed from our penchant for devising snap solutions to events we never seem able to foresee. If we do anticipate them we get bogged down in a morass of financial considerations and other extraneous issues. At the last minute we created a sector at Towang, with a Commander Artillery in charge and gave him the staff of a Brigade Commander who was soon to be given the task of evicting the Chinese![39]

Is the Sino-Indian war of 1962 a closed chapter in India's history? The history of the period 1959-62, and incidents such as the April-May 2013 intrusion of a Chinese army platoon into the Daulet Beg Oldi (DBO) area of Aksai Chin, show that the political and ground realities remain nearly the same as before. No agreement has been reached between India and China on the conflicting territorial claims of both countries and the resultant border issues. This is in spite of the general agreement reached during Indian Prime Minister Rajiv Gandhi's visit to Beijing in 1988, and the various subsequent various border management agreements with China, in 1993,[40] 1996[41] and 2005.[42]

Tibet continues to remain a 'core concern' of the PRC, second only to Taiwan, and more important than the recent addition of the South China Sea as another 'core concern.' The importance of Tibet to the People's Republic of China has been well explained by George Friedman in his article *Chinese Geopolitics and the Significance of Tibet,* of April 15, 2008, available on the Internet.

At the same time, the suitability of the Tibetan plateau as a location for the emplacement of long-range nuclear ballistic missiles, expressed by Lt. Gen. Sir Francis Tuker, the GOC-in-C of the Indian Army's Eastern Command in 1948, has been well utilised by China. The article by Hans M. Kristensen, *Extensive nuclear deployment area discovered in Central China,* of May 15, 2008, available on the Internet, gives details.

Tibet is now fairly well-connected by train to the Chinese heartland, as well as by road to Sichuan, and to Xinjiang provinces (through Aksai Chin). Logistical infrastructure in Tibet to support induction amd maintenance of large numbers of additional forces has increased greatly. The number of airfields capable of operation modern jet fighter aircraft has increased manifold. The logistical capabilities of the People's Liberation Army to move large numbers of troops and equipment across China has greatly increased. China has in recent years been practicing its armed forces in rapid deployment and reinforcement exercises to the Tibet Autonomous Region which adjoins the Indian borders. China's earlier weaknesses in projection of force over distances beyond its immediate border regions have been increasingly addressed. In the last few years China has greatly increased its force projection capability and movement capability within China. The PLA can no longer said to be a force with 'short arms and slow legs.' Its military philosophy now espouses an 'active defence' with pre-emptive thinking, under the most modern conditions of war. There is no nuclear deterrence stability between China and India as there is significant asymmetry between the ballistic missile forces of the two countries. Hence there remains the potential for conflict, for reasons of international relations which are beyond the scope of discussion of this study.

It is necessary, therefore, to study the Sino-Indian war of 1962 not merely as military history, organizational, logistical, operational, and tactical, but also a history of mistakes made in the past in the realm of geo-politics, and in the fields of diplomatic relations and intelligence appreciation.

Hawks among the India-watchers in China have reacted adversely to the Indian Government's greatly belated recognition, in October 2012, of the sacrifices of the Indian martyrs of the war. They have seen this as aggressive behavior on the part of India, and warned of dire consequences in case India does not remember the lessons of India's aggressive actions in 1959-1962, which led to their 'counter-attack in self-defence.'

Lt. Gen. Patabhiraman, who retired as the Vice-Chief of the Army Staff in December 2006, has given his views on both the 1962 war and the current situation in his 2012 article in the *USI Journal.* He believes that:

> Irrespective of the progress or non-progress in the boundary talks and increased bilateral engagements between China and India, the Indian Armed Forces, particularly the Army, can no longer ignore the growing asymmetry in the capacity to conduct operations between the PLA and the Indian military on our northern borders.[43]

NOTES

1. Wortzel, Larry M., 'Concentrating Forces and Audacious Action: PLA Lessons from the Sino-Indian War,' 2003, in *The Lessons of History: The Chinese People's Liberation Army at 75,* (US Army War College, Strategic Studies Institute, Carlisle, Penn, USA, 2003), p. 328, available on the Internet at www.strategicstudiesinstitute.army.mil/pdffiles/pub52.pdf.
2. *Ibid.,* pp. 339-340.
3. *Ibid.,* p. 341.
4. Maj. Gen. P.J.S. Sandhu, '1962—Battle of Se-La and Bomdi-La' in *USI Journal,* Vol. CXLI, No. 586, October-December 2011, pp. 577-578, and 1962—The Battle of Namka Chu and Fall of Tawang (A View from Other Side of the Hill) in *USI Journal,* Vol. CXLIII, No. 592, April-June 2013, pp.271-289.

5. *Ibid.*, p. 581.
6. *Ibid.*, pp. 578-579.
7. Brig. (later Maj. Gen.) D.K. Palit, Veer Chakra (1919-2008), has been painted as one of the villains of the 1962 Kameng fiasco by Neville Maxwell, the Australian author and commentator on this war. The highly-Anglicised, polo-playing and monocle-wearing, very British-officer-like Palit was an unlikely member of the 'Kaul team' in Army HQ. (He was the son of one of the few Indians who were earlier granted commissions in the Army by the British in the Indian Medical Service, the fore-runner of the Army Medical Corps, who had been in the First World War in France as a Captain). Brig. Palit was in style the very antithesis of Kaul himself. He was never a member of the *'Kaul-boys,'* as the Kaul coterie was referred to in a derogatory reference to the term 'call-girl' which had recently become well-known as a result of the Christine Keeler-Profumo affair in Britain. He was originally an officer of the Baluch Regiment, and had come into prominence after the wide success of his 1947 book, *The Essentials of Military Knowledge,* published in Aldershot, England, which somehow led to his 'Monty' nickname. He was awarded the Veer Chakra for gallantry while commanding the 3rd Battalion of the 9th Gorkha Rifles in an attack during the 1947-48 Kashmir war. He was probably selected for DMO by Kaul on the basis of his reputation as an intellectual professional soldier. He was later, as a Maj. Gen., Commandant of the Indian Military Academy. Widely-known and highly regarded in the world of equestrian sports, Palit died in Delhi at the age of 89, having refereed a polo match on horseback the day before, and was scheduled to judge an event at the National Equestrian Championship the day he died.
8. Sandhu, *op. cit.,* p. 582.
9. Seen by then-Maj. Ashok Kalyan Verma, BM of the Tawang brigade in 1968, Maj. Gen. Ashok Kalyan Verma, pers. comn., June 2013.
10. Wortzel, *op. cit.,* p. 345.
11. Sodhi, *Top Brass, op.cit.,* p. 35.
12. Xu Yan, *History of the Sino-Indian Border Self-Defensive War,* 1993.
13. Sandhu, *op. cit.* p. 585.
14. Praval, *op. cit.,* p. 236.
15. James Barnard Calvin, *The China-India Border War,* 1984.
16. Wortzel, Larry M., 'Concentrating Forces and Audacious Action: PLA Lessons from the Sino-Indian War,' in Laurie Burkilt, Andrew Scobell, Larry M. Wortzel, (Eds.), *The Chinese People's Liberation Army at 75,* 2003, p. 343.
17. *History, op. cit.,* p. 377-378.

18. *Ibid.,* p. 378.
19. According to media reports in 2003 the two Chinese prisoners, Yang Chen and Shih Liang, 'had been held as spies in a New Delhi jail for three years' before being transferred to the Central Institute of Psychiatry [CIP], a mental asylum in Ranchi. These two were eventually repatriated in July 2003 to their villages in Sichuan, China. Indian Foreign Ministry sources said that the release of the two POWs was conceived as a goodwill gesture and set in motion during a summit in China in June 2003 between Indian Prime Minister Atal Behari Vajpayee and his Chinese counterpart, Wen Jiabao.
20. Believed by many historians to be one of the best Allied generals of WW-II, his highest field command being GOC-in-C 14th Army, he was an Indian Army officer commissioned into the 6th Gurkha Rifles, though he later commanded 2nd/7th Gurkha Rifles [presently India's 3/11 Gorkha Rifles]. He rose to become the senior-most officer ever produced by the Indian Army of the British, rising to become Britain's Chief of the Imperial General Staff after WW-II, and eventually retiring from active life as Governor-General of Australia.
21. Field Marshal Sir William Slim, *'Defeat Into Victory,'* 1956, p. 290.
22. *Ibid.,* p. 289.
23. Dalvi, *op. cit.,* p. 70.
24. *Ibid.,* p. 65.
25. Sodhi, *Top Brass, op. cit.,* p. 44.
26. *History, op. cit.,* p. 424.
27. Praval, *op. cit.,* p. 238-239.
28. Sodhi, *Top Brass, op. cit.,* p. 44.
29. Pahwa, Lt. Gen. Pran, 'The Attack on Bomdi-La: A Personal Experience,' in *USI Journal,* Vol. CXLII, No. 590, October-December 2012, p. 601.
30. *Ibid.*
31. Forward Air Controllers: Air Force officers who are located on the ground with the forward troops, and over the radio guide the pilots of the ground-attack mission fighters onto the targets.
32. Bewoor, Gp Capt AG, in Close Air Support in 1962, on the Internet at www.bharat-rakshak.com/IAF/History/1962War/Bewoor.html.
33. Sodhi, *Top Brass, op. cit.,* p. 36.
34. Sodhi, *Significant Battles Since Independence, op.cit.,* p. 129.
35. Ministry of Defence, *History, op. cit.,* p. 426.
36. Dalvi, *op. cit.,* pp. 306-307.
37. Datta, *op. cit,* p. 139.
38. Dalvi, *op. cit.,* pp.172-173.
39. *Ibid.,* p. 173.

40. Agreement on the Maintenance of Peace and Tranquility along the Line of Actual Control in the China-India Border Areas, September 7, 1993.
41. Agreement on Confidence-Building Measures in the Military Field along the Line of Actual Control in the China-Indian Border Areas, November 29, 1996.
42. Protocol on the Modalities for the Implementation of Confidence-Building Measures in the Military Field along the Line of Actual Control in the China-India Border Areas, April 11, 2005.
43. Patabhiraman, Lt. Gen. S., 'Fifty Years after the 1962 Debacle,' in *USI Journal,* Vol. CXLII, No. 590, October-December 2012, p. 531.

Appendix A

The Henderson-Brooks Report: Report of the Inquiry into the 1962 Military Debacle

Present Status

The Henderson-Brooks report was the outcome of an inquiry ordered by the Indian Army to inquire into the causes for the October-November 1962 defeat in the war with China. Even though 50 years have passed since the events, this 'Top Secret' report has not yet been de-classified and made available, either to Parliament or the public.

After several failed attempts via the Parliament, in 2005 the veteran journalist Kuldip Nayar had approached the Government of India, Ministry of Defence (MoD), under ther Right to Information Act (RTI) asking for declassification of the document.[1] The request was turned down by the MoD on the grounds that the Report was an 'internal review' and therefore could not be placed in the public domain. When the matter was taken up with the Central Information Commission (CIC), the CIC, by its decision of 19th March 2009, rejected the demand for declassification of the report under the RTI, on the grounds that it would seriously compromise the country's security, and endanger relations with China.[2] On 10th May 2012 the Government of India informed Parliament accordingly.

The Inquiry

After the catastrophic events of October-November 1962 in the North-East Frontier Agency (NEFA), now known as Arunachal Pradesh, an Operations Review Committee was appointed in mid-December 1962 by the new Army Chief, Gen. J.N. 'Muchu' Chaudhuri, to inquire into the operations of 4 Corps. Lt. Gen. T. B. Henderson-Brooks, generally known as 'H-B,' was appointed Chairman of this committee, to be assisted by Brig. Premendra Singh Bhagat, Victoria Cross, then Commandant of the Indian Military Academy. 'H-B' was a competent but not outstanding officer, whose appointments and personality had kept him entirely outside the anti-Kaul and pro-Kaul (the so-called '*Kaul-boys*') fault-line which had divided the army's senior officers. Brig. P.S. Bhagat complemented 'H-B' by being a no-nonsense, fighting soldier, widely respected in the Army for both his professional competence and his professionalism.

The Government of India did not wish to institute an inquiry into the high-level policies, plans, and decisions that led to the outbreak of hostilities against the Chinese, and the committee was ordered to confine its inquiry only into 4 Corps' operations. Also, Lt. Gen. Henderson-Brooks was directed not to apportion responsibility for the reverses to specific individuals, most probably in order to protect Lt. Gen. Kaul's reputation. The inquiry tasks given were to examine:

- Training
- Equipment
- System of command
- Physical fitness of troops
- Capacity of commanders at all levels to influence the men under their command

Neville Maxwell, author of *India's China War* (1970) comments:

> The first four of those smacked of an enquiry into the sinking of the Titanic looking into the management of the shipyard where it was built and the health of the deck crew; only the last term has any immediacy and there the wording was distinctly odd—commanders do not usually 'influence' those they command, they issue orders and expect instant obedience. But Henderson-Brooks and Bhagat in effect ignored the constraints of their terms of reference and deliberately ignored other limits Chaudhuri had laid upon their investigation, especially his ruling that the functioning of Army HQ during the crisis lay outside their purview.[3]

THE AUTHORS AND THEIR REPORT

T.B. Henderson-Brooks was a second-generation Indian-domiciled English expatriate who had joined the Indian Army and was commissioned into the Maratha Light Infantry (MLI). In the early 1930's he had opted to be counted as an *Indian*, as opposed to a British, King's Commissioned Indian Army Officer, and had been so categorized in the Army List. During the Second World War, this had actually gone against him because his rank and seniority in the Indian Army would have entitled him to reasonably senior staff or command responsibilities, which the British were unwilling to give to Indian officers. In spite of his categorization, he was in looks, speech and manner as English as his hyphenated surname, and as English as the other British officers of the pre-1947 Indian Army. As a Lt. Col., he took over as Commanding Officer of 4th Marathas (4 MLI) in June 1947 at Ranchi, and was C.O. 4 MLI through its subsequent moves to Janshedpur and then to Lebong (Darjeeling) in 1948. In end-1962, Lt. Gen. T.B. Henderson-Brooks was G.O.C. 11 Corps in the Punjab.

This being a non-ministerial committee of inquiry, it could not examine a number of documents in the General Staff (Operations) branch of Army Headquarters, nor, because it was headed by a Corps Commander, could it question either the Eastern Army Commander, Lt. Gen. L.P. 'Bogey' Sen, or the Chief of Army Staff, Gen. V.N. Thapar, who were both senior to Lt. Gen. Henderson-Brooks. Lt. Gen. B.M. Kaul submitted two long statements to the Army Chief, and the Director of Military Operations, Brig D.K. 'Monty' Palit, also submitted a report to the Chief. In May 1963, Brig. J.P. Dalvi, who had been captured by the Chinese, was repatriated and submitted his report. None of these written reports were passed on to the Henderson-Brooks Committee. In spite of these handicaps in the constitution of the committee and the terms of reference given to it, it produced a comprehensive report which was submitted in mid-1963.

It is believed that two copies of the Henderson-Brooks Reports are officially kept: one kept in the cupboard containing 'Secret' documents in the office of the Defence Secretary, in the Ministry of Defence; the other in the Military Operations Directorate at the General Staff Branch in Army Headquarters. It was believed among knowledgeable Army circles in the latter half of the 1960's that Gen. Muchu Chaudhuri had shown it to the Australian historian Neville Maxwell, who was then researching the Sino-Indian border problem and the war. He had, it is believed, given the researcher permission to take notes, on the condition that his book (*India's China War,* 1970) would not expose its findings in detail. Maxwell's book thus mentions the report, but discusses it clinically in general terms at the end of the book (pp. 437-438). The author mentions the likelihood *'that the Henderson-Brooks Report will not be published until after the first non-Congress Government takes office in New Delhi'* (p. 439). During the Bharatiya Janta Party-led coalition government of 1999-2004, it was apparently shown to the temporarily officiating Defence Minister, Jaswant Singh, whose primary portfolio was External Affairs Minister, sometime during the period February to October 2002, with the intention of getting a decision on whether to officially release it or not. Jaswant Singh, himself a former Army officer who had been in the Armoured Corps with the tank regiment The Central India Horse, after studying the report and thinking about the issue, decided to let sleeping dogs lie, even though the Congress Party was now in the Opposition, possibly for political rather than national reasons.

Fortunately, the Henderson-Brooks Report had been made available to the Defence Ministry's Historical Division when it was tasked to research and write the official *History of the Conflict with China, 1962,* completed in 1992.[4] This history itself, however, has not yet been released, but is available on the Internet.

MAXWELL'S COMMENTS ON THE REPORT

Maxwell provides a useful introduction to the Report:

> When the Army's report into its debacle in the border war was completed in 1963, the Indian government had good reason to keep it Top Secret and give only the vaguest, and largely misleading, indications of its contents. At that time the

government's effort, ultimately successful, to convince the political public that the Chinese, with a sudden 'unprovoked aggression,' had caught India unawares in a sort of Himalayan Pearl Harbour was in its early stages and the report's cool and detailed analysis, if made public, would have shown that to be self-exculpatory mendacity.

But a series of studies, beginning in the late 1960s and continuing into the 1990s, revealed to any serious enquirer the full story of how the Indian Army was ordered to challenge the Chinese military to a conflict it could only lose. So by now only bureaucratic inertia, combined with the natural fading of any public interest, can explain the continued non-publication - the report includes no surprises and its publication would be of little significance but for the fact that so many in India still cling to the soothing fantasy of a 1962 Chinese 'aggression.'

It seems likely now that the report will never be released. Furthermore, if one day a stable, confident and relaxed government in New Delhi should, miraculously, appear and decide to clear out the cupboard and publish it, the text would be largely incomprehensible, the context, well known to the authors and therefore not spelled out, being now forgotten. The report would need an introduction and gloss - drawing upon the writer's research in India in the 1960s and material published later.

Two preambles are required, one briefly recalling the cause and course of the border war, the second to describe the fault-line, which the border dispute turned into a schism, within the Army's officer corps, which was a key factor in the disaster - and of which the Henderson Brooks Report can be seen as an expression.[5]

As per Maxwell, the report comprehensively reviewed the developments and events prior to the hostilities, and also the plans, posture and strength of the army in Ladakh as well as the 4 Corps zone of operations in NEFA. The Henderson Brooks Report is long (its main section, excluding recommendations and many annexures, covers nearly 200 foolscap pages), detailed and far-ranging. The report is a taut, unforgiving analysis which does credit to the professionalism of both the authors: *'It would have been convenient and logical,'* they note, *'to trace the events [beginning with] Army HQ, and then move down to Commands for more details, ... ending up with field formations for the battle itself.'*

Henderson-Brooks and Bhagat thus began from the genesis of the problem along the entire Sino-Indian border, and thus discovered a great deal that the Kaul camp and the government would have preferred to keep hidden. They quote Field Marshal Roberts:

> The art of war teaches us to rely not on the likelihood of the enemy not coming, but in our own readiness to receive him; not on the chance of his not attacking, but rather on the fact that we have made our position unassailable.

Maxwell, from his understanding of the report, notes that from the beginning of 1961, when the *'Kaulist putsch'* reshaped Army HQ:

> ... crucial professional military practice was abandoned. These appointments in General Staff are key appointments and officers were hand-picked by General Kaul to fill them. General Staff appointments are stepping stones to high command and correspondingly carry heavy responsibility. When, however, these appointments are looked upon as adjuncts to a successful career and the responsibility is not taken seriously, the results, as is only too clear, are disastrous. This should never be allowed to be repeated and the Staff as of old must be made to bear the consequences of their lapses and mistakes. Comparatively, the mistakes and lapses of the Staff sitting in Delhi without the stress and strain of battle are more heinous than the errors made by commanders in the field of battle.[6]

Regarding the 'Forward Policy' which was born and named at a meeting chaired by Nehru on November 2, 1961, which began the confrontation with China, among many other detailed comments the Report traces a contradictory duet between Army HQ and HQ Western Command. This difference of perception between Army HQ and Western Command was regarding the ordering the establishment of 'penny-packet' forward posts in Ladakh, specifying their location and strength, with Western Command protesting that it lacked the forces to carry out the allotted task, still less to face the grimly foreseeable consequences. Kaul [Chief of General Staff] and Palit [Director of Military Operations] *'time and again ordered in furtherance of the "forward policy" the establishment of individual posts, overruling protests made by Western Command.'*[7]

Maxwell opines that the report was by no means a whitewash, as its comments on the political demand for military action and victory, which were generated at top level meetings in Delhi, show:

The Defence Minister [Krishna Menon] categorically stated that in view of the top secret nature of conferences no minutes would be kept [and] this practice was followed at all the conferences that were held by the Defence Minister in connection with these operations.[8]

The Report comments:

> This is a surprising decision and one which could and did lead to grave consequences. It absolved in the ultimate analysis anyone of the responsibility for any major decision. Thus it could and did lead to decisions being taken without careful and considered thought on the consequences of those decisions.[9]

Maxwell onserves that the Henderson-Brooks Report comments scathingly on Army Headquarters issuing orders for tactical tasks directly to a forward brigade, rather than to the concerned Command HQ, and even by signal directly to individual battalions. The example cited was the order issued in mid-September 1962 to 7 Infantry Brigade then beneath Thagla Ridge to *'(a) capture a Chinese post 1,000 yards north-east of Dhola Post; (b) contain the Chinese concentration south of Thagla.'*

The Report comments:

> The General Staff, sitting in Delhi, ordering an action against a position 1,000 yards north-east of Dhola Post is astounding. The country was not known, the enemy situation vague and for all that there may have been a ravine in between [the troops and their objective], but yet the order was given. This order could go down in the annals of history as being as incredible as the order for 'the Charge of the Light Brigade.'[10]

THE OVERALL JUDGEMENTS

Maxwell's remarks on the Report itself are telling:

> Given the nature of the dramatic events they were investigating, it is not surprising that Henderson-Brooks' and Bhagat's cast of characters consisted in the main of fools and/or knaves on the one hand, their victims on the other. But they singled out a few heroes too, especially the jawans, who fought whenever their senior commanders gave them the necessary leadership, and suffered miserably from the latter's often gross incompetence.

As for the debacle itself, Maxwell comments:

> *'Efforts of a few officers, particularly those of Capt. N. N. Rawat'* to organise a fighting retreat, *'could not replace a disintegrated command,'* nor could the cool-headed Brigadier Gurbax Singh do more than keep his 48 Brigade in action as a cohesive combat unit until it was liquidated by the joint efforts of higher command and the Chinese.[11]

The new Defence Minister, Y.B. Chavan, who had taken over on 21st November 1962, after reading the Report, made a statement in Parliament in 1963, in which he ascribed the reasons for the debacle to leadership failures in the army and to the tactical mishandling of troops. He played the mistakes down by explaining that the troops had fought under severe geographical and tactical handicaps. Evidently the Congress Government wanted to divert criticism from itself, by putting the blame on geographical problems and the Chinese 'betrayal' of Indian friendship.

The Minister also summarized the main recommendations of the Report. These are:

1. The need for more realistic battle training, especially in mountain warfare.
2. The urgency of eliminating shortages of equipment.
3. The need for curbing the tendency among senior commanders to interfere in the tactical handling of troops at lower levels.

4. The requirement of preparing troops adequately before committing them to a theatre of operations.
5. The requirement of better communications (surface and signals).
6. The need for a better intelligence set-up.

The Defence Minister also gave out that while the performance of junior officers was 'fair,' at higher levels of command there had been lapses. The need for improvement in the work and procedures of the General Staff at all levels was also stressed.[12]

Maxwell's final comments on the Report are:

> Henderson-Brooks and Bhagat place the immediate cause of the collapse of resistance in NEFA in the panicky, fumbling and contradictory orders issued from corps HQ in Tezpur by a 'triumvirate' of officers they judge to be grossly culpable: General Sen, General Kaul and Brigadier Palit. Those were, however, only the immediate agents of disaster: Its responsible planners and architects were another triumvirate, comprised of Nehru, Mullik and again, Kaul.[13]

Dr. Bharatendu Kumar Singh, who has studied the issue of the Henderson-Brooks Report in detail, believes no purpose will be served by the declassification of the Report, as the perceived benefits to the country would be marginal. He believes, however, that India has still not adequately addressed some of the issues discussed in the Report, viz.:

- Logistics and infrastructure
- War-waging capacity
- Doctrine and strategy
- Confidence.[14]

NOTES

1. See 'Our governments have a tendency to keep things under wraps,' January 19, 2000, on the Internet at http://www.rediff.com.news/2000/jan/19/nayar.htm, and 'Lonely paper chase: the Government's refusal to declassify documents is shocking,' in the *Indian Express*, New Delhi, August 26, 2003.

2. The CIC decision is on the Internet at http://www.cic.gov.in/CIC-Orders/WB-19032009-04.pdf. Also see:'62 war to remain under wraps: CIC turns down appeal to make Henderson-Brooks Report public' in *The Tribune*, Chandigarh, March 22, 2009.
3. Maxwell, Neville, *Henderson-Brooks Report: An Introduction*, 2001, on the Internet at www.Stratmag.com. Also at other sites, including *Economic and Political Weekly*, Vol. 36, No. 14 & 15, April 7th-20th, 2001.
4. Sinha, P.B., and Athale, Col. A.A., *History of the Conflict with China, 1962* (New Delhi, Ministry of Defence, Government of India, 1993).
5. Maxwell, *op.cit.*
6. *Ibid.*
7. *Ibid.*
8. *Ibid.*
9. *Ibid.*
10. *Ibid.*
11. *Ibid.*
12. Praval, *op. cit.* p. 239-240
13. Maxwell, *Henderson-Brooks Report: An Introduction*, *Op. cit.*
14. Singh, Bhartendu Kumar, 'Henderson-Brooks Report and India's China Challenge,' in *USI Journal* Vol. CXLIII, No. 591, January-March 2013, pp. 73-74.

Appendix B

The Organisation of the Indian Army

THE ORGANISATION OF THE INFANTRY AND THE ARTILERY

The infantry is divided into socio-administrative groupings known as 'Regiments' which wear the same uniform details, such as the identifying cap badge, shoulder titles, and lanyard, and are generally drawn from the same area or social classes. These 'regiments' by which individual units of the infantry are identified, and by which they identify themselves, mostly have what is known as a 'fixed class composition' or are a 'single class' regiment. Examples of regiments are the 'Madras Regiment,' with men from all the communities of the four southern states, the 'Punjab Regiment' with Jat Sikhs and Dogra Rajputs of Himachal Pradesh and the Jammu region, the 'Maratha Light Infantry' which is predominantly a single-class regiment of Marathas but also has Deccani Muslims, the 'Garhwal Rifles' with Garhwalis from Uttarakhand state. The 'Grenadiers' is a 'fixed-class' regiment with Rajputs, Jats, Kaimkhani Muslims from Haryana, and Dogras from Himachal Pradesh and J&K.

The actual fighting units of an infantry regiment are its 'battalions,' which are numbered, generally from one onwards, such as 'Second Battalion, the Rajput Regiment' (or 2nd Rajput in spoken language), 'Fourth Battalion, the Grenadiers' (i.e., 4th Grenadiers), or 9th Punjab, for example. A regiment may have a large number of battalions.

Gorkha regiments have retained their pre-1947 naming system, in which ALL regiments had both a number and a name. Gorkhas have seven different regiments, which are numbered, eg, 1st Gorkha Rifles, 4th Gorkha Rifles, or 11th Gorkha Rifles, so their battalions have two numbers, the first being that of the individual battalion, the second that of the regiment, for example, '1st Battalion, the 9th Gorkha Rifles' (1st/9th Gorkha Rifles, or 1/9 Gorkhas, or 1/9 G.R.).

Infantry battalions are also named in writing in a particular abbreviated style which is generally used in the Army's Operation Orders, Situation Reports, and signal correspondence.* In this method, only the number of the battalion of the regiment to which it belongs, and an abbreviated form of the name of the regiment, are used. Only capital letters for individual units are used in this abbreviated system. (Such capitalized abbreviations are also used for other arms, e.g., the armoured corps and the artillery.) Some examples will illustrate the system.

- 9th Battalion, the Punjab Regiment, is written as '9 PUNJAB'; 13th Battalion, the Dogra Regiment is written as '13 DOGRA.'
- 1st Battalion, the Sikh Regiment, is written as '1 SIKH'; and 2nd Battalion, The Sikh Light Infantry, is written as '2 SIKH LI.' 19th Battalion, the Maratha Light Infantry is written as '19 MARATHA.'
- 4th Battalion, The Grenadiers, is written as '4 GRENADIERS'; while 5th Battalion, The Brigade of Guards, which is the name of the infantry regiment and is not a 'brigade' in the sense of a field formation, such as '7 Infantry Brigade,' is written as '5 GUARDS.'
- 4th Battalion, The Garhwal Rifles, is written as '4 GARH RIF'; 1st Battalion, the 9th Gorkha Rifles, also written as '1/9 Gorkha Rifles', is abbreviated to '1/9 G.R.'
- 3rd Battalion, The Jammu and Kashmir Rifles, a regiment of regular infantry, is written as '3 JAK RIF'; 14th Battalion, The Jammu and Kashmir Militia, which were not regular infantry in those days, was written as '14 J&K MILITIA.'
- '13th Battalion, The Kumaon Regiment' is written as '13 KUMAON,' and '1st Battalion, the 8th Gorkha Rifles' (or 1/8 Gorkha Rifles) is abbreviated as '1/8 GR.'
- 17th (Parachute) Field Artillery Regiment is written as '17 PARA

*This will, of course, be familiar to military readers.

FD'.

The civilian reader should be able to deduce the full names of other infantry units named in the text, but whose names have not been used as examples in this note. The spoken form or the layman's English form has also been used together with this wherever a doubt may arise in a non-military reader's mind as to whether the whole unit (i.e., the battalion) is meant, or only elements thereof.

Artillery units are individually called 'regiments,' such as '5 Field Regiment,' '17 Parachute Field Regiment,' '22 Mountain Regiment,' '36 Light Regiment,' '33 Heavy Mortar Regiment,' or '223 Medium Regiment' even though the formal name of the artillery branch as a whole is the 'Regiment of Artillery,' this name corresponding to the names of infantry regiments, which constitute a social 'family.' The artillery branch as a whole are informally known as 'Gunners.' In Operation Orders and the like, abbreviated forms are used, eg, '5 Fd Regt,' '17 Para Fd Regt,' '22 Mtn Regt,' '33 Hy Mor Regt,' or '223 Med Regt.' Sub-units of the artillery are known as 'batteries,' most have individual numbers, which are used in the abbreviated manner used in Operation Orders and the like, eg, '95 Fd Bty,' '52 Para Fd Bty,' '7 Mtn Bty' , '116 Hy Mor Bty,' and such-like.

All units of all of the arms and services are presently commanded by Colonels (though they were earlier commanded by Lieutenant Colonels, which is the world-wide norm), and have a standard complement of officers, men, arms and equipment, ranging from some 550 all ranks for an armoured regiment, to the approximately 900 all ranks of an infantry battalion. Below the unit are its functional sub-units, which actually do the fighting in the case of the combat arms: called the 'rifle companies,' named 'Company' of the infantry; the 'sabre squadrons' named 'Squadron' of the armour (i.e., the tank regiments), and the 'Battery' of the artillery. Sub-units are commanded by Majors, and are numbered alphabetically, the four rifle companies of an infantry battalion are 'A,' 'B,' 'C' and 'D,' and the three batteries of an artillery regiment are 'P,' 'Q,' and 'R.' These are invariably spoken of in the phonetic alphabet; thus there are 'Alpha' to 'Delta' Companies in infantry battalions, 'Alpha' to 'Charlie' Squadrons in armoured regiments, and 'Papa,' 'Quebec,' and 'Romeo' Batteries in every artillery regiment. As shown earlier, batteries of artillery regiments can also have formal numbers of their own, as do field companies of the combat engineers.

These sub-units are further broken down into smaller sub-units, 'platoons' in the case of infantry, and 'troops' in the case of the artillery. An infantry rifle company has about 135 all ranks, and basically has three platoons of 35 men each, plus other elements. An infantry platoon has three smaller sub-units, the 'sections.' The infantry section of ten men is commanded by a Havildar, who wears three stripes on his sleeve, though it used to be commanded by a Naik earlier, as is the world-wide norm. Naiks wear two stripes on their sleeves.

THE FIELD FORMATIONS

For the actual business of tactical military operations, battalions of various regiments, and units of the other arms and services are grouped together into 'field formations.' The smallest of these is the brigade, commanded by a Brigadier. (A brigadier is a 'one-star' general under the US Army system) The basic brigade is the infantry brigade or mountain brigade of three infantry battalions, almost invariably from three different regiments. A normal infantry brigade would have about 3,000 all ranks. The corresponding formation of the armoured corps, also broadly called the 'mechanized forces,' is the 'armoured brigade' or 'mechanized brigade,' with three or four units, such as two units (regiments) of tanks and one unit (battalion) of mechanized infantry for example, or vice versa. Artillery regiments are grouped together as an 'artillery brigade.'

The next higher field formation is the 'division,' which could be an 'infantry division,' a 'mountain division,' an 'armoured division,' a 'mechanized division,' or even an 'artillery division.' A division is commanded by a Major-General (a 'two-star' general), who is formally titled the General Officer Commanding (GOC) or informally known as the 'divisional commander.' An infantry division or mountain division would routinely consist of three infantry brigades and an artillery brigade, plus various other units of supporting arms and services. An infantry division would have between 15,000 and 17,000 all ranks, though some static infantry divisions in a defensive 'holding' role along the Line of Control in Jammu & Kashmir have much more, as a result of having more brigades, and also in some cases more battalions per brigade. (Chinese infantry divisions have about 10,000 all ranks).

Two or more divisions are grouped under a larger field formation known as a 'Corps,' each of which has a number, such as '16 Corps,' and is commanded by a Lieutenant-General, a 'three-star' general), who is the GOC of the Corps, or the 'Corps Commander.' (Three Chinese divisions are grouped together to form an Army, which is thus the equivalent of an Indian corps.)

An even larger fighting grouping is the 'field army' of two or more Corps, which in India's case are the static territorial 'commands,' such as 'Eastern Command' or 'Northern Command.' These are commanded by a Lieutenant-General who has other Lieut.-Generals who are GOC's under him, and so is a General Officer Commanding-in-Chief, or GOC-in-C of the command, but because it is the equivalent of a field army, he is also known as the 'Army Commander.' In this unusual case, a three-star general commands other three-star generals, who are always junior to him in service.

The senior-most officer of the Indian Army is a General (a 'four-star' general),while the senior-most formation commander is an Army Commander, the GOC-in-C of a regional command, such as Eastern Command, for example. In practical terms, the senior-most 'field formation' commander in India is a Corps Commander, such as GOC 33 Corps, since India's regional commands, though the equivalent of a 'field army' such as 14th Army, are unlikely to ever get fully mobilized to the extent of having to move themselves in fluid operations over long distances, as was the case in World War II.

Bibliography

1. Abitbol, Aldo D., 'Causes of the 1962 Sino-Indian War: A Systems Level Approach,' *Josef Korbel Journal of Advanced International Studies*, Vol 1, 2009, pp. 74-88, on the Internet at www.du.edu.korbel/jais/volume1_abitbol.pdf.
2. Ahmad, Lt. Col. Mustasad, *Living up to Heritage: The Rajput Regiment 1947-1970* (New Delhi, Lancer Publishers, 1997).
3. Amarinder Singh, Capt., *Lest We Forget* (Patiala, Regiment of Ludhiana Welfare Association, 1999).
4. Arpi, Claude, *The Fate of Tibet* (New Delhi, Har-Anand Publications, 2001).
5. Bajwa, Col. J.S., *Modernisation of the PLA: Gauging its Latent Future Potential* (New Delhi, Lancer Publications, 2002).
6. Bajwa, Maj. Gen. Kuldip Singh, *India's National Security: Military Challenges and Responses* (New Delhi, Har-Anand Publications, 2008).
7. Beckwith, Cristopher I., *The Tibetan Empire in Central Asia: A History of the Struggle for Great Power among the Tibetans, Turks, Arabs, and Chinese during the Early Middle Ages* (Princeton, USA, Princeton University Press, 1987).
8. Bewoor, Gp. Capt. A.G., Vayusena Medal, *Close Air Support in the 1962 War* on the Interrnet at www.bharat-rakshak.com/IAF/History/1962War/Bewoor.html.
9. Bhargava G. S., *The Battle of NEFA, The Undeclared War* (Bombay/New York, Allied Publishers, 1964).
10. Bhutani, Sudarshan, *A Clash of Political Cultures: Sino-Indian Relations 1957-1962* (New Delhi, Lotus Collection, 2004).
11. Brar, Brig. Kuldip S., *Through Wars and Insurgency – Diary of an Army Officer* (New Delhi, Pentagon Press, 2013).
12. Calvin, James Barnard, *The China-India Border War* (Quantico, Va., USA, Marine Corps Command and Staff College, 1984).
13. Chaturvedi, Gyaneshwar, *India-China Relations: 1947 to Present* (Agra, M.G. Publishers, 1991).
14. Chellaney, Brahma, 'The Lessons from a War,' in *Hindustan Times*, October 20, 2002.
15. Chellaney, Brahma, 'India's intractable border dispute with China,' in Elleman, Bruce A., Stephen Kotkin, and Clive Schofield (eds.), *Beijing's*

Power and China's Borders: Twenty neighbours in Asia (Armonk, New York, USA/London, England, M.E. Sharpe, 2013), pp. 46-59.

16. Chen Feng and Larry M. Wortzel, 'PLA Operational Principles and Limited War: The Sino-Indian War of 1962,' in Ryan, Mark A., David M. Finkelstein and Michael A. McDevitt (Eds.), *Chinese Warfighting: The PLA Experience Since 1949* (Armonk, NY, USA, M.E. Sharpe, 2003).
17. Clark, Gregory, *In Fear of China*, (Melbourne Lansdowne Press, 1967).
18. Cohen, S.P., *The Indian Army* (Berkeley, University of California Press, 1971).
19. Dalvi, Brig. J.P., *Himalayan Blunder* (Bombay, Hind Pocket Books/Thacker & Co, 1969).
20. Das, Gautam, *Unlearned Lessons: An Appraisal of India's Military Mistakes* (New Delhi, Har-Anand Publications, 2007).
21. Das, Gautam, *China-Tibet-India, the 1962 War and the Strategic Military Future* (New Delhi, Har-Anand Publications, 2009).
22. Dasgupta, Saibal, 'Paper blames Nehru for China-Tibet Discord,' in *The Times of India,* November 28, 2006.
23. Datta, Maj. Gen. J.S., *Recollections of the Se La-Bomdila Debacle 1962* (New Delhi, Knowledge World Publishers, 2013).
24. Dave, A.K., *The Real Story of China's War on India, 1962*, New Delhi, U.S.I. of India, Occasional Paper No. 1, 2006.
25. Deng Lifeng, *Zhang-Yin Bianzhong* ('The Sino-Indian Border War'), on the Internet at http://argo.virtualave.net/_private/wars/zhiyin.htm.
26. Diamond, Jared, *Guns, Germs and Steel, A Short History of Everybody for the Last 13,000 Years* (London, Jonathan Cape, 1997).
27. Durschmied, Erik, *Beware the Dragon: 1000 Years of Bloodshed* (London., Andre Deutsch Ltd., 2008).
28. Eipe, Ravi, Lt. Gen., *The 1962 War: Fighting in the Namkachu Region*, article of his interview to the South Asian Institute of Strategic Affairs, September 18, 2012, on the Internet at http://southasianidea.com/uncategorized/the-1962-war-fighting-in-the-namkachu-region/.
29. Elleman, Bruce A., Stephen Kotkin, and Clive Schofield (eds.), *Beijing's Power & China's Borders: Twenty neighbours in Asia* (Armonk, New York, USA/London, England, M.E. Sharpe, 2013).
30. Feng, Chen & Larry M. Wortzel, 'PLA Operational Principles and Limited War,' in Mark A. Ryan, David Michael Finkelstein, Michael A. McDevitt (Eds.), *Chinese Warfighting: The PLA Experience Since 1949*, pp. 179-181 (Watertown, Mass., USA, East Gate Books/New York, M.E. Sharpe, 2003).
31. Fisher, Margaret W., Rose, Leo E., and Huttenback, Robert A., *Himalayan Battleground: Sino-Indian Rivalry in Ladakh* (London, Pall Mall Press, 1963).

32. Friedman, George, 'Chinese Geopolitics and the Significance of Tibet,' April 15, 2008, in *STRATFOR, April 19, 2008, Geopolitical Weekly, Geopolitical Intelligence Report*, available on the Internet at http://stratfor.com/.
33. Garver, John W., *Protracted Conflict: Sino-Indian Rivalry in the Twentieth Century* (Seattle, Wa., University of Washington Press, 2001).
34. Garver, John W., *China's Decision for War with India in 1962*, on the Internet at http://www.people.fas.harvar.edu/~johnson/garver.pdf (published in Ross, Alastair Iain, and Ross, Robert S. (eds.), *New Directions in the Study of China's Foreign Policy*, 2006), accessed on April 22, 2008.
35. Government of India, *Chinese Aggression in War and Peace* (New Delhi, Ministry of Foreign Affairs, 1962).
36. Hoffman, Steven A., *India and the China Crisis* (Berkeley, University of California Press, 1990).
37. Howard, Russel D., *The Chinese People's Army: 'Short Arms and Slow Legs,'* USAF Institute for National Security Studies Occasional Paper 28, Regional Security Series (Colorado, USA, USAF Academy, 1999).
38. Jaspal Singh, Brig., *India's Land Forces: Structural Imperatives* (New Delhi, Manas Publications, 2003).
39. Jaswant Singh, *Defending India* (London, Palgrave Macmillan, 1999).
40. Jiang Siyi and Li Hui, *et al*, (eds.), *Zhong-yin bianjing ziwei fanji zuozhan shi* ('The history of China's counter-attack in self-defence on the Sino-Indian border') (Beijing, *Junshi Kexue Chubanshe* 'Military Academy Publication,' 1994), pp. 391-424.
41. Johri, Maj. Sitaram, *Chinese Invasion of NEFA* (Lucknow, Himalayan Publications, 1968).
42. Kadian, Rajesh, *India and its Army* (New Delhi, Vision Books, 1990).
43. Karnik, V.B., *China Invades India* (Bombay, Allied Publishers, 1963).
44. Kaul, Lt. Gen. B.M., *The Untold Story* (Bombay, Allied Publishers, 1967).
45. Kavic, Lorne, *India's Quest for Security* (Berkeley, University of California Press, 1967).
46. Keay, John, *China: A History* (London, HarperCollins Publishers, 2008).
47. Keay, John, *India: A History from the Earliest Civilsations to the Boom of the Twenty-First Century* (London, HarperCollins Publishers, 2010).
48. Khera, S.S., *India's Defence Problems* (New Delhi, Orient Longmans, 1968).
49. Khullar. Brig. Darshan, *When Generals Failed: The Chinese Invasion* (New Delhi, Manas Publications, 1999).
50. Kondapalli, Srikanth, *China's Military: The PLA in Transition* (New Delhi, Knowledge World, 1999).
51. Kler, Lt. Col. Gurdeep Singh, *Unsung Battles of 1962* (New Delhi, Lancer Publishers, 1995).

52. Kristensen, Hans M., 'Extensive nuclear deployment area discovered in Central China' on the Internet at http://www.fas.org/blog/2008/05/extensive_nuclear_deployment_area_discovered_in_central_china.php, May 15, 2008 accessed on June 7, 2008.
53. Lakshman Singh, Brig., *Letters from the Border and Other Less Told Stories: Op Leghorn Sino-Indian Conflict 8th October 1962 to 20th October 1962* (New Delhi, KW Publishers, 2003).
54. Lakshman Singh, Brig., *The Plastic Soldier*, April 1, 2010, on the Internet at http://signalsingh.blogspot.in/2010/04/plastic-soldier.html.
55. Lamb, Alastair, *The China-India Border: The Origins of the Disputed Boundaries* (London, Oxford University Press, 1964).
56. Liu, Xuecheng, *The Sino-Indian Border Dispute and Sino-India Relations* (New York, Lanham, 1994).
57. Ma Zhenfa (Chief Ed.), *Bianfanglun* [Border Defence Theory] (Beijing, Military Academy Publication, 1996) pp. 132-134.
58. Man, John, *Kublai Khan: The Mongol King Who Remade China* (London, Bantam Press, 2006).
59. Mankekar, D.R., *The Guilty Men of 1962* (Bombay, Tulsi Shah Enterprises, 1968).
60. Marozzi, Justin, *Tamerlane: Sword of Islam, Conqueror of the World* (London, HarperCollins Publishers, 2004).
61. Marston, Daniel P. and Chandar S. Sundaram, (Eds.), *A Military History of India and South Asia: From the East India Company to the Nuclear Era* (Bloomington, Indiana University Press, 2007).
62. Maxwell, Neville, *India's China War* (London, Jonathan Cape, 1970).
63. Maxwell, Neville, *Henderson-Brooks Report: An Introduction*, 2001, on the Internet at www.stratmag.com/issue2Dec-1/Kargil.htm, accessed on April 21, 2008.
64. McKay, Alex, *The History of Tibet* (London, RoutledgeCurzon, 2003).
65. Mehrotra, L.L., *India's Tibet Policy* (New Delhi, Tibetan Parliamentary and Policy Research Centre, 1997).
66. Mukherjee, L., *History of India (Hindu Period)* (27th Ed.) (Calcutta, Mondal Brothers, 1968).
67. Mullick, B.N., *My Years with Nehru: The Chinese Betrayal* (New Delhi, Allied Publishers, 1971).
68. McFarquhar, Roderick, *The Origins of the Cultural Revolution, Vol. 3, The Coming of the Cataclysm 1961-66*, (Oxford, Oxford University Press, 1997)
69. Menzies, Gavin, *1421, The Year China Discovered the World* (London, Bantam Press, 2002).
70. Michigan, Maj. Gen. A.H.E., *Right of the Line: The Grenadiers, A Historical Record* (Jabalpur, Grenadiers Association, 1995).

71. Mukherjee, L., *History of India*, 27th. Ed. (three vols.) (Kolkata, Mondal Brothers, 1963).
72. Nehru, Jawaharlal, *The Discovery of India* (Bombay, Asia Publishing House, 1961).
73. Noorani, A.G., 'The MEA's map phobia: India's territorial rights cannot be questioned on the basis of a map,' in *Hindustan Times*, April 1, 2003.
74. Noorani, A.G., 'Maps and Boundaries,' in *Frontline*, October 24, 2008, pp. 80-88.
75. Norbu, Dawa, 'Tibet in Sino-Indian Relations: The Centrality of Marginality,' in *Asian Survey*, Vol. 37, No. 11 (November 1997), pp. 1078-1095.
76. Pahwa, Lt. Gen. Pran, 'The Attack on Bomdi-La: A Personal Experience,' in *USI Journal*, Vol. CXLII, No. 590, October-December 2012, pp. 589-602.
77. Palit, Maj. Gen. D. K., *War in High Himalaya: The Indian Army in Crisis, 1962* (London, C. Hurst & Co., 1991).
78. Palsokar, Col. R.D., *The Grenadiers: A Tradition of Valour* (Jabalpur, Grenadiers Regimental Centre, 1980).
79. Parasnis, Wg. Cdr. R V, 'Remembering a War: The 1962 India-China Conflict,' in *The Rediff Special*, http://www.rediff.com/news/2002/dec/03chin.htm, accessed on May 05, 2008.
80. Patabhiraman, Lt. Gen. S., 'Fifty Years after the 1962 Debacle,' in *USI Journal*, Vol. CXLII, No. 590, October-December 2012, pp. 524-532.
81. People's Republic of China, Xinhua News Agency, *History of the Sino-Indian Border Self-Defensive War*, 1993, available on the Internet at http://big5.xinhuanet.com/gate/big5/news.xinhuanet.com/mil/2005-07/31/content_3279638.htm accessed on April 24, 2008.
82. People's Republic of China, *Documents on the Sino-Indian Boundary Question* (Beijing, Foreign Languages Press, 1960).
83. People's Republic of China, *The Sino-Indian Boundary Question* (Enlarged Edition) (Beijing, Foreign Languages Press, 1962).
84. Pillsbury, Michael, *China Debates the Future Security Environment* (Washington, DC, USA, National Defence University Press, 2000).
85. Prasad, Maj. Gen. Niranjan, *The Fall of Towang, 1962* (New Delhi, Palit and Palit, 1981).
86. Praval, Maj. K.C., *Indian Army after Independence* (New Delhi, Lancer Paperbacks, 1993).
87. Raghavan, Srinath, *War and Peace in Modern India: A Strategic History of the Nehru Years* (London, Palgrave MacMillan, 2010).
88. Raja Mohan, C, 'Soft Borders and Cooperative Frontiers: India's Changing Territorial Diplomacy Towards Pakistan and China' in *Strategic Analysis*, vol. 31, issue 1, pp. 1-23, January 2007.

89. Raman, B., 'Forgetting the Lessons of the 1962 War,' in *Asia Times Online*, http:www.atimes.com/South_Asia, February 2, 2003, accessed on March 21, 2003.
90. Richardson, H.E., *Tibet and its History* (London, Oxford University Press, 1962).
91. Rizvi, Janet, *Ladakh: Crossroads of High Asia* (Delhi, Oxford University Press, 1983).
92. Rowland, John. A., *History of Sino-Indian Relations: Hostile Coexistence* (Princeton, NJ, USA, D. van Nostrand, 1967).
93. Ryan, Mark A., David M. Finkelstein and Michael A. McDevitt (Eds.), *Chinese Warfighting: The PLA Experience since 1949*, (Watertown, Mass., USA, East Gate Books/New York, M.E. Sharpe, 2003).
94. Saigal, Lt. Col. J. R., *The Unfought War of 1962: The NEFA Debacle* (New Delhi, Allied Publishers, 1979).
95. Sandhu, Maj. Gen. P.J.S., '1962 – Battle of Se-La and Bomdi-La' in *USI Journal*, Vol. CXLI, No. 586, October-December 2011, pp. 575-594.
96. Sandhu, Maj. Gen. P.J.S., '1962—The Battle of Namka Chu and Fall of Tawang' in *USI Journal*, Vol. CXLIII, No. 592, April-June 2013, pp. 271-289.
97. Sawyer, Ralph D., *One Hundred Unorthodox Strategies: Battles and Tactics of Chinese Warfare* (New York, Westview Press, 1998).
98. Shahin, Sultan, 'Laying the ghost of the India-China war,' in *Asia Times Online*, http:www.atimes.com/South_Asia, November 1, 2002, accessed on March 21, 2003.
99. Shandilya, Charan, *Sino-Indian Relations: Reality of McMahon Line and Facts about the 'Chinese Aggression' in 1962* (Delhi, Supriya Art Press, 1998).
100. Singh, Bhartendu Kumar, 'Henderson-Brooks Report and India's China Challenge,' in *USI Journal* Vol. CXLIII, No. 591, January-March 2013, pp. 667-75.
101. Sinha, P.B., and Athale, Col. A.A., *History of the Conflict with China, 1962* (New Delhi, Ministry of Defence, Government of India, 1993).
102. Sodhi, Brig. H.S., *Top Brass—A Critical Appraisal of the Indian Military Leadership* (NOIDA, Trishul Publishers, 1993).
103. Sodhi, Brig. H.S., *Significant Battles since Independence* (New Delhi, Lancer Publishers, 2007).
104. Sridharan, Cdr. K., *A Maritime History of India* (New Delhi, Govt. of India, Ministry of Information and Broadcasting, Publications Division, 1965).
105. Subrahmanyam, T.G., *Famous Battles in Indian History* (Dehra Dun, Palit & Palit, 1969).
106. Sukhwant Singh, Maj. Gen. *India's Wars since Independence*, Vol. *III* (New Delhi, Lancer Publishers, 1982).

107. Sukumaran, Wg. Cdr. R., 'The 1962 India-China War and Kargil 1999: Restrictions on the Use of Airpower,' in *Strategic Analysis,* July 2003.
108. Sun Jinzhong, *Toushi ZhongYin guanxi jiuge* ('A Look at the Sino-Indian Disputes in Perspective') *Nanya Yanjiu Qikan* (South Asia Quarterly), Chengdu, Issue 1, Serial No. 108, 2002, pp. 49-53.
109. Thapliyal, Maj. Gen. S.V., 'China's Military Modernisation: A Perspective,' in *U.S.I. Journal,* vol. CXXXVII, no. 571, January-March 2008, pp. 79-86.
110. Thorat, Lt. Gen. S.P.P., *From Reveille to Retreat* (New Delhi, Allied Publishers, 1986).
111. Tuker, Lt. Gen. Sir Francis, *While Memory Serves* (London, Cassell, 1950).
112. Van Eckelen, W.F., *Indian Foreign Policy and the Border Dispute with China* (The Hague, Netherlands, Martinus Nijhoff, 1967).
113. Vedak, Harshvardhan, 'Tibet, China, Nehru and Pannikar,' 2001, on the Internet at http://vepa.us/dir00/tibet1.htm accessed on April 22, 2008.
114. Vedak, Harshvardan, and Chitre, Vikrant, 'The 1962 Sino-Indian War – A Historical Perspective,' on the Internet at http://orbat.com/site/sinoindianwar/index.htm accessed on April 22, 2008.
115. Verma, Maj. Gen. Ashok Kalyan, *Rivers of Silence* (New Delhi, Lancer Publishers, 1998).
116. Whiting, Allen S., *The Chinese Calculus of Deterrence: India and Indochina* (Ann Arbor, University of Michigan Press, 1975).
117. Wight, Martin, *Power Politics* (Harmondsworth, England, Penguin Books, 1979).
118. Woodman, Dorothy, *Himalayan Frontiers: A Political Review of British, Chinese, Indian and Russian Rivalries* (New York, Praeger Publishers, 1969).
119. Wortzel, Larry M., 'Concentrating Forces and Audacious Action: PLA Lessons from the Sino-Indian War,' in Laurie Burkilt, Andrew Scobell, Larry M. Wortzel, (Eds.), *The Chinese People's Liberation Army at 75,* (Carlisle, Penn., USA, US Army War College, Strategic Studies Institute, 2003) pp. 327-352. On the Internet at www.strategicstudiesinstitute.army.mil.
120. Xu Yan, *Zhong-Yin Bianjie Zhizhan Lishi Zhenxiang* ('The Historic Truth of the Sino-Indian Border War') (Hong Kong, Tian Di Publshing, 1993).
121. Yuan, Jing-dong, 'Foe or Friend?: The Chinese Assessment of a Rising India After Pokhran-II,' 2001, in Dittmer, Lowell (Ed.), *South Asia's Nuclear Security Dilemma* (New York, M.E. Sharpe, 2005).